The Flint Metro League

50 Years of
Sharing the Journey and
Leading the Way

Compiled by retired athletic director Gary Oyster

Preface

Compiling the Flint Metro League's history began when legendary Holly track coach Duane Raffin developed a list of Metro League individual track champions. Coach Raffin researched Flint Journal files dating to the league's first track season in 1969 and then printed and provided the results for anyone interested in them in time for the league's championship track meet in 2000.

Lapeer East assistant principal/athletic director Gary Oyster, the league's athletic director responsible for supervising track and cross  country at that time, continued compiling the list of league track champions, finding the handful of results that were missing from Flint Journal records in local weekly newspapers from the area, then keeping the list current as well as formatting the data in spreadsheet form to be sorted by year and event. He also compiled a complete list of the results of every Flint Metro League cross country championship.

Upon retiring as athletic director in 2003, Oyster continued working with the league on a voluntary basis before becoming the Metro's first executive director in 2005. One of his tasks was developing a league website that included historical records such as the track and cross country league  meet results and records from other sports provided by long-time Flint Journal sports reporter Greg Tunnicliff.

Oyster fully retired in 2016, turning the executive director reins over to Cathy North, and at that time the league asked him to compile a history of the Flint Metro League for its fiftieth anniversary in 1968. The first task was to complete a database of every first team all-league athlete in every sport. Beginning with the files already compiled accounted for half of the league's twenty-four sports, and Flint Journal archives were used as the primary source for the rest. The result was an alphabetical list that is over 99.8% complete containing more than 5,800 names, which may be found in the last section of this book. The all-league data in combination with lists of league team champions, MHSAA state champions, local newspaper articles, high school yearbooks, athletic director meeting minutes, and state coaches' association all-state recognitions all informed the compiling of the league's narrative history and highlights of its member schools, sport-by-sport highlights, and notable athletes, coaches and leaders.

While every effort has been made to be both thorough and objective, a few details over the fifty-year period could not be found. Anyone with reliable source information that might add to this compilation of the Flint Metro League's history is asked to contact an athletic director at a current league school.

Table of Contents

   The 56 athletes who have been named first-team all-Metro League in at least three sports.

Introduction

"Sharing the Journey...Leading the Way"

This was the league motto adopted by the Flint Metro League Student Council in the early 1980's. The league-wide student council, made up of student representatives from every Metro League school, is an example of the way that the league has done business for the first fifty years of its existence: collaborating and communicating to find the best practices used by member schools, so that doing "what's best for the kids" could occur at multiple levels throughout the league. Administrators, coaches, guidance counselors, teachers, and student leaders met regularly to share ideas that multiplied the effect of those practices up to ten-fold. In this way, the success of the Flint Metro League has gone far beyond athletic competition to touch academics, citizenship and social growth for students in communities around the greater Flint area, including Genesee, Lapeer, Shiawassee and northern Oakland counties.

This book is an attempt to share that half-century journey with those who participated in it or who are simply interested in how the Flint Metro League was created and why it continues to "Lead the Way".

NOTE: While every effort has been made to accurately record the fifty-year history of the Flint Metro League, some information may be missing or incomplete. Readers who can provide data that completes, corrects or adds to this league history are asked to contact the athletic director of their local high school with that information. Validated corrections will be placed on the Flint Metro League's official website as soon as practicable.

Founding the Flint Metro League

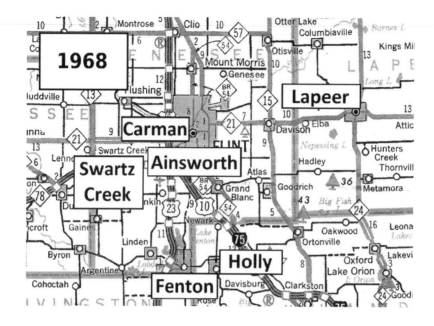

By the mid-1960's, most of the public school districts in Michigan had completed a period of consolidation, merging hundreds of tiny districts based around local one-room schoolhouses into single districts based around multi-classroom elementary schools and junior high schools feeding into one or more high schools. These high schools sponsored interscholastic athletic teams that competed against schools of similar populations in their geographic area, and leagues or conferences were formed to coordinate this competition.

In the greater Flint region, by 1966 there were five leagues serving area high schools that were generally based on the enrollment size of member schools. The Saginaw Valley Conference was made up of the largest schools in a four-county area, with the four Flint city high schools belonging to the SVC along with high schools in Bay City, Midland, Saginaw, and Pontiac. The Big Nine Conference, formed in 1960, served larger suburban school districts in Genesee County outside of Flint. The Genesee County "B" League and Flint Suburban

2

Conference (formerly the Genesee County "C" League) sponsored competition in the next largest groupings of schools by size, and the Flint Area Parochial League was made up of local parish high schools before the diocese created Powers Catholic High School in 1970.

The post-World War II "baby boom" meant that the adolescent population reaching high school age was exploding by the mid-1960's. The Carman School District, located in Flint Township south and west of the boundaries of the city of Flint, resulted from the consolidation of five smaller school districts. It opened newly-built Ainsworth High School in 1961, already overcrowded. While most school districts were able to accommodate increasing enrollments by adding on to existing buildings or replacing them with new, larger ones, the Carman district's population explosion (due in large part to being a community of auto workers commuting to GM plants) led it to building a second high school in 1967 to serve the northern half of its district while Ainsworth High School would serve the southern half. As part of the planning for the new high school, named Carman High School, a decision had to be made about what athletic conference its sports teams would compete in. To play a schedule of games independent of any league schedule would have meant greater travel distances, the inability for a team to compete for and win a league championship in its sport, the inability of its athletes to achieve all-conference honors, and an inordinate amount of time needed by the school's athletic director to schedule contests.

Pete Fornari was Carman HS's first athletic director and was a driving force behind the creation of the Flint Metro League.

League membership was generally based on school enrollment and geographic area, and each league governed its own game scheduling

3

and parameters of competition. Early on, the Genesee County Athletic Association had been formed by county superintendents to serve as the conduit for high schools to be added to leagues or change league affiliations. A process of petitioning to the GCAA for changes in league affiliations had been developed with approval based on consensus of all area leagues. The problem for the GCAA at the time of Carman High School's creation was that all Flint area leagues were playing full schedules in their sports.

The solution to Carman High School's dilemma was the formation of a new league; and while one option for doing so could simply have been reassignment of schools among the then-current Genesee County leagues, in the end the addition of two schools from outside Genesee County led to the original six-member makeup of the Flint Metro League.

Holly High School, located in northwestern-most Oakland County, was a member of the Wayne-Oakland County League, whose other member schools in the 1960's were Bloomfield Hills Andover, Brighton, Clarkston, Livonia Clarenceville, Milford, Northville and West Bloomfield. Lapeer High School belonged to the Tri-County League, made up of Oxford, Romeo, Waterford Kettering and Mt. Clemens L'Anse Creuse. Both Lapeer and Holly played the majority of their non-league contests against Genesee County schools, and Holly had a natural and long-lasting rivalry with neighboring Fenton.

With the approval of the Genesee County Athletic Association, the **Flint Metro League** began competition in the fall season of 1968 with **Ainsworth** and **Fenton** High Schools moving from the Genesee County "B" League, **Swartz Creek** from the Big Nine Conference, **Carman** High

School as a new school (after playing one year with an independent schedule with 9th to 11th graders in 1967-68), **Holly** and **Lapeer**. League competition was held and champions crowned in seven boys' sports in 1968-69: *football* and *cross country* in the fall; *basketball* and *wrestling* in the winter; and *baseball*, *golf* and *track* in the spring. Girls' sports were scheduled among league members in basketball, speedball, softball and track, but girls' sports did not fall under official Flint Metro League governance until 1973 after the passage of Title IX and the MHSAA's sponsorship of championships in girls' sports.

In the Flint Metro League's first year, administrators established an annual All Sports Award with a rotating trophy going to the school that had the best overall record in league competition. Points were given based on the final standings in each league-sponsored sport. The award was given based on seven sports in 1968-69, and by 1975-76 the award used standings in 12 sports. Carman and Fenton split the award over the first eight years of the Metro League, Fenton winning the award the first two years, followed by Carman the next four years.

The four-foot-tall All Sports Trophy was displayed at each of the league's member schools during the 1968-69 school year, after which the previous year's winner would be its caretaker. The result of the first year's All Sports competition was:

Fenton	32 ½ points
Carman	28 ½
Ainsworth	23 ½
Lapeer	22 ½
Swartz Creek	20
Holly	19

Five out of the six league schools won league championships in the Metro's first year of competition, and every league member won at least two championships in the conference's first three years. The league's competitive balance was demonstrated in football's first season: in the fall of 1968, Lapeer, with a 4-1 league record, nipped Carman for the league's first football crown. Carman finished at 3-1-1, with a scoreless tie against Holly in the final league game of the season preventing a co-championship. Despite finishing 0-5 in its inaugural league football season, Swartz Creek would improve to 3-2 in 1969 and then share two of the next three football championships.

Boys' basketball and baseball utilized ten-game schedules, and again competitive balance among league schools was demonstrated. Four different schools shared Metro boys' basketball championships in the league's first four years; while to this day no Metro League baseball team has ever gone undefeated, and no team went winless until 1999.

Four out of the original seven league boys' sports utilized "league meets" to determine at least a share of their league championships. Fenton dominated the first three years of boys' cross country, winning the initial 1968 league meet with a record 16 points after claiming six of the top seven individual finishes. Ironically, after 1970, Fenton would not win another boys' harrier title until 2003. Fenton also won the first boys' golf league meet, by ten strokes, and would win six of the first seven league boys' golf titles. Carman won the first Metro League wrestling championship by five points in a league meet that saw only three out of the twelve weight classes won by

Fenton's Don Keswick nips Holly's Tim White at the finish of the mile run in the Flint Metro League's first league championship meet in boys' track in 1969.

pins. (Carman would not win another Metro wrestling championship.) Holly claimed league titles in boys' track from 1969 through 1972 and won the Flint Metro League's first MHSAA state championship in 1971.

Once a majority of league schools sponsored them, **boys' swim** became an official league sport in 1970-71 and **boys' tennis** in 1972-73. **Mt. Morris** joined the Metro League as the seventh member school in the fall of 1972, coming from the Big Nine Conference.

With the passage of the federal equal opportunity legislation known as Title IX in 1972, high schools began to add girls' interscholastic sports to their extracurricular offerings. On September 6, 1973, Flint Metro League principals voted to approve by-laws for girls' sports and add them to the league constitution, also voting to include official girls' sports standings in tabulating the league all-sports trophy winner.

The MHSAA's first **girls' basketball** tournament was played in the fall of 1973, and that season the Flint Metro League crowned Carman (12-0) its first official league champion in the sport. **Softball** saw the first

Members of Carman High School's undefeated (15-0) softball team in 1973.

"official" league competition in the spring of 1973, two years before the first MHSAA state tournament. **Girls' track** teams had competed against other Metro League schools in an annual league meet starting in the league's first year, but became an "official" league sport in the spring of 1973, the same year the MHSAA sponsored its first state championship meet. MHSAA sponsorship standardized the events for girls' track; prior to that year, such "field day"-style events as the softball throw and the standing long jump were a unique part of girls' track competition in the league. In keeping with Metro League constitutional guidelines, once a majority of schools sponsored **volleyball** (winter 1976) and **girls' tennis** (fall 1977), they became official league sport offerings.

Even though it took until 1977 for a majority of schools in the Metro League to sponsor girls' tennis, this did not prevent girls interested in playing tennis from playing on boys' teams. The most successful girls to compete with the boys were the Serges sisters from Carman High School. Older sister Toni Serges teamed with a male teammate in 1973 to win the league tournament at #3 doubles, then paired with sophomore sister Kellie to take the 1974 title at #1 doubles. In 1975's league tournament, Kellie claimed the league title at #2 singles with Toni reigning at #4 singles, and Kellie won the league championship at #1 singles in 1976 before moving on to a stellar collegiate career at Cental Michigan University.

One girls' sport that did not become an official league-sponsored offering was speedball, a blend of soccer, basketball and football. Although popular in the greater Flint area, speedball never caught on as a sport offering for girls statewide and thus failed to become sanctioned by the MHSAA. Played in the fall, once the MHSAA placed girls' basketball in the fall season and volleyball in the winter, speedball became nothing more than a physical education class activity.

Speedball was a girls' fall sport activity that used a soccer ball, was scored like football and included passing elements like basketball. It was never sponsored by the majority of Flint Metro League schools nor the MHSAA, and thus was never an official league sport..

Amost immediatgely the Flint Metro League made a name for itself on a statewide level. Holly won the Class B state championship in boys' track in 1971, and that same spring Lapeer shared the Class A championship in boys' tennis (under a point system pre-dating the current team format). Fenton claimed back-to-back state Class B wrestling titles in 1971-72 and 1972-73.

Lapeer boys' tennis coach Rod McEachern along with team members John Greener, Rick Moore, Jim Cozens and Marty Stone with the Class A state championship trophy in 1971.
(Flint Journal photo provided by Greg Tunnicliff)

1976-1988: Adding Schools and Sports

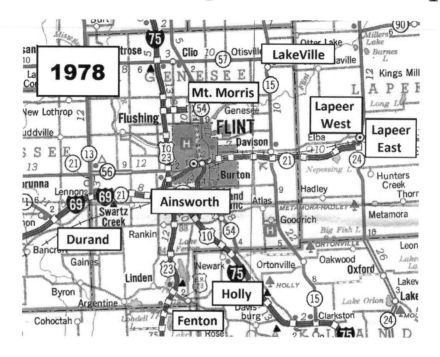

For fair competition in its state tournaments, the MHSAA divided its member schools into four "classes" of equal number based on the student enrollment of each school. By 1974 the Flint Metro League had three schools placed in Class A (Carman, Lapeer and Swartz Creek) and four in Class B (Ainsworth, Fenton, Holly, and Mt. Morris). When it came to state tournament competition the Class A schools found it harder to advance, coming up against schools with student populations that were many hundreds larger than them, and many located in large cities with well-developed recreation programs down to the elementary school level.

At the same time, some school districts had to deal with continuing rapid enrollment increases, many running two sessions or shifts of students through their high schools until a bond issue to build a bigger or second building could be passed. Fenton opened a new larger high school building in 1969, as did Mt. Morris in 1970. In Lapeer, by 1971

10

the district was running two shifts of students through its high school building every day: 11th and 12th graders attending morning classes from 7 a.m. to noon, sophomores and freshmen from around noon to 5 p.m. or later. Instead of doubling the size of its high school, Lapeer's school board decided to open a second high school once a bond issue was passed in 1973. Students in the west portion of the district would attend the original high school building, to be called **Lapeer West**; and students living east of M-24 attended the new building, Lapeer East High School. Like the Carman district had done when opening Carman High School, for the first year of Lapeer East's operation, 1975-76, only 9th through 11th grade students would attend the new building, allowing all the district's seniors to graduate together in 1976 from Lapeer West. **Lapeer East** would then join the Flint Metro League for athletic competition in 1976-77.

At a meeting of league principals and athletic directors on August 26, 1974, Carman High School administrators reported that they would be petitioning the Genesee County Athletic Association "to be reassigned". By the spring of 1975 the GCAA reached a consensus on Flint-area league realignment that would move Carman and Swartz Creek to the Big Nine Conference beginning in the 1976-77 school year, and move **LakeVille** High School to the Flint Metro League from the Genesee County B League at that time. The Metro League would still have seven members, with the new Lapeer East High School beginning league competition in the fall of 1976 as well. All seven Flint Metro schools would be in the MHSAA's Class B division for state tournament competition, with enrollments at the upper end of that classification.

An immediate effect of the change in league membership was the loss of boys' swimming and diving as a league-sponsored sport, because only Fenton, Holly and Mt. Morris sponsored swim/dive, and the other four league schools did not. However, with six schools sponsoring **volleyball** for the winter of 1976-77 it became a league sport offering, followed by **girls' tennis** in the fall of 1977. **Hockey** was added as an official league sport in 1978-79, after many years of Metro teams playing within the Genesee County High School Hockey League without playing each other consistently.

Durand had petitioned the Genesee County Athletic Association for admission to the Flint Metro League at the same time as LakeVille, but had been turned down. Two years later Durand, located in Shiawassee County, was approved to join the Metro, giving the league eight schools in four counties. By that time the Genesee County Athletic Association was no longer involved in decisions regarding league membership, and those decisions were now left up to individual leagues, to which local school districts would apply for admission. In the fall of 1979 Ortonville-Brandon and Oxford applied separately to join the Flint Metro League for the 1980-81 school year, but were declined due to the league's administrators preferring the scheduling advantages of an eight-member league.

A school millage failure in the LakeVille school district and the resulting budget shortfall caused LakeVille to cancel sports for the 1980-81 school year. Other districts during this period dealt with budget constraints by either implementing participation fees known as "pay-to-play" or cancelling individual sports with low participation numbers. These financial uncertainties caused league administrators to look more favorably on adding schools to the league's membership. **Linden** High School was admitted to the Flint Metro League beginning with the 1982-83 school year; and **Oxford** High School was admitted and began league competition in the spring season of 1983 as it transitioned from an Oakland County league that was down to four members. Metro League administrators overlooked the fact that neither Linden or Oxford sponsored boys' or girls' tennis; on the other hand, both new members had strong cross country programs at a time when some league schools were cancelling the sport.

Girls began competing in cross country as individuals, running races held concurrently with boys' races, in 1978; by 1981 enough schools sponsored **girls' cross country** to allow a league team championship. Unfortunately, even with the participation of Linden and Oxford, not enough schools sponsored girls' cross country to keep it an official league sport in the fall of 1985 and 1986 before resuming in 1987. It would not be until 1992 that every league school sponsored both boys' and girls' cross country. With the addition of **boys' soccer** in the fall of 1985 and **girls' soccer** in the spring of 1988, the Flint Metro League was sponsoring league competition and championships in 17 sports.

The admission of Oxford as a league member in the spring of 1983 made the Flint Metro League a ten-member conference. This created the need for scheduling changes for some sports. The length of a sport's season, and the need for some flexibility in a school's ability to schedule non-league competition, required innovations in scheduling league contests and determining league champions in basketball, volleyball and football. Basketball's season was 20 games long, and 14 of those games were scheduled within the league by dividing the league into two five-team divisions (an East Division and a West Division); playing each division opponent twice and non-division league members once; and holding a final cross-over game at the end of the league season based on division standings, meaning the first-place team from each division played for the league championship. Because volleyball's season was limited to 18 dates, each league school played a single round-robin schedule against league opponents concluded by a seeded season-ending tournament, combining the tournament outcome with the dual-match records of each school to determine the league championship and final standings. In football, some league schools had inter-league rivalry games scheduled for the first game of the season. To maintain these traditional rivalry games within a nine-game schedule, it was decided that league schools would play only eight of their nine league opponents, with the league opponent not to be played rotated every other year.

One thing that remained a constant throughout this period of financial uncertainty and expansion of league members was the outcome of the All Sports Award championship. Fenton began an 18-year hold on winning the All Sports Trophy in the 1974-75 school year. Fenton's most dominant sports were boys' golf with ten league championships in a twelve-year period; volleyball with eight titles in twelve years; wrestling with nine in twelve years; boys' tennis winning 11 league trophies in twelve years; and Fenton's softball teams claiming nine league championships in a ten-year span that also included state championships in 1978, 1979 and 1980.

Holly also won consecutive state championships in boys' cross country in 1977 and 1978. Holly, like the rest of the Metro League members, was still competing in Class B in state tournaments, but this would soon change as the MHSAA enrollment numbers it used for competition classification adjusted lower for the dividing line between Class A and Class B, while most Metro high schools had steady or slowly rising student enrollments. By 1980 Holly moved to Class A for state tournaments, followed soon after by Lapeer West and Lapeer East. While this made state team championships harder to attain for the Class A schools, Ainsworth claimed the 1982 Class B boys' track championship and Mt. Morris won the Class B crown in softball in 1984.

The 1984 Mt. Morris Softball Team, State Champions coached by Tom Stasik (back row far left)

The Flint Metro League had at least one individual Class B state wrestling champion every year between 1978 and 1987, along with 11 individual state champions in track and field, 8 in boys' swimming and two in boys' cross country during that span in both Class A and Class B.

There was one exception to the number of league schools maintaining steady enrollment during this period. The Carman-Ainsworth school district was hit especially hard by the closure of large automotive plants in Flint, and by the end of the 1985-86 school year, Ainsworth High School was closed; all of its high school students would attend the Carman building, now to be called Carman-Ainsworth High School. The Flint Metro League returned to being a nine-school conference for the 1986-87 school year.

1988-2002: Sharing and Leading

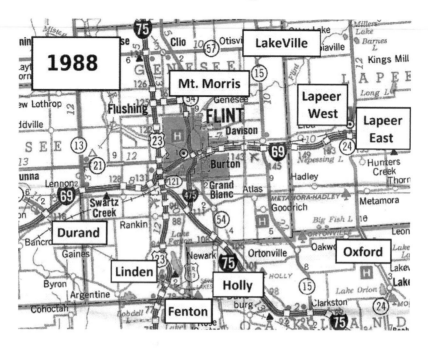

The Flint Metro League now entered its longest period of membership stability, with the same member schools from 1986-87 through 1996-97. Sport offerings were also stable during this time, with no new sports attaining league sponsorship until a majority of league schools sponsored girls' golf in the spring of 2002. One thing that did change

Flint Metro League Logo from the 1990's era

during this era was Fenton's dominance in the All Sports Award. Its string of winning 18 consecutive All Sports Trophies was ended by Lapeer East in 1992-93. Five different schools would win the All Sports award over the next decade: Lapeer East, Fenton and Oxford three times each, and Holly and Lapeer West once each.

Competitive league races strengthened Metro schools for state tournament success. In 1990 Fenton won its third state wrestling championship in Class B. Holly won the girls' cross country state title in

1990 in Class A despite being nipped by Class B LakeVille that fall for the league trophy. LakeVille's girls and Oxford's boys both won Class B track and field championships in the spring of 1991. Oxford won the Metro League's first football state championship in 1992 in Class BB, followed by Lapeer West winning the Class A gridiron trophy in 1995. Lapeer West followed up by claiming the state Division 2 wrestling championship back-to-back in 2000 and 2001.

During this time the MHSAA was changing the way it classified schools for its state tournaments. For sports that were sponsored by fewer schools statewide, the MHSAA divided those schools into equally-sized divisions for competition, rather than use one single classification statewide for all sports. The effect on Metro League schools was that most member schools were placed in Division 2 for sports like cross country, golf, soccer, tennis, track and wrestling. Metro schools met more often at the district level of state tournaments under this system.

League principals and athletic directors mirrored the MHSAA's focus on educational athletics being an "extension of the classroom". In the 1990's Flint Metro League administrators standardized recognition of the league's scholar-athletes, providing certificates for varsity athletes who maintained cumulative grade point averages of 3.5 or higher through their season of competition.

Scholar-Athlete Certificate

Another initiative taken on by the MHSAA during the 1990's was sportsmanship. Flint Metro League athletic directors embraced this initiative strongly. The league was not having difficulty with the sportsmanship between its schools, but wanted to remain proactive in the face of increasing publicity given to displays of poor sportsmanship by professional and college teams and players. In August 1998 the league sponsored its first "sportsmanship jamboree", each member school sending representative student-athletes to meet at Oxford High School for workshop activities designed to define and promote good sportsmanship. MHSAA Executive Director Jack Roberts was the keynote speaker at the first sportsmanship summit, which became a traditional annual event centered on student leadership as well as sportsmanship.

Attendees of the first Flint Metro League Sportsmanship Jamboree in August 1998 sat for a group photo.

Students who attended the first Flint Metro League Sportsmanship Jamboree signed T-shirts to be displayed at each member school.

Also by 1998 a sportsmanship initiative started by one school was adopted league-wide. Athletic directors sent congratulatory letters to the coach, AD and principal of the school whose varsity team displayed the best sportsmanship in each sport every season. Eventually, with the technology provided by e-mail and the development of a league website on the internet, the process of recognizing the teams showing the best sportsmanship was both streamlined and made highly publicized.

As the twenty-first century approached, changes in the relative enrollments of member schools again dictated league membership changes. In 1997 Durand, the conference's westernmost member, left the Metro League for the Mid-Michigan B League. In 2001 the next smallest high schools, LakeVille and Mt. Morris, announced that they were accepted into an expanding Genesee Area Conference for the 2002-03 school year. Neither school had won a Metro League championship in any sport since 1997; each of the other six member schools had won at least one league title every year since then.

Not wanting to have only six member schools, the Flint Metro League's administrators began looking for new members, for the first time using a structured application process. **Brandon** High School, located in Ortonville directly between Holly and Oxford, had expressed interest in joining the Metro several times over the previous twenty years, and after applying again was accepted to join the league for the 2002-03 school year. This meant that only two of the seven league member schools would be located in Genesee County, but this would soon change.

2002-2018: Changing Membership, Continued Excellence

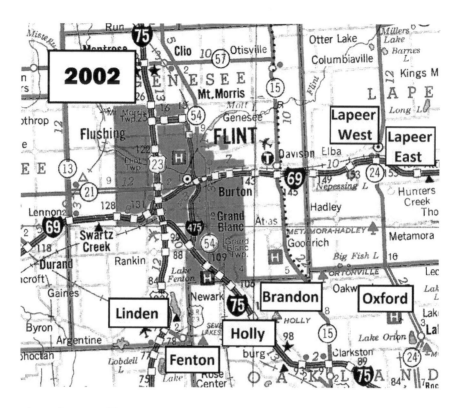

Changing school enrollment patterns had always led to changes in league affiliations, and by the start of the twenty-first century the driving force for high school sizes was a state-wide decline in birth rate and the resulting reduction in school enrollment numbers. For a league to maintain steady membership, all of its member schools would need to see similar rises or falls in attendance numbers; if any schools remained steady or increased in size while others fell, competitive balance would be affected. In Genesee County this greatly affected the Big Nine Conference, traditionally made up of the larger Class A high schools in the area along with highly-competitive parochial high school Powers Catholic. The Big Nine's smallest schools were more affected by enrollment decline than the largest, and as those smaller Class A schools became less competitive within their league, they saw participation numbers in their sports teams decline.

Five former Big Nine schools joined the Flint Metro League over a twelve-year period starting in 2005. **Clio** applied to and was accepted into the Metro in 2005; **Swartz Creek** rejoined the league in 2006; **Kearsley** was accepted in 2008; and **Flushing** in 2014. **Owosso** had left the Big Nine in 2007 and spent ten years in the Lansing area-based CAAC Conference before applying to and joining the Flint Metro for the 2017-18 season.

During that same period, changes in student enrollment led Oxford and Lapeer to other leagues. Oxford's growth compared to other league schools led it to move to the Oakland Activities Association in 2010. Enrollment decline in Lapeer caused its school board to merge its two high schools into a single Lapeer High School, and it left the Metro League for the Saginaw Valley Conference in 2014.

This period also saw an increase in the number of sports sponsored by the Flint Metro League. Attempting to improve the overall quality of education, Michigan's legislature promoted open enrollment and choice of school while increasing the number of charter schools allowed to operate. This, along with the trend of declining school enrollment brought about by the decline in the birth rate, created an environment of competition between school districts, and sports offerings were a means of attracting students in this competitive environment.

The Metro League added *girls' golf* in the spring of 2002, as soon as the requisite number of member schools sponsored it. *Competitive cheerleading* became an official league sport in 2003-04; the MHSAA had developed competitive cheer as a full-fledged sport with a state tournament in 1994. *Swim/dive* for *girls* became a league sport in the fall of 2004, followed by the return of *boys' swim/dive* that winter. *Boys'* and *girls' bowling* were sponsored by a majority of Flint Metro League schools beginning in the winter of 2008-2009, and *girls' lacrosse* completed its first season of Metro competition in the spring of 2016.

Like all high school athletic conferences in Michigan, in the 2007-2008 school year the Flint Metro League had to deal with major changes in when certain boys' and girls' sports were played. The MHSAA had been taken to court over the issue of whether girls who played volleyball in the winter season were at a disadvantage when it came to college recruitment, compared with players in other states who played volleyball in the fall season. After several years of litigation, the MHSAA's loss in the federal court decision meant that the MHSAA tournaments in volleyball, girls' basketball, golf and tennis would change their season of play, and therefore the entire playing seasons for those sports would have to move. Volleyball became a fall sport, and girls' basketball moved to be played in the winter, with its season beginning and ending one week before boys' basketball. Girls' golf shifted from the spring to the fall season, trading seasons with boy's golf (which had moved from spring to fall in the 1971-1972 season). Girls' and boys' tennis also exchanged seasons, with the boys playing in the fall starting in 2007.

Regardless of the seasons when sports were played, the Flint Metro League found continued success in MHSAA tournaments. Linden was crowned state champion in boys' cross country in 2008, and was runner-up in that sport in 2012. Kearsley began a dominant run in Division II bowling in 2010 by finishing as girls' state runner-up before winning the MHSAA championships in 2012, 2014, 2015, 2016, 2017

and 2018, the greatest success in MHSAA finals in Metro League history. After Lapeer West's boys' bowling team finished second in the state in 2013, Kearsley's boys' team claimed its own state titles by winning championships in 2014 and 2015 and taking runner-up honors in 2016. In

Kearsley's first state girls' bowling champions

the spring

of 2014, Swartz Creek won the Metro League's first MHSAA golf championship when its boys' team claimed the Division I title. The girls' basketball team from Flushing won the Class A championship in 2017. Near misses came in baseball, with Lapeer West finishing as state runner-up

Swartz Creek's state championship boys' golf team

in 2002 and Linden getting to the championship game before losing in 2004 and 2016; wrestling, with Lapeer West as state runner-up in 2003 and Oxford in 2009; and girls' soccer, where Fenton bowed out in the last game of the 2015 season.

Overall in its 50 year history, 12 Flint Metro League schools have won 29 MHSAA state championships in 13 sports, and another 28 teams representing nine schools have been state runners-up in 12 sports. In addition, Flint Metro athletes have claimed 151 individual state championships in wrestling, track and field, swimming and diving, cross country, tennis, golf and bowling.

Supplementing the scope of its athletic competition, the Flint Metro League continued a progressive course of action in promoting academics and good citizenship. Outside of athletics, the league's principals sponsored quiz bowl and science/math competitions between league member schools; continued having representative students meet as a league-wide student council; and hosted meetings of member school guidance counselors to help plan best-practice based state testing procedures.

Unique among Michigan athletic conferences, the Flint Metro League has had five years since 2009 with at least half of its athletic departments led by female athletic directors. From 2009-10 through

Holly AD Deb VanKuiken received the MHSAA's Women in Sports Leader-Ship Award in 2009.

2011-12, Deb VanKuiken (Holly), Sharon Miller (Lapeer East), Mary Haslinger (Lapeer West), Cathy North (Linden) and Sue Calvo (Swartz Creek) filled the athletic leadership positions at their schools. During the 2014-15 and 2015-16 school years, VanKuiken, North and Calvo were joined by Lisa Taylor, AD at Clio High School.

League athletic directors continued hosting an annual student leadership summit, begun in 1998, at which student-athletes from every league school participated in leadership development and sportsmanship-enhancing activities facilitated by state- and nationally-renowned motivational speakers. Additionally, over 500 students are recognized every year by the league as Scholar-Athletes for maintaining grade point averages over 3.5 while participating in varsity sports.

Participants in the 2015 Flint Metro
League Student Leadership Summit

In 2013, the league began recognizing a Coach of the Year in each sport, with that honor being presented at an annual Coaches Summit held at the end of the school year in June.

The 2013 Flint Metro League
Coach of the Year recipients

Over the first 50 years of its existence, the Flint Metro League has grown from offering competition in seven sports to overseeing 23 sports, emphasizing the educational value of quality competition with fair play, good sportsmanship, and the development of life-long habits of body and mind that will continue to benefit the communities the league serves.

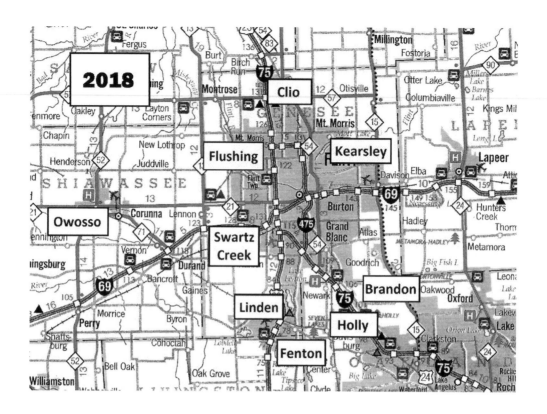

SCHOOLS

HISTORY OF FLINT METRO LEAGUE MEMBERSHIP

1968-1972: The Original Six
Fenton   (Gen. Co. B)
Flint Ainsworth (Big Nine)
Flint Carman   (New school)
Holly   (Wayne-Oakland)
Lapeer   (Tri-County)
Swartz Creek   (Gen. Co. B)

1972-1976
Fenton
Flint Ainsworth
Flint Carman
Holly
Lapeer
Mt. Morris   (from Big Nine)
Swartz Creek

1976-1978
Fenton
Flint Ainsworth
Holly
Lapeer East   (new school)
Lapeer West
Mt. Morris
Otisville-LakeVille   (from Gen. Co. B)
(Carman & Sw. Ck. To Big Nine)

1978-1982
Durand   (from Gen. Co. B)
Fenton
Flint Ainsworth
Holly
Lapeer East
Lapeer West
Mt. Morris
Otisville-LakeVille

1982-1983
Durand
Fenton
Flint Ainsworth
Holly
Lapeer East
Lapeer West
Linden   (from Genesee 8)
Mt. Morris
Otisville-LakeVille

1983-1986
Durand
Fenton
Flint Ainsworth
Holly
Lapeer East
Lapeer West
Linden
Mt. Morris
Otisville-LakeVille
Oxford   (from North Oakland)

1986-1997
Durand
Fenton
Holly
Lapeer East
Lapeer West
Linden
Mt. Morris
Otisville-LakeVille
Oxford

(Ainsworth closed)

1997-2002
Fenton
Holly
Lapeer East
Lapeer West
Linden
Mt. Morris
Otisville-LakeVille
Oxford
(Durand to Mid-Mich. B)

2002-2005
Fenton
Holly
Lapeer East
Lapeer West
Linden
Ortonville-Brandon   (from OAA)
Oxford
(LakeVille & Mt. Morris to GAC)

2005-2006
Brandon
Clio (from Big Nine)
Fenton
Holly
Lapeer East
Lapeer West
Linden
Oxford

2006-2008
Brandon
Clio
Fenton
Holly
Lapeer East
Lapeer West
Linden
Oxford
Swartz Creek (from Big Nine)

2008-2010
Brandon
Clio
Fenton
Holly
Kearsley (from Big Nine)
Lapeer East
Lapeer West
Linden
Oxford
Swartz Creek

2010-2014
Brandon
Clio
Fenton
Holly
Kearsley
Lapeer East
Lapeer West
Linden
Swartz Creek
         (Oxford to OAA)

2014-2017
Brandon
Clio
Fenton
Flushing (from Sag. Valley)
Holly
Kearsley
Linden
Swartz Creek
      *(Lapeer East & West
       merge and join SVC)*

2017-
Brandon
Clio
Fenton
Flushing
Holly
Kearsley
Linden
Owosso (from CAAC)
Swartz Creek

Ainsworth High School Spartans
Charter Member: 1968 to 1986

Merged with Carman HS to form Carman-Ainsworth HS (Big Nine Conference, then SVC) in 1986

League Championships (* = shared):

Baseball	3 (1972, 1977, 1985*)	Football	5 (1975, 1976, 1977*, 1980, 1981*)
Boys' Basketball	2 (1969-70, 1970-71*)	Hockey	7 (1978-79, 1980-81 to 1985-86)
Girls' Basketball	6 (1968-69 to 1972-73, 1974*)	Softball	2 (1975*, 1986)
Boys' Cross Country	3 (1976*, 1979, 1982)	Boys' Track	1 (1982)
		Girls' Track	2 (1982, 1983)
Girls' Cross Country	1 (1982)	Volleyball	1 (1977)
		Wrestling	1 (1983-84)

MHSAA State Championships:

Boys' Track	1982

MHSAA State Runners-up:

Hockey	1977
Volleyball	1978

Individual State Champions

Steve Powers	1975	Wrestling (Class B)
Rex Hart	1981	Wrestling (Class B)
Scott Savoie	1981	Wrestling (Class B)
Tim Fellows	1982	Track & Field (Class B) Shot Put and Discus
Jim Featherston	1982	Track & Field (Class B) 330 Hurdles

Rick Walt	1983	Wrestling (Class B)
Dave Ketter	1983	Wrestling (Class B)
Tim Fellows	1983	Track & Field (Class B) Discus
Dave Walt	1984	Wrestling (Class B)
Rick Walt	1984	Wrestling (Class B)
Walt Pannick	1984	Wrestling (Class B)
Craig Sheeran	1985	Wrestling (Class B)

Athletic Directors:
Carlo Lubiato   1968 to 1970
Jack Baldwin, 1970 to 1985-86

Carlo Lubiato
Ainsworth athletic director for its first two years in the Flint Metro League

Jack Baldwin
Served as Ainsworth's athletic director from 1970-71 through its merger with Carman HS in 1986, then continued as Carman-Ainsworth AD through 1994. He served as Ainsworth's baseball coach from its opening in 1961 to 1985, and was inducted into the Greater Flint Area Sports Hall of Fame in 2001

Brandon High School Blackhawks
League Member 2002 to Present

League Championships (* = shared):

Boys' Basketball	1 (2005-06)	Baseball	1 (2013-14*)
Girls' Basketball	1 (2002)	Softball	2 (2003*, 2015)
Competitive Cheer	9 (2007-8 through 2015-16)	Boys' Swim/Dive	2 (2009-10, 2010-11)
		Girls' Swim/Dive	1 (2012*)
Girls' Cross Country	3 (2004, 2005, 2006*)	Girls' Track	5 (2005, 2006, 2007, 2012*, 2013*)
Boys' Golf	1 (2005)		
Hockey	5 (2004-05, 2005-06, 2006-07;	Wrestling	2 (2013-14, 2014-15*)
as co-op team KBH:	2011-12*, 2014-15*)	Boys' Bowling	1 (2014-15*)
Boys' Soccer	4 (2008, 2015, 2016*, 2017)		

Athletic Directors:

Larry Lamphere, to Feb. 2006
Tom Rodenbaugh, April 2006 to 2007-08
Jam Meagher, August 2008 to Sept. 2008

Wayne Thompson, Oct. 2008 to 2010-11
Don Watchowski 2011-12 to 2015-16
Chris Deines, 2016-17 to present

Larry Lamphere
As AD, guided Brandon's first few
years in the Flint Metro League;
MIAAA regional AD of the Year 2014
for his work as AD at Lapeer, Brandon
and Clio

Don Watchowski
5 years as Brandon AD

Dr. Mike Ferguson
Principal
Led Brandon's transition to the Flint
Metro League;
as league president guided the
process for adding new schools

Carman High School Cougars
Charter Member: 1968 to 1976

Merged with Ainsworth HS to form Carman-Ainsworth HS (Big Nine Conference, then SVC) in 1986

All Sports Championships: 4 (1970-71 through 1973-74)

League Championships (* = shared):

Baseball	5 (1969, 1971, 1973, 1974, 1976)	Softball	2 (1973, 1974)
		Boys' Swim/Dive	3 (1970-71, 1971-72, 1975-76)
Boys' Basketball	2 (1970-71, 1972-73)	Boys' Tennis	2 (1975, 1976)
Girls' Basketball	3 (1973, 1974*, 1975)	Boys' Track	2 (1972*, 73)
		Girls' Track	2 (1974*, 75*)
Boys' Cross Country	1 (1971)	Wrestling	1 (1968-69)
Football	5 (1969, 1970*, 1971, 1972*, 1973)		

Individual State Champion

Rob Cummings	1976	Track & Field (Class A) 120 Hurdles

Athletic Directors:

Pete Fornari	1968 to 1975
Pat Fields	1975-1976

Pete Fornari

Carman's athletic director for all but one year of its tenure in the Flint Metro League; under his leadership the Carman athletic program won four All Sports championships (from 1970-71 through 1973-74); he was inducted into the Greater Flint Area Sports Hall of Fame in 2000

Clio High School Mustangs
League Member 2005 to Present

League Championships (* = shared):

Baseball	3 (2006, 2008*, 2013*)
Girls' Basketball	2 (2010-11, 2012-13)
Boys' Cross Country	1 (2015)
Hockey	3 (co-op with Swartz Creek: 2011-12*, 2012-13; with SC and Flushing: 2015-16)
Softball	1 (2017*)
Wrestling	1 (2014-15*)

Individual State Champions

Vince Lahar	2007	Wrestling (Division 2)
Mason Smith	2013	Wrestling (Division 2)
Mason Smith	2014	Wrestling (Division 2)

Athletic Directors:

Gary Langdon, 1998-99 to 2007-08
Ron Maygar, 2008-09 to Dec. 2010
*Tony Leonardo, Dec. 2010 to Feb. 13, 2011
Larry Lamphere, Feb. 14, 2011 to Jan. 28, 2014

*Joe Beckwith, Jan. 29, 2014 to June 30, 2014
Lisa Taylor, 2014-15 to 2015-16
John Darga, July 1, 2016 to present

*Interim athletic directors

Gary Langdon
Athletic Director who led Clio's
transition into the Flint Metro
League; MIAAA regional AD of the
Year 2006

Lisa (Hillman) Taylor
Former Fenton All-state pitcher;
Clio athletic director and current
principal

Fletcher Spears
Oxford HS graduate, principal at Linden,
assistant superintendent for Swartz Creek and Clio
before becoming Clio superintendent

Durand High School Railroaders
League Member 1978 to 1997

League Championships (* = shared):

Baseball	3 (1978-79*, 1982-83, 1988-89)	Football	3 (1981-82*, 1982-83, 1983-84*)
Boys' Basketball	3 (1978-79*), 1982-83*, 1985-86)	Softball	1 (1994-95)
		Wrestling	4 (1981-82, 1986-87*, 1993-94*, 1994-95)
Boys' Cross Country	1 (1987-88)		
Girls' Cross Country	1 (1996-97)		

MHSAA State Runners-up:

Wrestling (B)   1982

Individual State Champions

Greg Sargis	1979	Wrestling (Class B)
Jeff Ellis	1980	Wrestling (Class B)
Melanie Deters	1980	Track & Field (Class B) 400 Dash
Mark Clough	1982	Wrestling (Class B)
Alan Tyler	1989	Wrestling (Class B)
Kari Karhoff	1994	Track & Field (Class B) 400 Dash
Kari Karhoff	1996	Track & Field (Class B) 300 Hurdles
Kari Karhoff	1997	Track & Field (Class B) 300 Hurdles

Athletic Directors:

Lloyd Lamphere 1978-79 to 1980-81
Conlin Smith 1981-82 to March 1995
Rick Carsten 1995-1996
Joe Guyski 1996-1997

Conlin Smith

14 year tenure as Durand AD,
also won 3 league titles as boys'
basketball coach

Fenton High School Tigers
Charter Member: 1968 to Present

All Sports Championships: 37

League Championships:

Baseball	11 (5 shared)	Boys' Soccer	6 (2 shared)
Boys' Basketball	16 (6 shared)	Girls' Soccer	10 (4 shared)
Girls' Basketball	13 (2 shared)	Softball	23 (7 shared)
Boys' Cross Country	10 (2 shared)	Boys' Swim/Dive	7
Girls' Cross Country	3 (1 shared)	Girls' Swim/Dive	14 (1 shared)
Football	16 (9 shared)	Boys' Tennis	13
Boys' Golf	25 (2 shared)	Girls' Tennis	7 (3 shared)
Girls' Golf	6 (1 shared)	Boys' Track	9 (3 shared)
Hockey	6 (1 shared)	Girls' Track	17 (5 shared)
Girls' Lacrosse	3 (co-op with Linden)	Volleyball	25 (4 shared)
		Wrestling	16 (2 shared)

MHSAA State Championships:

Wrestling	1972, 1973, 1990
Softball	1978, 1979, 1980

MHSAA State Runners-up:

Wrestling (B)	1971
Girls' Basketball	1982
Baseball	1985, 1989

Individual State Champions

Marv Pushman	1969	Wrestling (Class B)
Don Keswick	1971	Track & Field (Class B) 880 Run
Mark Wiesen	1972	Wrestling (Class B)
Joseph Varney	1972	Wrestling (Class B)
Randall Chene	1973	Wrestling (Class B)
Dave Karns	1973	Track & Field (Class B) 880 Run
Mike Pickhover	1974	Wrestling (Class B)
Scott Burdick	1974	Swim/Dive (Class B) 50 and 100 Yd. Freestyle
Robin Sweetman	1975	Wrestling (Class B)
Mike Helms	1975	Track & Field (Class B) 880 Run
Dennis Schumaker	1976	Wrestling (Class B)
Katie Anderson, Angie	1977	Track & Field (Class B) Mile Relay
Pitman, Susan Ambler, Sue Hintz		
Jeff Merrill	1978	Wrestling (Class B)
Randy Walker	1978	Swim/Dive (Class B) 100 Yd. Backstroke
Dean Ammon	1982	Swim/Dive (Class B) 100 Yd. Backstroke
Mark Harris	1982	Swim/Dive (Class B) 200 and 500 Freestyle
Melanie Nelson	1985	Swim/Dive (Class B) 100 Yd. Breaststroke
Melanie Nelson	1986	Swim/Dive (Class B) 100 Yd. Breaststroke
Marty Spees	1987	Swim/Dive (Class B) 200 Ind. Medley
Melanie Nelson	1987	Swim/Dive (Class B) 100 Yd. Breaststroke
Teena Spees, Melanie	1987	Swim/Dive (Class B) 200 Medley Relay
Nelson, Diedra Schepler, Brigitte Hansen		
Brian Lambert	1988	Swim/Dive (Class B) Diving
Dave Caslmon	1990	Wrestling (Class B)
Jeff Nichols	1990	Wrestling (Class B)
Dru Bishop	1997	Track & Field (Class B) 800 Run
Scott Pushman	1998	Wrestling (Division 2)
Dru Bishop	1998	Track & Field (Class B) 800 Run
Scott Pushman	1999	Wrestling (Division 2)
Liz Korsedal	1999	Swim/Dive (Class B) 100 Yd. Butterfly
Lambros Kottalis	2000	Wrestling (Division 2)
Liz Korsedal	2000	Swim/Dive (Class B) 100 Yd. Butterfly
Amber Shalla	2000	Swim/Dive (Class B) 500 Yd. Freestyle
Jon Herstein	2001	Wrestling (Division 2)
Mike Pickhover	2002	Wrestling (Division 2)
Michael Peck, Shawn	2004	Track & Field (Division 2) 400 Relay
Debo, Matt Temple, Matt Maygar		
Amy Morrison	2006	Track & Field (Division 1) Pole Vault
Alex Ralston, Joe Kryza,	2007	Track & Field (Division 2) 3200 Relay
Jesse Anderson, Joe Dimambro		
Amy Morrison	2007	Track & Field (Division 2) Pole Vault
Jacob Lee	2016	Track & Field (Division 1) 3200 run
Dominic Dimambro	2017	Track & Field (Division 1) 3200 run

Athletic Directors:
Ivan Williams to 1970-71
Ken Wegner 1971-72 to 1973-74
Ken Wensel 1974-75 to 1984-85
Chuck Pilar 1985-86 to 1987-88

Kirk Louis 1988-89 to 1993-94
Scott Thurlow 1994-95 to 2003-04
Mike Bakker, 2004-05 to present

Ivan Williams
Long-time AD and namesake for
Fenton athletic stdium

Dr. Ken Wensel
Athletic Director, Principal

Ken Wegner
Athletic Director, Principal

Kirk Louis
Six-year tenure as AD followed
successful years as tennis and swim
coach

Scott Thurlow
LakeVille grad, ten years as Fenton
athletic director

Mark Suchowski
Principal since 2004

Peggy Yates
Principal, Superintendent

Mike Bakker
Longest-serving Fenton AD since
Tigers joined the Flint Metro League;
MIAAA regional AD of the Year 2010

Flushing High School Raiders
League Member 2014 to present

All Sports Championship: 1 (2014-15)

League Championships (* = shared):

Baseball	1 (2015)
Boys' Basketball	3 (2015-16, 16-17, 17-18*)
Girls' Basketball	4 (2014-15, 15-16, 16-17, 17-18)
Boys' Golf	2 (2015, 2016)
Girls' Cross Country	1 (2014)
Girls' Golf	2 (2014, 2015*)
Hockey	1 (2015-16*)
Boys' Track	2 (2016, 2018*)
Girls' Track	2 (2015, 2018*)
Volleyball	1 (2014-15)

MHSAA State Championship: Girls' Basketball 2016-17

Individual State Champions

Ben Cushman	2017	Wrestling (Division 1)
Breanna Perry	2017	Track & Field (Division 1) High Jump
Ben Cushman	2018	Wrestling (Division 1)

Athletic Directors:
Paul Brieger 2014 to 2017
Kevin Foltz 2017 to 2018

Paul Brieger

Athletic Director, oversaw Flushing's
transition to Flint Metro League; won
Metro's all-sports trophy in 2015,
state championship in girls'
basketball in 2017

Holly High School Bronchos
Charter Member: 1968 to Present

All Sports Championship: 1 (1993-94)

League Championships (* = shared):

Baseball	2 (1969-70, 2012-13*)	Boys' Soccer	1 (2010-11)
Boys' Basketball	5 (2000-01*, 03-04, 08-09*, 13-14, 14-15)	Softball	1 (2017*)
Girls' Basketball	4 (1980-81*, 83-84, 93-94*, 2013-14)	Boys' Swim/Dive	5 (2004-05 to 2009-10)
Boys' Bowling	2 (2008-09*, 09-10*)	Boys' Tennis	28 (1 shared)
Boys' Cross Country	18 (3 shared)	Girls' Tennis	34 (2 shared)
Girls' Cross Country	14 (6 shared)	Boys' Track	20 (5 shared)
Football	1 (2011-12*)	Girls' Track	8 (4 shared)
Boys' Golf	3 (1975-76, 06-07*, 07-08)	Volleyball	1 (1993-94*)
Hockey (KBH co-op)	2 (2011-12*, 14-15)	Wrestling	8 (1982-83, 91-92, 04-05, 06-07*, 10-11, 11-12, 12-13, 17-18)

MHSAA State Championships:

Boys' Track	1971
Boys' Cross Country	1977, 1978
Girls' Cross Country	1990

Individual State Champions

Mike Moses	1975	Track & Field (Class B) Long Jump
Ralph Smith	1975	Track & Field (Class B) High Jump
Jeff Lewis	1978	Track & Field (Class B) 880 Run
Matt Stack	1980	Cross Country (Team Race) Class A

Ed Lumm	1982	Track & Field (Class B) Pole Vault
Steve Yobuck	1987	Wrestling (Class A)
Stan Boyd	1989	Wrestling (Class A)
Justin Torres	1999	Wrestling (Division 2)
Rob Fiorillo	2004	Track & Field (Division 1) 110 Hurdles
Josh Houldsworth	2009	Wrestling (Division 1)
Jake Hyde	2009	Wrestling (Division 1)
Jonathon Beeler	2009	Track & Field (Division 1) High Jump
Anthony Gonzales	2010	Wrestling (Division 2)
Josh Houldsworth	2010	Wrestling (Division 2)
Jonathon Beeler	2010	Track & Field (Division 1) High Jump
Justin Gaumer	2010	Track & Field (Division 1) Discus
Anthony Gonzales	2012	Wrestling (Division 2)
Shawn Scott	2012	Wrestling (Division 2)
Andrew Anderson	2013	Bowling (Division 2)
Nicole Johnson	2018	Tennis (Division 2) #2 singles

Athletic Directors:

Elmer Rose 1968-69 to 1971-72
Bob Bloomer 1972-73 to ?
Leroy Millis ? to 1980-81
Pat Koeske (admin. Asst.)1981-82 to ?
Leroy Millis 1984-85 to 1991-92
Denise Barber 1992-93

Anne Doriean 1993-94
Mike Vanderlip 1994-95 to Jan. 1997
George Lovich (interim) Jan. to June 1997
Tim Dode, 1997-98 to 2001-02
Deb VanKuiken, 2002-03 to present

Elmer Rose

Leroy Millis

Tim Dode

As AD, led development of league's sportsmanship initiatives

Deb VanKuiken

AD tenure included receiving the MHSAA's Women in Sports Leadership Award, and work with numerous local, state and national athletic organizations; regional AD of the Year in 2005 and statewide AD of the Year in 2014

Dave Nuss

Principal, Superintendent

Kearsley High School Hornets
League Member 2008 to Present

League Championships (* = shared):

Baseball	1 (2008-09)	Boys' Golf	2 (2008-09, 09-10)
Boys' Bowling	6 (2009-10*, 10-11, 13-14, 14-15*, 16-17, 17-18)	Hockey	3 (2008-09; as KBH co-op: 2011-12*, 14-15)
		Softball	2 (2010-11*, 16-17*)
Girls' Bowling	9 (2009-10 to 17-18)	Boys' Track	1 (2014-15*)
Competitive Cheer	2 (2016-17, 17-18)	Wrestling	2 (2015-16, 16-17)

MHSAA State Championships:

Girls' Bowling	2012, 2014, 2015, 2016, 2017, 2018
Boys' Bowling	2014, 2015

State Runners-up:

Boys' Bowling	2016
Girls' Bowling	2010

Individual State Champions

Lindsay Ploof	2011	Bowling (Division 2)
Chad Stephen	2015	Bowling (Division 2)
Hannah Ploof	2016	Bowling (Division 2)

Athletic Director:
Paul Gaudard 2008 to 2018

Paul Gaudard
Athletic Director during Kearsley's move to and first ten years of membership; MIAAA regional AD of the Year 2011

LakeVille High School Falcons
League Member 1976 to 2002

League Championships (* = shared):

Baseball	1 (1990)	Girls' Track	10 (1985*, 1989 - 96, 1997*)
Girls' Cross Country	2 (1989, 1990)	Volleyball	4 (1987-88, 88-89, 93-94*, 94-95)
Football	2 (1978, 1979)		
Softball	1 (1997*)	Wrestling	3 (1987-88*, 92-93, 93-94*)
Boys' Track	6 (1980, 1992*, 1994 - 1997)		

MHSAA State Championships:
   Girls' Track   1991

State Runners-up:
   Girls' Track   1995

Individual State Champions:

Ed Brown	1979	Track & Field (Class B) 330 Hurdles
Brian Hittle	1980	Wrestling (Class B)
Jim Bailey	1986	Wrestling (Class B)
Karri Kuzma	1990	Track & Field (Class B) Shot Put
Laura Bell	1990	Track & Field (Class B) 3200 Run
Karri Kuzma	1991	Track & Field (Class B) Shot Put
Laura Bell	1991	Track & Field (Class B) 1600 Run
Scott Gavan	1992	Track & Field (Class B) Discus
Stan Marshall	1995	Wrestling (Class B)
Stan Marshall	1996	Wrestling (Division 2)
Terresha Derossett	1996	Track & Field (Class B) High Jump
Stan Marshall	1997	Wrestling (Division 2)
Terresha Derossett	1997	Track & Field (Class B) 110 Hurdles

Athletic Directors:

Darrel Morton 1976-77 to 1980-81
Lorna Kelly 1981-82 to 1997-98
Rod Studaker 1998-99
Ed Rodden 1999-2000 to 2000-01
Rod Studaker 2001-02

Darrell Morton
Athletic director from LakeVille's entry into Metro League until 1981, when a millage failure led to cancellation of athletics for one year

Lorna Kelly
17-year tenure as athletic director is tied for longest in Metro League

Lapeer High School Panthers
Charter Member: 1968 to 1975
(split into Lapeer West and Lapeer East in 1975, West students attended former Lapeer HS building and competed as "Lapeer West")

League Championships:

Boys' Cross Country	3 (1972, 1974, 1975)	Boys' Golf	1 (1971)
Football	2 (1968, 1974)	Boys' Tennis	2 (1973, 1974)

MHSAA State Championship:

Boys' Tennis   1971 (prior to Boys' Tennis becoming an official league sport)

Athletic Director:

Jack Fitzpatrick 1968-69 to 1976-77

Henry Smith
Principal

Jack Fitzpatrick
Athletic Director

Lapeer East High School Eagles
League Member 1976 to 2014

All Sports Championships: 3 (1992-93, 1994-95, 1999-2000)

League Championships (* = shared):

Baseball	7 (1981, 82, 84, 85*, 2010, 11, 12)	Hockey	2 (1989-90, 2013-14* as co-op)
Boys' Basketball	14 (1978-79*, 79-80, 80-81, 81-82, 83-84, 90-91, 92-93, 94-95*, 97-98, 1999-2000, 01-02, 02-03, 04-05*, 07-08)	Boys' Soccer	2 (2007, 2011)
		Girls' Soccer	16 (1990 to 2000, four shared; 2002*, 06, 07, 09, 11*)
		Softball	1 (1999*)
		Boys' Tennis	1 (1993)
Girls' Basketball	10 (1985, 86*, 90, 91*, 92, 93*, 94, 95, 96, 97*)	Girls' Tennis	1 (1977*)
		Boys' Track	2 (1999, 2000)
		Volleyball	10 (76-77*, 80-81, 81-82*, 95-96, 96-97*, 99-00*, 2000-01, 03-04, 04-05, 05-06*)
Boys' Bowling	1 (2011*)		
Girls' Cross Country	2 (1995*, 1997)		
Football	2 (2004, 2011*)		
Boys' Golf	2 (1980*, 1984)		

Individual State Champions:

Justin Joseph	2006	Wrestling (Division 2)
Phillip Joseph	2009	Wrestling (Division 2)

Athletic Directors:
Bill DesJardins, 1975-76 to 1982-83; district-wide AD 1980 to 2001
Dave Rowe, 1983-84 to 1985-86
Gary Oyster, 1986-87 to 2002-03

Mike Butterfield, 2003-04 (also district athletic coordinator)
Jack Lindell 2004-05 to 2007-08
Sharon Miller, 2008-09 to 2012-13
Brian Shelson, 2013-14

Barrie Fell

First Lapeer East Principal 1975-1988

Bill DesJardins

First Athletic Director for Lapeer East; Served over 20 years as Lapeer's district-wide director of athletics

Mike Linton

Principal 1988-2001
Later Superintendent for Central Lake schools

Gary Oyster

Athletic Director at Lapeer East for 17 years (tied for longest AD tenure in league); MIAAA regional AD of the Year 2004

Lapeer West High School Panthers
League Member 1975 to 2014
(1975-76 Included All 12th Graders in District)

All Sports Championship: 1 (1996-97)

League Championships (* = shared):

Baseball	8 (1991, 92, 93*, 96, 2001*, 03, 04, 05*)	Girls' Golf	1 (2009)
Boys' Basketball	6 (1984-85, 86-87, 96-97, 2000-01*, 04-05*, 06-07)	Hockey	4 (1990-91, 2002-03, 03-04, 13-14* as co-op)
		Boys' Soccer	4 (1997-98, 98-99*, 1999-2000, 12-13)
Girls' Basketball	2 (2005-06*, 11-12)	Girls' Soccer	1 (2011-12)
Competitive Cheer	3 (2004-05, 05-06, 06-07)	Softball	11 (1987 to 91, 2003*, 04, 05, 08, 09, 11*)
Football	8 (1995, 96, 97, 2000*, 01, 03, 07*, 14*)	Boys' Tennis	1 (1999*)
		Girls' Tennis	2 (1979, 80)
		Boys' Track	1 (1998)
Boys' Golf	5 (1976, 88, 96, 2000, 03)	Volleyball	1 (2005-06*)
		Wrestling	5 (1999-2000 to 03-04)

MHSAA State Championships:

Football	1995
Wrestling	2000, 2001

State Runners-up:

Baseball	1992, 2002
Wrestling	2003
Boys' Bowling	2013

Individual State Champions:

Shelly Dagley	1979	Track & Field (Class B) Shot Put
Chris Boehmer	1980	Track & Field (Class B) Long Jump
Chris Boehmer	1982	Track & Field (Class A) Long Jump

Monica Rincon	1997	Tennis (Division 2)
Rory Medina	2000	Wrestling (Division 2)
James Kish	2000	Wrestling (Division 2)
Roger Kish	2000	Wrestling (Division 2)
Jason Fellows	2001	Wrestling (Division 2)
James Kish	2001	Wrestling (Division 2)
Roger Kish	2001	Wrestling (Division 2)
Roger Kish	2002	Wrestling (Division 2)
Justin Chrzanowski	2003	Wrestling (Division 2)
Roger Kish	2003	Wrestling (Division 2)
Justin Chrzanowski	2004	Wrestling (Division 2)

Athletic Directors:

Jack Fitzpatrick to 1976-77
Bob Keefe 1977-78 to 1979-80
Bill DesJardins (district-wide AD) 1980-1983
Dennis Jager 1983 to 1986
Bill Townsend 1986 to 1994
Ray Miller 1994-95 to 1996-97
Dick Valentine, 1997-98 to Dec. 2000

Mike Smith, Jan. 2001 to 2003-04
Rob Belous, 2004-05
Tim Zeeman, 2005-06 to 2008-09
Mary Haslinger, 2009-10 to 2011-12
Aaron Shinn, 2012-13 to 2013-14

Jack Fitzpatrick

Bill Townsend

Tim Zeeman

Linden High School Eagles
League Member 1983 to Present

League Championships (* = shared):

Baseball	5 (1986, 87, 2014*, 16, 18*)	Boys' Golf	4 (1993, 97, 98, 99)
Boys' Basketball	4 (1991-92, 93-94, 94-95*, 95-96)	Girls' Golf	7 (2002 to 05, 2006-07, 07-08, 08-09)
Girls' Basketball	1 (2003-04)	Hockey	11 (1988-89, 1992-93 to 2001-02, shared in 98-99)
Boys' Cross Country	9 (1990, 91, 97*, 2007-08, 08-09, 09-10, 10-11*, 11-12, 12-13)	Girls' Lacrosse	3 (co-op with Fenton)
		Boys' Soccer	6 (2000, 2003*, 04, 05, 14, 15)
Girls' Cross Country	9 (1992-93, 93-94*, 2003-04, 07-08, 09-10*, 10-11, 12-13, 13-14, 15-16)	Girls' Soccer	7 (2001, 02*, 03, 04, 10, 14, 15)
		Softball	1 (1998)
		Boys' Track	3 (2001, 04*, 13*)
Football	8 (1986*, 2002, 05, 06, 08*, 09, 10, 12*)	Girls' Track	1 (2003)
		Wrestling	1 (2005-06)

MHSAA State Championships:

Boys' Cross Country   2008

State Runners-up:

Baseball	2004, 2016
Boys' Cross Country	2012

Individual State Champions:

Amy Warner	1987	Track & Field (Class B) High Jump
Corey Kalo	1994	Wrestling (Class B)
Ryan Norman, Jordan Norman, Jeff Krause, Matt Keenan		
	2003	Track & Field (Division 2) 800 Relay

Missy Ward	2004	Golf (Division 1)

Jack Hord, Kyle LeMieux, Dylan Ryan, Brendan Sage   2009 Track & Field (Division 2) 3200 Relay

Athletic Directors:

Joe Piwowarczyk 1982-83 to 1993
Pete Maas 1993 to 1995-966
Robyn Deighton 1996-1997
Francie Novar, 1997-98 to 1998-99
Jim Robinson, 1999-March 2000
Brian Boudreau March to June 2000
Jon Chapman, 2000-01 to 2002-03

Russ Ciesielski, 2003-04 to 2004-05
Darin Dreasky, 2005-06 to 2006-07
Kraig Enders, 2007-08
Dallas Lintner, 2008-09
Cathy North, 2009-10 to 2015-16
Greg Durkac, 2016-17 to

Joe Piwowarczyk

Cathy North

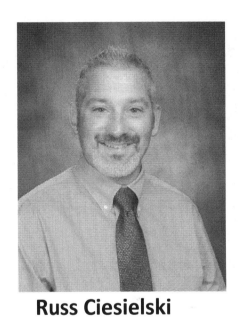

Russ Ciesielski

The only individual
with experience as a
Flint Metro League
athlete, coach, athletic
director, principal and
superintendent
(all at Linden)

Mt. Morris High School Panthers
(Elizabeth Ann Johnson HS)
League Member 1972 to 2002

League Championships (* = shared):

Baseball	6 (1979*, 80, 88, 93*, 94, 95)	Boys' Golf	2 (1989, 90)
		Softball	4 (1981, 83*, 84*, 85)
Boys' Basketball	1 (1994-95*)	Volleyball	2 (1979-80, 82-83*)
Girls' Basketball	1 (1977)	Wrestling	4 (1986-87*, 90-91, 95-96, 96-97)
Football	1 (1988-89)		

MHSAA State Championship:
Softball   1984

Individual State Champions:

Ron Gamble, Shelton Pinnix, Tim Tucker, Don Gamble	1973	Track & Field (Class B) 440 Relay
Mike Anderson	1986	Wrestling (Class B)
Mike Anderson	1987	Wrestling (Class B)
Tony Holifield	1997	Wrestling (Division 2)
Tony Holifield	1998	Wrestling (Division 2)
Frank Garofalo	1998	Track & Field (Class B) Discus

Athletic Directors:

Don Koleber 1972-73 to 1973-74	John Burtrum 1982-83 to 1988-89
Phil Taylor 1974-75 to 1976-77	John Sekenger 1989-90 to 1990-91
Paul Street 1977-78 to 1978-79	Rich Burdis Dec. 1991 to 1997-98
Kevin White 1979-80 to 1980-81	Doug Fillmore 1997-98 to 1999-2000
Ed Broillet 1981-82	Jack Lindell 2000-01 to 2001-02

Don Kolebar

AD for Mt. Morris's first two years in
Flint Metro League

Rich Burdis

Received 2004 MHSAA Allen W. Bush
Award for athletic leadership at
Mt. Morris and Flushing; MIAAA
regional AD of the Year 2000

Lisa Hagel

Mt. Morris Principal and Superintendent
Became superintendent of Genesee Intermediate Schools in 2010

Owosso High School Trojans
Joined League in 2017-18

Athletic Director:
Dr. Dallas Lintner

Brad Van Pelt

Owosso's best-known athlete with stellar 3-sport high school & college career, seven varsity letters at MSU and 5 Pro Bowls with NY Giants football

JoEllen Smith

Winningest softball coach in greater Flint area, with over 730 wins through 2018

Dr. Dallas Lintner

As AD, led Owosso's transition to the Flint Metro League

Oxford High School Wildcats
League Member 1983 to 2010

All Sports Championships: 3 (2000-01, 2001-02, 2002-03)

League Championships (* = shared):

Baseball	4 (1998, 2002, 07, 08*)	Football	12 (1986*, 89*, 91 to 95, 98*, 99, 2000*, 07*, 08*)
Girls' Basketball	9 (1986*, 87, 88, 89, 91*, 97*, 99, 2000, 01)	Boys' Golf	2 (2001, 02)
		Boys' Soccer	12 (1986 to 93, 95, 96, 98*, 2006)
Boys' Bowling	1 (2008-09*)	Girls' Soccer	2 (1989, 96*)
Girls' Bowling	1 (2008-09)	Softball	1 (2010)
Competitive Cheer	1 (2003-04)	Boys' Track	5 (1984, 87, 88*, 91, 93)
Boys' Cross Country	9 (1992, 94*, 97*, 98, 99, 2000, 01, 02, 03*)	Girls' Track	9 (1984, 87*, 88, 97*, 2001, 02*, 08, 09*, 10)
Girls' Cross Country	5 (1983, 84, 88, 2000, 10*)	Volleyball	4 (1996-97*, 2002, 03, 08)
		Wrestling	5 (1998-99, 2006-07*, 07-08, 08-09, 09-10)

MHSAA State Championships:

Boys' Track	1991
Football	1992

State Runners-up:

Football	1990, 1993
Wrestling	2009

Individual State Champions:

Mike Goodfellow	1987	Cross Country (Individual Race) Class B
Cari Byrd	1988	Track & Field (Class B) 800 Run
Mike Goodfellow	1988	Cross Country (Individual Race) Class B

Mike Goodfellow	1989	Track & Field (Class B) 1600 and 3200 Run
Vidal Fragoso, Kniffen, Derney, Erik Welch	1990	Track & Field (Class B) 1600 Relay
Vidal Fragoso, Steve McCracken, Cliff Wells, Erik Welch	1991	Track & Field (Class B) 800 Relay
Mark Goodfellow, Kurt Stephenson, Vidal Fragoso, Erik Welch	1991	Track & Field (Class B) 3200 Relay
Erik Welch	1991	Track & Field (Class B) 400 dash
Mark Goodfellow	1993	Track & Field (Class B) 1600 run
Eric Ghiaciuc	2000	Wrestling (Division 2)
Willie Breyer	2001	Wrestling (Division 2)
Tim Breyer	2003	Wrestling (Division 2)
Tony Lyssiotis	2003	Wrestling (Division 2)
Dylan Smith	2009	Wrestling (Division 2)

Athletic Directors:

Lee Noftz, 1983 to 1991-1992
John Voorheis 1992-93
Don Maskill, 1993-94 to 1997-98

Pat Ball, 1998-99 to 2008-09
Mike Watson, 2009-10

Lee Noftz

Don Maskill

Pat Ball

MIAAA regional AD of
the Year 2009

Swartz Creek High School Dragons
Charter Member: 1968 to 1976; 2006 to Present

League Championships (* = shared):

Boys' Basketball	5 (1971-72, 73-74, 74-75*, 2009-10*, 17-18*)	Hockey	5 (2007-08, 10-11; as co-op: 11-12*, 12-13*, 15-16*)
Girls' Basketball	1 (2006)	Girls' Soccer	1 (2017)
Boys' Bowling	4 (2011-12*, 12-13, 13-14*, 15-16)	Softball	3 (2012, 13, 18)
		Boys' Swim/Dive	1 (1972-73)
Girls' Cross Country	1 (2008*)	Boys' Track	6 (1974*, 75*, 76, 2007, 10, 12)
Football	2 (1970*, 72*)		
Boys' Golf	4 (2006*, 11, 12*, 14)	Girls' Track	4 (1969-1972)
Girls' Golf	2 (2010, 12)	Wrestling	3 (1969-70, 73-74, 75-76)

MHSAA State Championship:

Boys' Golf   2014

MHSAA State Runners-up:

Wrestling   1972

Individual State Champions:

Brad Tucker	1972	Wrestling (Class A)
Mark Whaley	1973	Wrestling (Class A)
Dave Priest	2007	Wrestling (Division 2)
Kevin Weiler	2012	Track & Field (Division 1) Shot Put
Jackson Maxwell	2014	Swim/Dive (Division 2) Diving
Kevin Weiler	2014	Track & Field (Division 1) Shot Put and Discus

Athletic Directors:

Dave Kittell   1968 to ?   Sue Calvo   2006-07   to present
Jim Stableford   ? to 1976

Dave Kittell   **James Stableford**   **Sue Calvo**
MIAAA regional AD of
the Year 2013

SPORTS

SPORTS SPONSORED BY THE FLINT METRO LEAGUE

To be considered an official sport of the Flint Metro League, a majority of the member schools must sponsor the sport and the MHSAA must hold a championship tournament in that sport. The following is a list of league sports and the years the league has sponsored each one:

Baseball	1968-69 to present
Boys' Basketball	1968-69 to present
Girls' Basketball	1968-69 to present
Boys' Bowling	2008-09 to present
Girls' Bowling	2008-09 to present
Competitive Cheer	2003-04 to present
Boys' Cross Country	1968-69 to present
Girls' Cross Country	1981-82 to 1984-85; 1987-88 to present
Football	1968-69 to present
Boys' Golf	1968-69 to present
Girls' Golf	2001-02 to present
Hockey	1978-79 to 2015-16
Girls' Lacrosse	2015-16 to present
Boys' Soccer	1986-87 to present
Girls' Soccer	1987-88 to present
Softball	1972-73 to present
Boys' Swim/Dive	1970-71 to 1975-76; 2004-05 to present
Girls' Swim/Dive	2004-05 to present
Boys' Tennis	1972-73 to present
Girls' Tennis	1977-78 to present
Boys' Track	1968-69 to present
Girls' Track	1968-69 to present
Volleyball	1976-77 to present
Wrestling	1968-69 to present

FLINT METRO LEAGUE BASEBALL CHAMPIONS

1969	Carman	1994	Mt. Morris
1970	Holly	1995	Mt. Morris
1971	Carman	1996	Lapeer West
1972	Ainsworth	1997	Fenton
1973	Carman	1998	Oxford
1974	Carman	1999	Fenton
1975	Fenton	2000	Fenton
1976	Carman	2001	Fenton, Lapeer West
1977	Ainsworth	2002	Oxford
1978	Fenton	2003	Lapeer West
1979	Durand, Fenton, Mt. Morris	2004	Lapeer West
1980	Mt. Morris	2005	Fenton, Lapeer West
1981	Lapeer East	2006	Clio
1982	Lapeer East	2007	Oxford
1983	Durand	2008	Clio, Oxford
1984	Lapeer East	2009	Kearsley
1985	Ainsworth, Fenton, Lapeer East	2010	Lapeer East
1986	Linden	2011	Lapeer East
1987	Linden	2012	Lapeer East
1988	Mt. Morris	2013	Clio, Holly
1989	Durand	2014	Brandon, Linden
1990	LakeVille	2015	Flushing
1991	Lapeer West	2016	Linden
1992	Lapeer West	2017	Fenton
1993	Lapeer West, Mt. Morris	2018	Fenton, Linden

MHSAA State Runners-up:

Fenton, 1985 Class B

Fenton, 1989 Class B

Lapeer West, 1992 Class A

Lapeer West, 2002 Division 2

Linden, 2004 Division 2

Linden, 2016 Division 2

Four-time First Team All-League

Mike Carson, Lapeer East	2006-09

Three-time First Team All-League

Mitch King, Lapeer East	1979-81	Tom McCarter, Lapeer East	2010-12
Scott McNiel, Ainsworth	1984-86	Jack Hranec, Brandon	2011-13
David Dodge, Mt. Morris	1991-93	Joel Perry, Holly	2012-14
Will Jostock, Lapeer West	2002-04	Austin Buerkel, Linden	2013-15
Ryan Pender, Lapeer East	2003-05	Jim Ziobro, Clio	2013-15
Jeremy Bukowski, Oxford	2005-07	Chase Coselman, Fenton	2015-17
Chad Carson, Lapeer East	2010-12	Tyler Randick, Flushing	2015-17

Larry Lamphere, Durand
Inducted in CMU Hall of Fame;
Drafted by Houston Astros, played as
high as AA level;
Athletic Director career included
Lapeer, Brandon and Clio

Scott Winterlee, Mt. Morris
First team All-Metro in three sports;
Univ. of Michigan starting shortstop
for 3 years, MVP 1991, NCAA 3rd team
All-American 1992

Brandon Reed, Lapeer West
Drafted by Detroit Tigers;
Pitched AAA for Tigers & Yankees

Mike Carson, Lapeer East
Only 4-time First Team All-Metro
League baseball player

FLINT METRO LEAGUE BOYS BASKETBALL CHAMPIONS

1969	Ainsworth		1995	Lapeer East, Linden and Mt. Morris
1970	Ainsworth and Fenton		1996	Linden
1971	Carman		1997	Lapeer West
1972	Swartz Creek		1998	Lapeer East
1973	Carman		1999	Fenton
1974	Swartz Creek		2000	Lapeer East
1975	Fenton and Swartz Creek		2001	Holly and Lapeer West
1976	Fenton		2002	Lapeer East
1977	Fenton		2003	Lapeer East
1978	Fenton		2004	Holly
1979	Durand, Fenton and Lapeer East		2005	Lapeer East and Lapeer West
1980	Lapeer East		2006	Brandon
1981	Lapeer East		2007	Lapeer West
1982	Lapeer East		2008	Lapeer East
1983	Durand and Fenton		2009	Fenton and Holly
1984	Lapeer East		2010	Fenton and Swartz Creek
1985	Lapeer West		2011	Fenton
1986	Durand		2012	Fenton
1987	Lapeer West		2013	Fenton
1988	Fenton		2014	Holly
1989	Fenton		2015	Holly
1990	Fenton		2016	Flushing
1991	Lapeer East		2017	Flushing
1992	Linden		2018	Flushing & Swartz Creek
1993	Lapeer East			
1994	Linden			

Three-time First Team All-League

Darby Decker, Fenton   1975-77

Dylan Hickoff, Fenton   2010-12

Scored 1,000+ Career Points

Cullen Turczyn, Lap. East/West	2009-13	1,358		Dustin DeShais, Brandon	2006-09	1,087
Doug Shepherd, Holly	1991-94	1,198		Paul Adas, Kearsley	2008-12	1,049
Brandon Fisher, Lapeer East	1991-93	1,195		Jon Champagne, Linden	1993-96	1,048
Kyle Woodruff, Holly	2012-16	1,175		Scott Timmons, Lap. East	1977-80	1,034
Scott Winterlee, Mt. Morris	1986-89	1,133		Tim Zeeman, Swartz Ck.	1972-75	1,024
Ryan Hickoff, Fenton	2008-12	1,108		Dylan Hickoff, Fenton	2008-12	1,001

Tim Zeeman, Swartz Creek
1973-75: First career 1,000 pt. scorer
in league games

Darby Decker, Fenton
Played on three league champions:
1975-77
First 3-time 1st Team All-Metro
League boys' basketball player

Brandon Fisher, Lapeer East
Three of top four best scoring games
(48, 47 and 43 points)
1,195 career points in league games:
1991-93

Doug Shepherd, Holly
Second on career scoring list with
1,198 points in league games
1992-94

Dylan & Ryan Hickoff,
Fenton
2009-12
Dylan: Second 3-time First Team All-Metro boys' basketball player; 1,001 career points in league games
Ryan: 1,108 career points in league games

Cullen Turczyn
Lapeer East 2009-10
Lapeer West 2010-13
All-time career scoring leader with 1,358 points in league games

FLINT METRO LEAGUE GIRLS BASKETBALL CHAMPIONS

1968-69	Ainsworth	1993-94	Holly and Lapeer East
1969-70	Ainsworth	1994-95	Lapeer East
1970-71	Ainsworth	1995-96	Lapeer East
1971-72	Ainsworth	1996-97	Lapeer East
1972-73	Ainsworth	1997-98	Lapeer East and Oxford
1973-74	Carman	1998-99	Fenton
1974-75	Ainsworth & Carman	1999-2000	Oxford
1975-76	Carman	2000-01	Oxford
1976-77	Fenton	2001-02	Oxford
1977-78	Mt. Morris	2002-03	Brandon
1978-79	Fenton	2003-04	Linden
1979-80	Fenton	2004-05	Fenton
1980-81	Fenton and Holly	2005-06	Fenton and Lapeer West
1981-82	Fenton	2006-07	Swartz Creek
1982-83	Fenton	2007-08	Fenton
1983-84	Holly	2008-09	Fenton
1984-85	Fenton	2009-10	Fenton
1985-86	Lapeer East	2010-11	Clio
1986-87	Lapeer East and Oxford	2011-12	Lapeer West
1987-88	Oxford	2012-13	Clio
1988-89	Oxford	2013-14	Holly
1989-90	Oxford	2014-15	Flushing
1990-91	Lapeer East	2015-16	Flushing
1991-92	Lapeer East and Oxford	2016-17	Flushing
1992-93	Lapeer East	2017-18	Flushing

MHSAA State Champions: Flushing   2017   Class A

MHSAA State Runners-up: Fenton   1982   Class B

Four-time First Team All-League
Christina Rivette, Fenton   2005-09   Gabrielle Rivette, Fenton   2008-11

Three-time First Team All-League

Sue Williams, Ainsworth	1976-78	Alyssa Copley, Holly	2012-14
Dru Bishop, Fenton	1996-98	Kaitlyn Smith, Holly	2014-16
Payge Salquist, Oxford	1999-2000	Jacara Thompson, Sw. Creek	2015-17
Savannah Stedman, Brandon	2004-06	Lauren Newman, Flushing	2015-17
Marisa Liburdi, Lapeer West	2010-12	Chloe Idoni, Fenton	2016-18
Breanna Pennington, Clio	2011-13		(9th to 11th grade)

Roz VanGuilder, Oxford
1984-86
1,256 career points in league games;
38-point game in 1986

Amanda Behrenbrinker,
Lapeer East
1991-93
1,179 career points in league games;
36- and 34-point games in 1993

Jenny White, Oxford
1994-97
1,188 career points in league games;
40 points in 1997 game, also had 35-
and 31-point games that year

Dru Bishop, Fenton
1995-98
1,182 career points in league games
3-time first team all-league

Katie Moore, Clio
2005-09
1,079 career points in league games;
36- and 31-point games

Christina Rivette, Fenton
2005-09
All-time career leader with 1,439
points in league games; 4-time first
team all-league

Gabrielle Rivette, Fenton
2007-11
1,140 career points in league games;
4-time first team all-league

Kaitlyn Smith, Holly
2012-16
1,243 career points in league games

Jacara Thompson, Sw. Creek
2015-17
1,241 career points in league games

Chloe Idoni, Fenton
2015-
First team all-league in 9th, 10th and
11th grade, over 1,000 career points

FLINT METRO LEAGUE BOYS BOWLING CHAMPIONS

2009	Holly and Oxford	2014	Kearsley
2010	Holly and Kearsley	2015	Brandon, Kearsley and
2011	Kearsley		Swartz Creek
2012	Lapeer East and Swartz	2016	Swartz Creek
	Creek	2017	Kearsley
2013	Swartz Creek	2018	Kearsley

MHSAA State Champions: Kearsley 2014, 2015

MHSAA State Runners-up:

Lapeer West   2014   Kearsley   2016

MHSAA Individual State Champions

Andrew Anderson, Holly   2013   Chad Stephen, Kearsley   2015

Andrew Anderson, Holly

State Champion, 2013
Bowled first perfect
300 game in league
competition

Chase Kaufman, Swartz Creek

Only three-time All-
Metro 1st team boys'
bowler

Chad Stephen, Kearsley

State Individual
Champion, 2015

FLINT METRO LEAGUE GIRLS BOWLING CHAMPIONS

2009	Oxford		2014	Kearsley
2010	Kearsley		2015	Kearsley
2011	Kearsley		2016	Kearsley
2012	Kearsley		2017	Kearsley
2013	Kearsley		2018	Kearsley

MHSAA State Champions: Kearsley 2012, 2014-18

MHSAA State Runners-up: Kearsley 2010

MHSAA Individual State Champions

Lindsey Ploof, Kearsley	2011	Hannah Ploof, Kearsley	2016

Four-time First Team All-League

Hannah Ploof, Kearsley   2013-16

Three-time First Team All-League

Lindsey Ploof, Kearsley	2010-12	Alexis Roof, Kearsley	2016-18
Barbara Hawes, Kearsley	2016-18		

Lindsey Ploof, Kearsley

State Individual Champion 2011;
3-time All-Metro first team selection

Hannah Ploof, Kearsley

State Individual Champion 2016;
Only 4-time All-Metro first team
selection

Alexis Roof, Kearsley

3-time All-Metro first team selection

Barbara Hawes, Kearsley

3-time All-Metro first team selection

FLINT METRO LEAGUE COMPETITIVE CHEER CHAMPIONS

2004	Oxford	2012	Brandon
2005	Lapeer West	2013	Brandon
2006	Lapeer West	2014	Brandon
2007	Lapeer West	2015	Brandon
2008	Brandon	2016	Brandon
2009	Brandon	2017	Kearsley
2010	Brandon	2018	Kearsley
2011	Brandon		

Sierra Coughlin, Brandon

Four-time All-Metro League 1st team cheerleader 2013-16

McKayla Launius, Clio

Four-time All-Metro League 1st team cheerleader 2015-18

Hailey Baltosser, Kearsley

Four-time All-Metro League cheerleader; 2nd team 2014 1st team 2015-17

FLINT METRO LEAGUE BOYS CROSS COUNTRY CHAMPIONS

1968	Fenton	1993	Holly
1969	Fenton	1994	Holly and Oxford
1970	Fenton	1995	Holly
1971	Carman	1996	Holly
1972	Lapeer	1997	Oxford and Linden
1973	Holly	1998	Oxford
1974	Lapeer	1999	Oxford
1975	Lapeer West	2000	Oxford
1976	Ainsworth and Holly	2001	Oxford
1977	Holly	2002	Oxford
1978	Holly	2003	Fenton and Oxford
1979	Ainsworth	2004	Fenton
1980	Holly	2005	Fenton
1981	Ainsworth and Holly	2006	Fenton
1982	Ainsworth	2007	Linden
1983	Holly	2008	Linden
1984	Holly	2009	Linden
1985	Holly	2010	Fenton and Linden
1986	Holly	2011	Linden
1987	Durand	2012	Linden
1988	Holly	2013	Holly
1989	Holly	2014	Holly
1990	Linden	2015	Clio
1991	Linden	2016	Fenton
1992	Oxford	2017	Fenton

MHSAA State Champions: Holly (Class B) 1977 1978   Linden (Div. 2) 2008

MHSAA State Runners-up: Fenton (Class B) 1970   Linden (Div. 2) 2012

Three-time Individual League Champions
Don Keswick, Fenton   1968-70   Donnie Richmond, Oxford   2001-03
Mike Goodfellow, Oxford   1986-88
MHSAA Individual State Champions
Matt Stack   Holly   1980   Class A team race
Mike Goodfellow   Oxford   1987, 1988   Class B individual race

Don Keswick, Fenton
League Champion 1968-70

Mike Goodfellow, Oxford
League Champion 1986-88
State Champion 1987-88

Matt Stack, Holly
State Champion 1980
League Champion 1979-80

Donnie Richmond, Oxford
League Champion 2001-03

FLINT METRO LEAGUE GIRLS CROSS COUNTRY CHAMPIONS

1981	Holly	2000	Oxford
1982	Ainsworth	2001	Holly
1983	Oxford	2002	Fenton and Holly
1984	Oxford	2003	Linden
1985	Not a league sport	2004	Brandon
1986	Not a league sport	2005	Brandon
1987	Holly	2006	Brandon and Holly
1988	Oxford	2007	Linden
1989	LakeVille	2008	Holly and Swartz Creek
1990	LakeVille	2009	Holly, Linden and Oxford
1991	Holly	2010	Linden
1992	Linden	2011	Holly
1993	Holly and Linden	2012	Linden
1994	Holly	2013	Linden
1995	Holly and Lapeer East	2014	Flushing
1996	Durand	2015	Linden
1997	Lapeer East	2016	Fenton
1998	Holly	2017	Fenton
1999	Holly		

MHSAA State Champions: Holly (Class A) 1990

Four-time Individual League Champions
Jackie Bucholz, Holly	1993-96
Rachel Gutierrez, Linden	2000-03

Three-time Individual League Champions
Laura Bell, LakeVille	1988-90
Sydney Elmer, Linden	2011-13

Laura Bell, LakeVille
League Champion 1988-90

Rachel Gutierrez, Linden
League Champion 2000-03

Jackie Bucholz, Holly
League Champion 1993-96

Sydney Elmer, Linden
League Champion 2011-13

FLINT METRO LEAGUE FOOTBALL CHAMPIONS

1968	Lapeer	1993	Oxford
1969	Carman	1994	Oxford
1970	Carman and Swartz Creek	1995	Lapeer West
		1996	Lapeer West
1971	Carman	1997	Lapeer West
1972	Carman, Fenton and Swartz Creek	1998	Fenton and Oxford
		1999	Oxford
1973	Carman	2000	Lapeer West and Oxford
1974	Lapeer	2001	Lapeer West
1975	Ainsworth	2002	Linden
1976	Ainsworth	2003	Lapeer West
1977	Ainsworth and Fenton	2004	Lapeer East
1978	LakeVille	2005	Linden
1979	LakeVille	2006	Linden
1980	Ainsworth	2007	Lapeer West and Oxford
1981	Ainsworth and Durand	2008	Fenton, Linden and Oxford
1982	Durand		
1983	Durand and Fenton	2009	Linden
1984	Fenton	2010	Linden
1985	Fenton	2011	Fenton, Holly and Lapeer East
1986	Oxford and Linden		
1987	Fenton	2012	Fenton and Linden
1988	Mt. Morris	2013	Fenton and Lapeer West
1989	Fenton, Lapeer West and Oxford	2014	Fenton
		2015	Fenton
1990	Oxford	2016	Fenton
1991	Oxford	2017	Fenton
1992	Oxford		

MHSAA State Champions: Oxford (Class BB) 1992   Lapeer West (Class A) 1995
MHSAA State Runners-up: Oxford (Class BB) 1990 1993

Three-year First Team All-League

Ed Rykulski, Carman	1971-73		Roger Kish, Lapeer West	2000-02
Lloyd McClelland, Ainsworth	1975-77		Tim North, Linden	2002-04
Tim Pierce, Durand	1983-85		Tyler Hamilton, Fenton	2007-09
Carl Reaves, Oxford	1990-92		Preston Haggadone, Lap. West	2007-09
Eric Raab, Oxford	1992-94		Cody Marks, Linden	2007-09
Matt Green, Oxford	1994-96		Josh Czarnota, Fenton	2015-17
Doug Kress, Lapeer West	1999-01		Cade Dickson, Linden	2015-17
Jason Edwards, Linden	2000-02			

Flint Metro League Alumni with Significant Football Careers

**Kemp Rasmussen,
Lapeer West**
Indiana University
Carolina Panthers 4 seasons
Played in Super Bowl XXXVIII

**Glen Pakulak,
Lapeer East**
University of Kentucky
NCAA All-American Punter
2002 Mosi Tatupu Award & Ray Guy
Finalist

**Eric Ghiaciauc,
Oxford**
Central Michigan University
Drafted in 4th round
Cincinnati Bengals 4 seasons

87

Dave Rayner,
Oxford
Michigan State University
All-time scoring leader upon graduation
6th round draft choice by Indianapolis
PK for 11 NFL teams

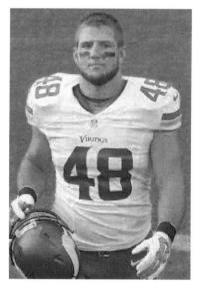

Zach Line,
Oxford
Southern Methodist University
1,000-yard rusher in three seasons
Minnesota Vikings and New Orleans Saints

Jake Long,
Lapeer East
University of Michigan
All-American Offensive Tackle
First Draft Choice in 2008 NFL Draft
Selected for 4 Pro Bowls with Miami

FOOTBALL TEAM RECORDS

Most consecutive victories:
43 – Oxford, 1989-1994 (Lost 24-14 to Lapeer West on Sept. 29, 1989 and lost 21-6 to Mt. Morris on Sept. 1, 1995)

Most consecutive home victories:
25 – Oxford, 1988-94 (ended in 21-6 loss to Mt. Morris on Sept. 1, 1995)

Most consecutive road victories:
27 – Oxford, 1989-96 (Began with 13-6 win at Fenton on Oct. 20, 1989, ended with 14-7 loss at Linden on Oct. 4, 1996)

Most points in game by one team:
77 – Swartz Creek 77, Kearsley 61 (Sept. 13, 2013)

Most points in game by two teams:
138 -- Swartz Creek 77, Kearsley 61 (Sept. 13, 2013)

Fewest points in game by two teams:
0 – Holly 0, Carman 0 (Nov. 1, 1968)
0 – Lapeer 0, Fenton 0 (Oct. 29, 1971)
   Note: Ainsworth beat Mt. Morris 7-0 in overtime on Oct. 18, 1985 and Lapeer West beat Holly 6-3 in double overtime after 0-0 through four quarters on Sept. 3, 1993.

Most points scored in season:
393 – Linden, 2009 (9 games)

Fewest points allowed in season:
21 – Lapeer, 1974 (6 games)

Most shutouts in season:
5 – Linden, 2005 (7 games)

Most consecutive games without being shut out:
119 – Oxford, 1985-2001

Most consecutive shutouts:
4 – Linden, 1986; Lapeer West, 2001; Linden, 2005

Most consecutive shutout quarters:
19 – Lapeer West, 2001

Most points in one half by two teams:
81 – Swartz Creek 56, Kearsley 25 at halftime, Sept. 13, 2013

Most points in one quarter by two teams:
56 – Fenton 42, Flushing 14 in second quarter, Oct. 17, 2014

Most rushing yards in game by one team:
557 – Lapeer West vs. Holly, Oct. 20, 1989 (58 att.)

Most passing yards in game by one team:
606 – Swartz Creek vs. Kearsley, Sept. 13, 2013 (Brendon Fitch 606)

Most total yards in game by one team:
836 – Swartz Creek (233 rush, 603 pass) vs. Kearsley, Sept. 13, 2013

Most total yards in game by two teams:
1,587 – Swartz Creek 836, Kearsley 751, Sept. 13, 2013

Most rushing yards in game by two teams:
767 – LakeVille 514, Holly 253, Oct. 25, 1996

Most 100-yard rushers in game:
3 – Ainsworth vs. Swartz Creek, Oct. 17, 1975 (Marty Halverson 146, Mark Reaves 127, Tim Zamora 102)
3 – Mt. Morris vs. Holly, Sept. 19, 1980 (Jim Larkin 8-129, Mike Robinson 5-109, Steve Goff 14-102)
3 – Lapeer West vs. Holly, Oct. 20, 1989 (Mike Currie 22-166, Nate Miller 14-132, Dave Bernard 15-129)

Most interceptions in game by one team:
6 – Mt. Morris vs. Lapeer West, Sept. 9, 1988

Most two-point conversions in game by one team:
4 – LakeVille vs. Holly, Oct. 26, 1979
4 – Lapeer West vs. Lapeer East, Oct. 28, 1994

Biggest comebacks:
22 – LakeVille trailed 28-6 vs. Holly, won 56-34, Oct. 25, 1996
22 – Clio trailed 41-19 vs Kearsley after three quarters, Clio won 47-41 on Oct. 16, 2009.

Longest overtime game:
4 OT – Mt. Morris 27, Ainsworth 26 (Oct. 3, 1981; 7-7 after 4 quarters)

INDIVIDUAL FOOTBALL RECORDS

Most touchdowns in game:
6 – Darrell Thomas (Lapeer East) vs. Holly, Oct. 20, 1978 (6 rushing)
6 – Johnny Williams (Holly) vs. Lapeer East, Oct. 19, 2012 (5 rushing and 1 kickoff return)

Most 2-point conversions in game:
4 – Chris Piliafas (Lapeer West) at Lapeer East, Oct. 28, 1994 (all runs)

Most rushing yards in game:
358 – Darrell Thomas (Lapeer East) vs. Holly, Oct. 20, 1978

Most rushing yards in half:
241 – John Ciesielski (Linden) vs. Mt. Morris, Sept. 15, 1995 (15 carries, 2nd half)

Most rushing attempts in game:
45 – Jack Achtabowski (Lapeer) vs. Holly, Oct. 26, 1973 (235 yards)

Longest TD run:
99 – Evan Papuga (Holly) vs. Linden, Aug. 30, 2012

Most rushing yards by QB in game:
291 – Tyler Hamilton (Fenton) vs. Brandon, Oct. 2, 2009 (31 att.)

Most touchdown passes in game:
6 – Mike Templeton (Lapeer West) vs. LakeVille, Sept. 10, 1993
6 – Dustin Mayner (Linden) vs. Clio, Sept. 29, 2006
6 – Brendon Fitch (Swartz Creek) vs. Kearsley, Sept. 13, 2013

Most passing yards in game:
606 – Brendon Fitch (Swartz Creek) vs. Kearsley, Sept. 13, 2013 (26-41)

Most pass completions in game:
35 – Shaye Brown (Linden) vs. Holly, Aug. 30, 2012 (43 att)

Most 2-point passes in one game:
3 – Jeff Crace (LakeVille) vs. Holly, Oct. 26, 1979

Most receiving yards in game:
208 – Max Cummings (Swartz Creek) vs. Fenton, Oct. 12, 2012 (12 catches)

Most receptions in game:
12 – Craig Kirbitz (Clio) vs. Holly, Oct. 2, 2009 (133 yards)
12 – Max Cummings (Swartz Creek) vs. Fenton, Oct. 12, 2012 (208 yards)

Longest TD catch:
98 – Kevin Baker (Linden) from Travis Marsh at Brandon on Oct. 14, 2011

Longest field goals:
52 – Ken Coon (LakeVille) vs. Holly, Oct. 29, 1976
52 – Noel Miller (Linden) vs. Holly, Sept. 23, 2006
52 – Isaac Joseph (Lapeer East) vs. Holly, Aug. 27, 2010

Most extra points in game:
11 – Jackson Maxwell (Swartz Creek) vs. Kearsley, Sept. 13, 2013

Most field goals in season:
9 – Fletcher Spears (Clio), 2008

Most points kicked in game:
12 -- Jacob Matus (Flushing) vs. Clio 9/19/14 (6 XP, 2 FG)

Most kicking points in season:
50 -- Kenny Allen (Fenton), 2011

Longest punt return TD:
85 – Robert Oginsky (Mt. Morris) at Lapeer West, Oct. 2, 1987

Longest kickoff return TD:
99 – Justin Benner (Lapeer East) vs. Lapeer West, Sept. 28, 2007
99 – Luke Lozano (Clio) vs Brandon Oct. 14, 2016

Most punt return TDs in game:
2 – Tim Rossiter (Ainsworth) vs. Holly, Sept. 23, 1977

Longest interception return:
107 – Robert Oginsky (Mt. Morris) vs. Oxford's Kirk Mudd, Oct. 14, 1988

Longest fumble return for TD:
103 – Aaron Steedman (Linden) vs Kearsley, 2014

Most career league wins by quarterback:
24 – Mike Gardner (Oxford), 1991-93 (24-0 record)

FLINT METRO LEAGUE BOYS GOLF CHAMPIONS

1968-69	Fenton	1993-94	Linden
1969-70	Fenton	1994-95	Fenton
1970-71	Lapeer	1995-96	Fenton
1971-72	Fenton	1996-97	Lapeer West
1972-73	Fenton	1997-98	Linden
1973-74	Fenton	1998-99	Linden
1974-75	Fenton	1999-2000	Linden
1975-76	Holly	2000-01	Lapeer West
1976-77	Lapeer West	2001-02	Oxford
1977-78	Fenton	2002-03	Oxford
1978-79	Fenton	2003-04	Lapeer West
1979-80	Fenton	2004-05	Fenton
1980-81	Fenton and Lapeer East	2005-06	Brandon
1981-82	Fenton	2006-07	Holly and Swartz Creek
1982-83	Fenton	2007-08	Holly
1983-84	Fenton	2008-09	Kearsley
1984-85	Lapeer East	2009-10	Kearsley
1985-86	Fenton	2010-11	Swartz Creek
1986-87	Fenton	2011-12	Fenton and Swartz Creek
1987-88	Fenton	2012-13	Fenton
1988-89	Lapeer West	2013-14	Swartz Creek
1989-90	Mt. Morris	2014-15	Flushing
1990-91	Mt. Morris	2015-16	Flushing
1991-92	Fenton	2016-17	Fenton
1992-93	Fenton	2017-18	Fenton

MHSAA State Champions: Swartz Creek (Class A) 2014

Six-time League Tournament Medalist: Heath Fell, Lapeer East (two pre-season, four league tournaments) 1985-88

Four-time First Team All-League

Heath Fell, Lapeer East	1985-88	Ben Zyber, Swartz Creek	2011-14
Chris Osentoski, Lapeer West	2001-04	John Lloyd, Fenton	2012-15
Tyler Nunn, Fenton	2006-10		

Kevin Burch, Swartz Creek

Three-time league tournament
medalist 1970-71 (spring) 1971 (fall)

Heath Fell, Lapeer East

Six-time league tournament medalist
(two pre-season); four-time first
team all-league 1985-88

Ben Zyber, Swartz Creek

Four-time first team all-league 2011-
14; two-time league tournament
medalist; member of team state
champions 2014

John Lloyd, Fenton

Four-time first team all-league 2012-
15; three-time league tournament
medalist (one pre-season)

FLINT METRO LEAGUE GIRLS GOLF CHAMPIONS

2001-02	Linden
2002-03	Linden
2003-04	Linden
2004-05	Linden
2005-06	Fenton
2006-07	Linden
2007-08	Linden
2008-09	Linden
2009-10	Lapeer West
2010 -11	Swartz Creek
2011-12	Swartz Creek
2012-13	Fenton
2013-14	Fenton
2014-15	Flushing
2015-16	Fenton and Flushing
2016-17	Fenton
2017-18	Fenton

Five-time League Tournament Medalist: Missy Ward, Linden (two pre-season, three league tournaments) 2002-04

MHSAA Individual State Champion

Missy Ward   Linden   2004   Division 2

Four-time First Team All-League

Katae Iordanou, Linden   2003-06
Laura Kwiatkowski, Brandon 2003-06
Haylee Zyber, Swartz Creek   2008-11

**Catherine Benscoter,
Lapeer West**
League tournament medalist
2007-09

Laura Kwiatkowski, Brandon
4-time first team all-league 2003-06
Medaled at two pre-season and one
league tournament

Missy Ward, Linden
State Individual Champion 2004
League tournament medalist 2002-04
Pre-season tournament medalist
2003-04

Kerrigan Parks, Flushing
Medaled at two pre-season (2014-15)
& two league tournaments 2015-16

FLINT METRO LEAGUE HOCKEY CHAMPIONS

1979	Ainsworth	2000	Linden
1980	Fenton	2001	Linden
1981	Ainsworth	2002	Fenton
1982	Ainsworth	2003	Lapeer West
1983	Ainsworth	2004	Lapeer West
1984	Ainsworth	2005	Brandon
1985	Ainsworth	2006	Brandon
1986	Ainsworth	2007	Brandon
1987	Fenton	2008	Swartz Creek
1988	Fenton	2009	Kearsley
1989	Linden	2010	Fenton
1990	Lapeer East	2011	Swartz Creek
1991	Lapeer West	2012	Kearsley/Brandon/Holly United and Swartz Creek/ Clio
1992	Linden		
1993	Linden		
1994	Linden	2013	Swartz Creek/Clio
1995	Linden	2014	Lapeer
1996	Linden	2015	Kearsley/Brandon/Holly United
1997	Linden		
1998	Linden	2016	Swartz Creek/ Clio/ Flushing
1999	Fenton and Linden		

Three-time First Team All-League

Mark Wiley, Holly	1975-77
Scott McNeill, Ainsworth	1984-86
Keith Kuzmich, Linden	1984-86
Matt Sohlden, Lapeer East	1984-86
Marc Percola, Fenton	1991-93
Blake Blackmer, Fenton	1999-2001
Justin Peter, LakeVille	2000-02

**Mark Wiley, Holly
1975-77**

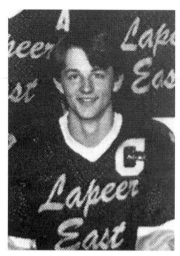

**Matt Sohlden,
Lapeer East 1984-
86**

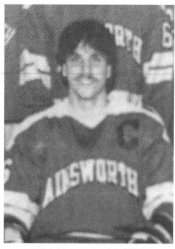

**Scott McNeill,
Ainsworth 1984-86**

**Keith Kuzmich,
Linden 1984-86**

**Marc Percola,
Fenton 1991-93**

**Blake Blackmer,
Fenton 1999-2001**

**Justin Peter,
LakeVille 2000-02**

FLINT METRO LEAGUE GIRLS LACROSSE CHAMPIONS

2016   Fenton/Linden
2017   Fenton/Linden
2018   Fenton/Linden

Kyle Bliss, Fenton (FLax Heat)
First team All-League 2017-18

Jasmine McDonald, Swartz Creek
First team All-League 2016-17

Ellie Reuschlein, Fenton (FLax Heat)
First team All-League 2016-17

Natalie Miller, Fenton (FLax Heat)
First team All-League 2016-17

Sara Reuschlein, Fenton (FLax Heat)
First team All-League 2017-18

FLINT METRO LEAGUE BOYS SOCCER CHAMPIONS

1986	Oxford		2002	Fenton
1987	Oxford		2003	Fenton and Linden
1988	Oxford		2004	Linden
1989	Oxford		2005	Linden
1990	Oxford		2006	Oxford
1991	Oxford		2007	Lapeer East
1992	Oxford		2008	Brandon
1993	Oxford		2009	Fenton
1994	Fenton		2010	Holly
1995	Oxford		2011	Lapeer East
1996	Oxford		2012	Lapeer West
1997	Lapeer West		2013	Linden
1998	Lapeer West and Oxford		2014	Linden
1999	Lapeer West		2015	Brandon
2000	Linden		2016	Brandon and Fenton
2001	Fenton		2017	Brandon

Four-time First Team All-League

Shawn Wagoner, Fenton	1991-94
Matt Green, Oxford	1993-96
Anthony Sanchez, Lapeer West	1996-99
Zach Bakos, Linden	2010-13

Scott Fouracre, Oxford

97 career goals
Three-time First team All-league
1990-92

Shawn Wagoner, Fenton

First team All-league 1991-94

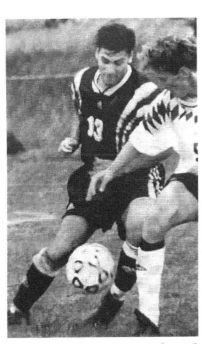

Matt Green, Oxford

First team All-league 1993-96

**Anthony Sanchez,
Lapeer West**

First team All-league 1996-99

Kellen Kalso, Oxford
First team All-league 1996-98
Played on national team 1999

Colin Owen, Lapeer East
43 career shutouts
17 shutouts in 2011

Zach Bakos, Linden
First team All-league 2010-13

FLINT METRO LEAGUE GIRLS SOCCER CHAMPIONS

1988	Fenton	2004	Linden
1989	Oxford	2005	Fenton
1990	Fenton and Lapeer East	2006	Lapeer East
1991	Fenton and Lapeer East	2007	Lapeer East
1992	Lapeer East	2008	Fenton
1993	Fenton and Lapeer East	2009	Lapeer East
1994	Lapeer East	2010	Linden
1995	Lapeer East	2011	Fenton and Lapeer East
1996	Lapeer East and Oxford	2012	Lapeer West
1997	Lapeer East	2013	Fenton
1998	Lapeer East	2014	Linden
1999	Lapeer East	2015	Linden
2000	Lapeer East	2016	Fenton
2001	Linden	2017	Swartz Creek
2002	Lapeer East and Linden	2018	Fenton
2003	Linden		

MHSAA State Runners-up: Fenton (Div. 2) 2015

Four-time First Team All-League

Tiffany Green, Fenton	1990-93
Megan Burns, Oxford	1992-95
Sarah Courtright, Oxford	1995-98
Jessica Hoppe, Lapeer East	1996-99
Julie Valentine, Lapeer West	1996-99
Jessica Morgan, Lapeer East	1997-2000
Krystn Freeman, Linden	1998-01
Katy Ghilardi, Lapeer East	2004-07
Mikki Nuccio, Brandon	2005-08
Tori Bailey, Fenton	2007-10
Mary-Kathryn Fiebernitz, Linden	2008-11
Francesca Ortega, Lapeer West	2011-14
Lauren Lawrence, Swartz Creek	2013-16
Katie Wilkowski, Linden	2013-16

**Kristen McCormack,
Lapeer East**

85 career league goals
43 single season goals
First team All-Metro 1990-92;
Lapeer East won league titles all
three years she played

Tiffany Green, Fenton

First team All-Metro 1990-93, first to
make first team all four years;
Fenton won three league titles during
her career

Sarah Courtright, Oxford

First team All-Metro 1995-98; only
four-time first-team all-league
goalkeeper; first team All-State 1998;
Oxford won a league title in 1996

Jessica Hoppe, Lapeer East

First team All-Metro 1996-99,
first team All-State 1998-99;
Lapeer East won four league titles in
her career

Jessica Morgan, Lapeer East

First team All-Metro 1997-2000;
Eagles won league titles every year of
her career

Krystyn Freeman, Linden

First team All-Metro 1998-2001;
110 career goals (in all games); four-
time All State selection;
Linden won its first league title her
senior year

Katy Ghilardi, Lapeer East

First team All-Metro 2004-07;
Lapeer East won two league titles
during her career

Tori Bailey, Fenton

First team All-Metro 2007-10
2nd team All-State 2007-08, first team
2009-2010, Dream Team 2009;
Fenton took the league title in 2008

**Mary-Kathryn Fiebernitz,
Linden**

First team All-Metro 2008-11
Four years All-State, first team 2009-
11, Dream Team 2010-11;
Linden won league title her junior
year

**Francesca Ortega,
Lapeer West**

First team All-Metro 2011-14
All State second team 2013,
first team 2014;
Lapeer West won its only league title
in 2012

Bri Costigan, Fenton

First team All-Metro 2014-16
All State second team 2014,
first team 2015-16;
Fenton won the league title 2015

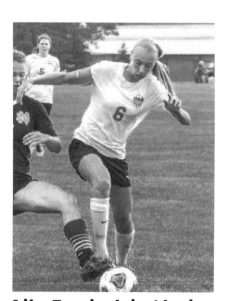

Alia Frederick, Linden

First team All-Metro 2015-17
All State first team 2015 and 2017;
Linden took league title in 2016

FLINT METRO LEAGUE SOFTBALL CHAMPIONS

1973	Carman	1997	Fenton and LakeVille
1974	Carman	1998	Linden
1975	Ainsworth and Fenton	1999	Fenton and Lapeer East
1976	Fenton	2000	Fenton
1977	Fenton and Holly	2001	Fenton
1978	Fenton	2002	Fenton
1979	Fenton	2003	Brandon & Lapeer West
1980	Fenton	2004	Lapeer West
1981	Mt. Morris	2005	Lapeer West
1982	Fenton	2006	Fenton
1983	Fenton and Mt. Morris	2007	Fenton
1984	Fenton and Mt. Morris	2008	Lapeer West
1985	Mt. Morris	2009	Lapeer West
1986	Ainsworth	2010	Oxford
1987	Lapeer West	2011	Fenton, Kearsley and
1988	Lapeer West		Lapeer West
1989	Lapeer West	2012	Swartz Creek
1990	Lapeer West	2013	Swartz Creek
1991	Lapeer West	2014	Fenton
1992	Fenton	2015	Brandon
1993	Fenton	2016	Fenton
1994	Fenton	2017	Clio, Holly and Kearsley
1995	Durand	2018	Swartz Creek
1996	Fenton		

MHSAA State Champions: Fenton (Class B) 1978, 1979, 1980   Mt. Morris (Class B) 1984

MHSAA State Runners-up: Fenton (Class B) 1993

Four-time First Team All-League

Tracy Carr, Lapeer West	1989-92
Dana Blugerman, Holly	2000-03
Nicole Fick, Lapeer West	2002-05
Mallory Miller, Lapeer West	2002-05
Katie Dreyer, Lapeer West	2003-06

Carman 1973

First league softball champions
Perfect regular season (15-0)
L-R: Marilyn Hollier, Frances Jewell,
Janell Crane, Marsha Olds, and
Shelly Medemar

Jeanne Mathews, Fenton

44-16 overall, 31-11 league as pitcher
1973-76; batted .476 in Metro (.531
overall) in four years; two-time
league champion

Barb Barclay, Fenton

62-5 over three years, pitched Tigers
to state championships in 1978 &
1979

Deanne Moore, Fenton

2B on 1979 title team, All-State
pitcher for 1980 state champions;
Player of the Decade at Michigan
State University

Connie Rolison, Mt. Morris
Pitched Mt. Morris to state
championship in 1984 and three
league titles

Tracy Carr, Lapeer West
Set national record with 136 wins in
four-year pitching career, leading
Lapeer West to league titles in 1989,
1990 and 1991

Lisa Hillman, Fenton
Took Fenton to state championship
game in 1993, losing in 20 innings; led
Fenton to league titles in 1992 and
1993

Dana Blugerman, Holly
Only four-time 1st team All-Metro
Catcher 2000-03

**Nicole Fick,
Lapeer West**
Infielder, 2002-05

**Mallory Miller,
Lapeer West**
Pitcher, 2002-05

**Katie Dreyer,
Lapeer West**
Infielder, 2003-06

Forming the core of a strong Lapeer West team, each of these three players earned first-team all-league honors all four years they played, and led Lapeer West to league titles in 2003, 2004 & 2005.

FLINT METRO LEAGUE BOYS SWIM/DIVE CHAMPIONS

1971	Carman		1974	Fenton
1972	Carman		1975	Fenton
1973	Swartz Creek		1976	Carman

League rules require that at least half of the member schools must sponsor a sport in order for it to be considered an official league sport. Not enough FML schools sponsored boys swim/dive between 1976-77 and 2004-05 for it to be considered a league sport with a championship, all-league honors, etc.

2005	Holly		2012	Fenton
2006	Holly		2013	Fenton
2007	Holly		2014	Fenton
2008	Holly		2015	Fenton
2009	Holly		2016	Fenton
2010	Brandon		2017	Fenton
2011	Brandon		2018	Fenton

Four-year League Champions
Jake Quinnan, Holly   2008-11

MHSAA Individual State Champions

Scott Burdick	Fenton	1974	50 and 100 Yd. Freestyle	Class B
Randy Walker	Fenton	1978*	100 Yd. Backstroke	Class B
Dean Ammon	Fenton	1982*	100 Yd. Backstroke	Class B
Mark Harris	Fenton	1982*	200 and 500 Freestyle	Class B
Marty Spees	Fenton	1987*	200 Ind. Medley	Class B
Brian Lambert	Fenton	1988*	Diving	Class B
Jackson Maxwell	Swartz Creek	2014	Diving	Division 2

*- Swim/dive was not a Metro League sport in these years

FLINT METRO LEAGUE BOYS SWIM RECORDS

League records are best winning times/score at league championship meet

Event	Name	School	Time/Score	Year
200 Yd Medley Relay		Swartz Creek/Flushing	1:43.18	2018
	I Barbour, J. Stemczynski, P. Adams, D Burkhardt			
200 Yd Freestyle	Zac Miceli	Fenton	1:45.78	2016
200 Yd IM	Evan Bartow	Fenton	2:03.61	2018
50 Yd Freestyle	Brant Cassidy	Fenton	21.81	2014
1 M Diving	Bill Schaible	Swartz Creek	494.70	1973
100 Yd Butterfly	Zach Balitzkat	Holly	53.86	2009
100 Yd Freestyle	Zac Miceli	Fenton	48.54	2015
500 Yd Freestyle	Kyle Banner	Fenton	4:57.49	2017
200 Yd Freestyle Relay		Holly	1:31.94	2009
	M O'Connor, A Lipiec, N Keller, Z Balitzkat			
100 Yd Backstroke	Joel Diccion	Fenton	55.63	2018
100 Yd Breaststroke	Noel Nowacki	Kearsley	1:00.52	2017
400 Yd Freestyle Relay		Fenton	3:24.21	2015
	A Landis, Z Miceli, M Fabatz, K Banner			

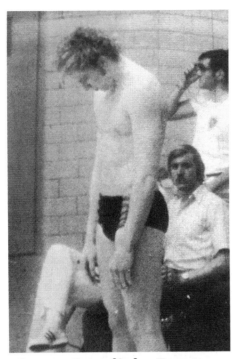

Scott Burdick, Fenton

1974 State Champion
50 & 100 Freestyle
1973 and 1974 League Champion

Jake Quinnan, Holly

Four-year League Champion
2008-11

Randy Walker, Fenton

1978 State Champion
100 Backstroke
1976 League Champion (200 MR)

Jackson Maxwell, Swartz Creek

2014 State Diving Champion
Three-year League Diving Champion
2012-14

FLINT METRO LEAGUE GIRLS SWIM/DIVE CHAMPIONS

2004	Fenton
2005	Fenton
2006	Fenton
2007	Fenton
2008	Fenton
2009	Fenton
2010	Fenton
2011	Fenton
2012	Brandon and Fenton
2013	Fenton
2014	Fenton
2015	Fenton
2016	Fenton
2017	Fenton

Four-year League Champions

Lauren Campbell, Fenton	2004-07
Amanda Kleinert, Fenton	2005-08
Deanna Hooper, Fenton	2007-10
Kendal Mykietuik, Fenton	2007-10
Breanna Konopitski, Brandon	2008-11
Haley Shaw, Fenton	2009-12
Gabrielle Haaraoja, Fenton	2010-13
Elise Cassidy, Fenton	2013-16

MHSAA Individual State Champions

Melanie Nelson	Fenton	1985*, 1986*, 1987*	100 Yd. Breaststroke	Class B
Teena Spees, Melanie Nelson, Diedra Schepler, Brigitte Hansen				
	Fenton	1987*	200 Medley Relay	Class B
Liz Korsedal	Fenton	1999*, 2000*	100 Yd. Butterfly	Class B
Amber Shalla	Fenton	2000*	500 Yd. Freestyle	Class B

*- Swim/dive was not a Metro League sport in these years

FLINT METRO LEAGUE GIRLS SWIM RECORDS

League records are best winning times/score at league championship meet

Event	Name	Team	Time	Year
200 Yd Medley Relay		Fenton	1:55.19	2016
E Cassidy, L Gruber, C Dailey and G Siefker				
200 Yd Freestyle	Sara Heines	Brandon	1:58.21	2014
200 Yd IM	Emily Shallman	Lapeer	2:10.94	2011
50 Yd Freestyle	Ashley Corriveau	Lapeer	23.94	2008
1 mtr Diving	Taylor Shegos	Fenton	460.55	2015
100 Yd Butterfly	Emily Shallman	Lapeer	57.41	2011
100 Yd Freestyle	Ashley Corriveau	Lapeer	52.71	2008
500 Yd Freestyle	Sara Heines	Brandon	5:12.38	2014
200 Yd Freestyle Relay		Fenton	1:41.94	2011
H Shaw, G Haaraoja, K Kidd, S Wujciak				
100 Yd Backstroke	Haley Shaw	Fenton	58.77	2012
100 Yd Breaststroke	Emily Shallman	Lapeer	1:09.23	2012
400 Yd Freestyle Relay		Fenton	3:46.02	2012
G Haaraoja, M Cassner, L Davis, H Shaw				

Melanie Nelson, Fenton
Three-time state champion in 100
breaststroke 1985, 1986, 1987

Liz Korsedal, Fenton
State champion 100 butterfly
1999, 2000

Ashley Corriveau, Lapeer
Record holder in 50 and 100
freestyle; won three league titles in
100 freestyle, 2006-08, and back-to-
back 50 freestyle titles in 2007-08

Emily Shallman, Lapeer
Holds league records in 200 IM, 100
butterfly, and 100 breaststroke; six
league titles in three years in those
events 2010-2012

Haley Shaw, Fenton

Four-time league champion in 100 backstroke, 2009-2012; set league record of 58.77 in 2012

Sara Heines, Brandon

Eleven league titles (six individual and five relays) 2012-2014; holds records in 500 free and 200 free (2014)

Gabrielle Haaraoja, Fenton

Twelve league titles (six individual) in four years 2010-2013

FLINT METRO LEAGUE BOYS TENNIS CHAMPIONS

1972-73	Lapeer	1996-97	Holly
1973-74	Lapeer	1997-98	Holly
1974-75	Carman	1998-99	Holly and Lapeer West
1975-76	Carman		
1976-77	Fenton	1999-2000	Holly
1977-78	Fenton	2000-01	Holly
1978-79	Fenton	2001-02	Holly
1979-80	Fenton	2002-03	Holly
1980-81	Fenton	2003-04	Holly
1981-82	Fenton	2004-05	Holly
1982-83	Fenton	2005-06	Holly
1983-84	Holly	2006-07	Holly
1984-85	Fenton	2007-08	Holly
1985-86	Fenton	2008-09	Holly
1986-87	Fenton	2009-10	Holly
1987-88	Fenton	2010 -11	Holly
1988-89	Holly	2011-12	Holly
1989-90	Holly	2012-13	Fenton
1990-91	Fenton	2013-14	Holly
1991-92	Holly	2014-15	Holly
1992-93	Lapeer East	2015-16	Holly
1993-94	Holly	2016-17	Holly
1994-95	Holly	2017-18	Holly
1995-96	Holly		

MHSAA State Champions: Lapeer (Class A co-champion) 1971 (old format)

Four-time League Champions (any flight)

Jim Gatza, Fenton	1978-81	Steve Wilson, Holly	2002-05
John Schenk, Fenton	1978-81	Spencer Navarre, Brandon	2009-12
David Taylor, Holly	1993-96	Zac Goodrich, Holly	2010-13
Tony Hernandez, Holly	1997-2000	Taylor Mills, Holly	2010-13
Ryan Ward, Holly	1997-2000	Craig Richards, Holly	2010-13
Keith Johnson, Holly	2002-05		

Glen Koeske, Holly

3-time League Champion at #1 singles
1985-87

Carlos Rincon, Lapeer West

3-time League Champion at #1 singles
2000-02

Brennan Brown, Holly

3-time League Champion at #1 singles
1992-94

Spencer Navarre, Brandon

Only 4-time Metro League boys'
champion at #1 singles, 2009-2012

"A night and a day in Ortonville"

Sept. 21, 2010 and Sept. 24, 2010

(Flint Journal article written by Greg Tunnicliff, used by his permission)

Ortonville Brandon 4, Holly 4

Ortonville, Michigan – It was supposed to be a normal high school tennis match, but there was no way it was going to be anything but special.

Night matches and 50 dual-meet winning streaks can hardly be considered normal. After one night and one day of competition, Brandon sophomore Nick Skinsacos (pictured on the right being carried off the court by his teammates) edged Holly junior Colton Richards 7-6 (10-8), 2-6, 7-5 at No. 4 singles, knotting the final score at 4-4.

The tie ended the Bronchos' Flint-area record 50 dual-meet winning streak. Holly had not left a dual without a victory since a 6-2 loss to Brighton on April 20, 2004, The Bronchos had won a Metro League record 62 straight duals, with their last blemish being a 4-3 loss at Lapeer West on April 29, 1999.

Holly and Brandon were forced to play the first night tennis dual in Flint-area history on Sept. 21, 2010 because of prior scheduling conflicts. The Bronchos and the Blackhawks each had matches scheduled that day – Holly hosted Lapeer West and Brandon hosted Clio – before playing each other.

The Holly-Brandon dual was moved from Brandon High to the school district's Harvey Swanson Elementary School because its eight-court facility is equipped with lights. The match began at 6:45 p.m. and it didn't take long for it to become a legend.

With both teams pulling off upsets, the teams were tied 3-3 after the first six matches came off the courts. Holly assured itself of at least a tie when junior Sam Caldwell (photo on the left) upset Brandon senior McKenzie Walsh, 4-6, 7-6 (8-6), 6-2, at No. 2 singles to give thet Bronchos a 4-3 lead.

With Skinsacos leading Richards late in the third set in the dual's final match, the lights clicked off at 10 p.m., forcing the dual to be postponed. The lights at Harvey Swanson Elementary School are hooked up to a timer that is set to go on at 7:30 p.m. and go off at 10 o'clock sharp.

The match was supposed to be completed on Sept. 22, but it ended up being pushed back to Sept. 24 because Holly was not able to get a bus on Sept. 22. When play resumed on Sept. 24, Skinsacos lost the first game and then won the next two to win the match and tie the final score. The tie put both teams at 6-0-1 in the Metro.

Brandon 4, Holly 4

Singles — Spencer Navarre (B) d. Jeff Sophiea 6-2, 6-4; Sam Caldwell (H) d. McKenzie Walsh 4-6, 7-6 (8-6), 6-2; Nathan Navarre (B) d. Connor Bilkos 6-1, 6-1; Nick Skinsacos (B) d. Colton Richards 7-6 (10-8), 2-6, 7-5
Doubles — Erik Kahn-Zach Goodrich (H) d. Zach Duff-Noah Rice 6-3, 6-1; Quinton Trudell-Matt Jones (B) d. Jake Quinnan-Craig Richards 7-5, 1-6, 6-1; Ricky Slemons-Taylor Mills (H) d. Jesse Lutz-Jeremy Mullin 6-1, 6-3; Mark Retka-Travis Kerton (H) d. Mike Olsen-Andrew Weitz 6-1, 6-0.

Records: Brandon 8-0-1, 6-0-1 Metro League. Holly 6-0-1 Metro League

FLINT METRO LEAGUE GIRLS TENNIS CHAMPIONS

1977-78	Fenton and Lapeer East		1998-99	Holly
1978-79	Fenton		1999-2000	Holly
1979-80	Lapeer West		2000-01	Holly
1980-81	Lapeer West		2001-02	Holly
1981-82	Fenton		2002-03	Holly
1982-83	Holly		2003-04	Holly
1983-84	Holly		2004-05	Holly
1984-85	Holly		2005-06	Holly
1985-86	Fenton and Holly		2006-07	Holly
1986-87	Holly		2007-08	Holly
1987-88	Holly		2008-09	Holly
1988-89	Holly		2009-10	Holly
1989-90	Holly		2010 -11	Holly
1990-91	Holly		2011-12	Fenton
1991-92	Holly		2012-13	Holly
1992-93	Holly		2013-14	Fenton
1993-94	Holly		2014-15	Holly
1994-95	Holly		2015-16	Holly
1995-96	Fenton and Holly		2016-17	Holly
1996-97	Holly		2017-18	Holly
1997-98	Holly			

MHSAA State Individual Champion

Monica Rincon, Lapeer West	#1 singles	1997	Division 2
Nicole Johnson, Holly	#2 singles	2018	Division 2

Four-time League Champions (any flight)

Amy Glowaz, Holly	1984-87	Michelle Leone, Holly	2003-06
Heidi Owens, Holly	1986-89	Morgan Baylis, Holly	2011-14
Amy Cook, Holly	1989-92	Leah Moller, Holly	2011-14
Emily Barton, Holly	1992-95	Carley Postma, Holly	2011-14
Taylor Matlock, Holly	1996-99	Madison Ballard, Fenton	2012-15
Amy Palmgren, Holly	2000-03	Jenna Pepper, Holly	2013-16
Christi Hernandez, Holly	2001-04	Sydney Renehan, Holly	2013-16
Courtney Yee, Holly	2002-05	Paige Reid, Holly	2014-17
Ginny Blakely, Holly	2003-06	Megan Lesperance, Holly	2015-18

Toni Serges, Carman

Before girls' tennis had enough participation to be its own sport, girls were
allowed to play on boys' tennis teams starting in 1973. Toni paired with Jim
Ecklund to win the league's #3 doubles in 1973; won at #1 doubles with her sister
Kellie in 1974; and was #4 singles champion in 1975

Kellie Serges, Carman

Kellie also played on Carman's boys' tennis team in 1974-76
Metro League #1 doubles champion with her sister Toni in 1974; #2 singles
champion in 1975; and won the league championship at #1 singles in 1976

Monica Rincon, Lapeer West

MHSAA State Champion
at #1 Singles 1997
League champion #1 Singles
1996 and 1997

Kristen Fettig, Holly

League Champion #1 Singles
1998 and 1999
Runner-up at #1 Singles 1997
League Champion at #2 Singles 1996

Casey Spooner, Lapeer West

League Champion at #1 Singles
2008 and 2009 (spring)
Runner-up at #1 Singles 2006 (fall)

Madison Ballard, Fenton
Only 4-time Metro League girls'
champion at #1 singles
2012-15

Nicole Johnson, Holly
State Champion at #2 singles 2018

Taylor Barrett, Holly
League Champion at #1 Singles
2016-18
(9th through 11th grade)

FLINT METRO LEAGUE BOYS TRACK CHAMPIONS

1969	Holly	1994	LakeVille
1970	Holly	1995	Lakeville
1971	Holly	1996	LakeVille
1972	Carman and Holly	1997	LakeVille
1973	Carman	1998	Lapeer West
1974	Holly and Swartz Creek	1999	Lapeer East
1975	Holly and Swartz Creek	2000	Lapeer East
1976	Swartz Creek	2001	Linden
1977	Holly	2002	Fenton
1978	Holly	2003	Fenton
1979	Holly	2004	Fenton and Linden
1980	LakeVille	2005	Fenton
1981	Holly	2006	Fenton
1982	Ainsworth	2007	Swartz Creek
1983	Holly	2008	Holly
1984	Oxford	2009	Holly
1985	Holly	2010	Swartz Creek
1986	Holly	2011	Holly
1987	Oxford	2012	Swartz Creel
1988	Fenton and Oxford	2013	Holly and Linden
1989	Fenton	2014	Holly
1990	Holly	2015	Holly and Kearsley
1991	Oxford	2016	Flushing
1992	LakeVille and Linden	2017	Fenton
1993	Oxford	2018	Fenton and Flushing

MHSAA State Champions: Holly (Class B) 1971
Ainsworth (Class B) 1982
Oxford (Class B) 1991

Four-year League Champions:

Craig Thomas, Swartz Creek	1971-74	Donnie Richmond, Oxford	2001-04
Jared Maxwell, Holly	1993-96	John Williams, Holly	2010-13
Vinnie Candela, LakeVille	1994-97		

MHSAA Individual State Champions

Year	Name	School	Event	Class
1971	Don Keswick	Fenton	880 Run	Class B
1973	Ron Gamble, Shelton Pinnix,Tim Tucker, Don Gamble, Mt. Morris		440 Relay	Class B
1973	Dave Karns	Fenton	880 Run	Class B
1975	Mike Moses	Holly	Long Jump	Class B
1975	Ralph Smith	Holly	High Jump	Class B
1975	Mike Helms	Fenton	880 Run	Class B
1976	Rob Cummings	Carman	120 Hurdles	Class A
1978	Jeff Lewis	Holly	880 Run	Class B
1979	Ed Brown	LakeVille	330 Hurdles	Class B
1982	Tim Fellows	Ainsworth	Shot Put/Discus	Class B
1982	Ed Lumm	Holly	Pole Vault	Class B
1982	Jim Featherston	Ainsworth	330 Hurdles	Class B
1983	Tim Fellows	Ainsworth	Discus	Class B
1989	Mike Goodfellow	Oxford	1600/3200 Run	Class B
1990	Vidal Fragoso, Kniffen, Derney, Erik Welch	Oxford	1600 Relay	Class B
1991	Vidal Fragoso, Steve McCracken, Cliff Wells, Erik Welch, Oxford		800 Relay	Class B
1991	Mark Goodfellow,Kurt Stephenson,Vidal Fragoso,Erik Welch, Oxford, 3200 Relay, Class B			
1991	Erik Welch	Oxford	400 dash	Class B
1992	Scott Gavan	LakeVille	Discus	Class B
1993	Mark Goodfellow	Oxford	1600 run	Class B
1998	Frank Garofalo	Mt. Morris	Discus	Class B
2003	Ryan Norman, Jordan Norman, Jeff Krause, Matt Keenan, Linden		800 Relay	Div. 2
2004	Rob Fiorillo	Holly	110 Hurdles	Div. 1
2004	Michael Peck, Shawn Debo, Matt Temple, Matt Maygar, Fenton		400 Relay	Div. 2
2007	Alex Ralston, Joe Kryza, Jesse Anderson, Joe Dimambro, Fenton		3200 Relay	Div. 2
2009	Jonathon Beeler	Holly	High Jump	Div. 1
2009	Jack Hord, Kyle LeMieux, Dylan Ryan, Brendan Sage, Linden		3200 Relay	Div. 2
2010	Jonathon Beeler	Holly	High Jump	Div. 1
2010	Justin Gaumer	Holly	Discus	Div. 1
2012	Kevin Weiler	Swartz Creek	Shot Put	Div. 1
2014	Kevin Weiler	Swartz Creek	Shot Put/Discus	Div. 1
2016	Jacob Lee	Fenton	3200 run	Div. 1
2017	Dominic Dimambro	Fenton	3200 run	Div. 1

FLINT METRO LEAGUE BOYS TRACK AND FIELD RECORDS

Event	Name	School	Mark	Year
100 Meter Dash	Vinnie Candela	LakeVille	10.7	1997
	Mike Peck	Fenton	10.7	2003
200 Meter Dash	Mike Peck	Fenton	21.9	2003
400 Meter Dash	Brendan Lagios	Holly	49.34	2009
800 Meter Run	Jeremy Dickie	Swartz Creek	1:56.86 FAT	2010
1600 Meter Run	Jeremy Dickie	Swartz Creek	4:24.0	2010
3200 Meter Run	Jacob Lee	Fenton	9:42.58	2014
110 Meter Hurdles	Rob Fiorello	Holly	14.1	2003
300 Meter Int. Hurdles	Rob Fiorello	Holly	38.8	2003
Discus	Justin Gaumer	Holly	173' 5"	2010
High Jump	Jonathon Beeler	Holly	6' 10"	2010
Long Jump	Mike Moses	Holly	23' 3 ½"	1974
Pole Vault	Josh Fiedor	Holly	15' 0"	2010
	Justin McKenzie	Linden	15' 0"	2014
Shot Put	Kevin Weiler	Swartz Creek	57' 10"	2013
400 Meter Relay		Flushing	43.12 (FAT)	2018

Nick Morrison, Jesse McLemore, Ry'lon Roberts, Aidan Harrison

800 Meter Relay		Fenton	1:29.64	2018

John Sage, Noah Sage, Ryan Miller, Brandon Miller

1600 Meter Relay		Holly	3:25.6	2009

Andy Lipiec, Brendan Lagios, Robert Linson, Jonathon Beeler

3200 Meter Relay		Brandon	8:04.43	2014

Sam Toward, Taras Thronson, Colin Hooker, Kyle Doyon

BOYS RETIRED RECORDS   (events or distances no longer used)

Event	Name	School	Mark	Year
100 Yard Dash	Cottrell Williams	Holly	9.9	1971
	Todd Powell	LakeVille	9.9	1984
220 Yard Dash	Cottrell Williams	Holly	22.3	1970
440 Yard Dash	Jeff Lewis	Holly	49.9	1978
880 Yard Run	Jeff Lewis	Holly	1:54.9	1978
Mile Run	Chris Gilbert	Fenton	4:20.5	1976
Two Mile Run	Chris Gilbert	Fenton	9:39.1	1977
120 Yd. High Hurdles	Rob Cummings	Carman	14.3	1976
180 Yd. Low Hurdles	Roger Downing	Holly	20.1	1970
330 Yd. Low Hurdles	Kurt Ebert	Holly	38.4	1977
300 Meter Low Hurdles	Jim Featherston	Ainsworth	37.3	1982
440 Yard Relay		Fenton	44.4	1984

Jeff Cislo, Dave Dort, Mike Wade, Chris Sweetman

880 Yard Relay		Holly	1:31.1	1976

Chris Brooks, Craig Brooks, Jim Fultz, John Lueb

Mile Relay		Holly	3:26.2	1976

Chris Brooks, Kurt Ebert, Joe Herronen, Jeff Lewis

Two Mile Relay		Holly	8:18.5	1985

Bill Reynolds, Alex Bothwell, Steve Cassar, Bob Jacobs

Cottrell Williams, Holly
1969-71

Won six league titles in 100 and 220 yard dash, sweeping both events three straight years

Craig Thomas, Swartz Creek
1971-74

Won seven individual league titles and set four records; four-time league champion in pole vault; also won titles in long jump, high jump and high hurdles

Jim Featherston, Ainsworth
1981-82

Won five league titles in four different events (200 m, 400 m, 110 and 300 hurdles); in 1982 league meet, set records in three events and missed a fourth by 0.1 seconds; 1982 Class B state champion in 330 yard hurdles

Tim Fellows, Ainsworth
1981-83

Won five league titles in shot put and discus; 1982 state Class B champion in shot put and discus and in 1983 repeated as state discus champion; his league shot put record lasted 32 years and his discus league record for 27 years

Jeff Loria, Fenton 1981-83

Five league titles in long jump and high jump; his high jump record of 6' 5 5/8" stood for 27 years

Mike Goodfellow, Oxford
1987-89

Won six league titles in 800m, 1600m and 3200m, winning all three in 1988; 1989 state champion in 1600m and 3200m

Erik Welch, Oxford 1989-91

Three-time league champion in 400m and won 200m once; at 1991 state meet, anchored winning 800 and 3200 relays and won 400m as Oxford won the state championship

Jon Beeler, Holly 2009-10

State Division 1 and Metro League champion in high jump, 2009 and 2010; smashed league high jump record in 2010 by over 4" with leap of 6' 10"

Kevin Weiler, Swartz Creek 2012-14

Five league titles in shot put and discus; two-time state champion in shot put (2012 and 2014), and won state title in discus in 2014

FLINT METRO LEAGUE GIRLS TRACK CHAMPIONS

1975	Carman and Fenton		1997	LakeVille and Oxford
1976	Fenton		1998	Fenton
1977	Fenton		1999	Fenton
1978	Fenton		2000	Holly
1979	Fenton		2001	Oxford
1980	Holly		2002	Fenton and Oxford
1981	Holly		2003	Linden
1982	Ainsworth		2004	Fenton
1983	Ainsworth		2005	Brandon
1984	Oxford		2006	Brandon
1985	Holly and LakeVille		2007	Brandon
1986	Fenton		2008	Oxford
1987	Fenton and Oxford		2009	Holly and Oxford
1988	Oxford		2010	Oxford
1989	LakeVille		2011	Holly
1990	LakeVille		2012	Brandon and Holly
1991	LakeVille		2013	Brandon and Holly
1992	LakeVille		2014	Fenton
1993	LakeVille		2015	Flushing
1994	LakeVille		2016	Fenton
1995	LakeVille		2017	Fenton
1996	LakeVille		2018	Fenton and Flushing

MHSAA State Champions: LakeVille (Class B) 1991

MHSAA State Runners-up: Fenton (Class B) 1977   LakeVille (Class B) 1995

Four-year League Champions:

Robin Pruitt, Carman	1973-76		Kelli Hammond, LakeVille	1988-91
Sue Ambler, Fenton	1975-78		Emily Kaiser, LakeVille	1989-92
Chris Boehmer, Lapeer West	1979-82		Erin Hagstrom, Linden	1992-95
Julie Brooks, Holly	1979-82		Cynthia Smith, LakeVille	1992-95
Mary Brown, Ainsworth	1982-85		Jackie Bucholz, Holly	1994-97
Connie Johnson, Fenton	1987-90		Teressha DeRosset, LakeVille	1994-97
Val Kage, Oxford	1987-90		Kari Karhoff, Durand	1994-97
Laura Bell, LakeVille	1988-91		Shelly Maruszak, LakeVille	1994-97

Dru Bishop, Fenton	1996-99	Hannah George, Oxford	2006-09
Karen LeRoy, Oxford	1997-2000	Shannon Seeley, Oxford	2007-10
Caryn Inman, Oxford	2000-03	Kate Wolanin, Oxford	2007-10
Rachel Gutierrez, Linden	2001-04	Mariah Ridal, Holly	2009-12
Amy Morrison, Fenton	2004-07	Sydney Elmer, Linden	2011-14
Jacqui Sylva, Oxford	2005-08	Madison Pierce, Brandon	2012-15

MHSAA Individual State Champions

Year	Name	School	Event	Class
1977	Katie Anderson, Angie Pitman, Susan Ambler, Sue Hintz, Fenton		Mile Relay	Class B
1979	Shelly Dagley	Lapeer West	Shot Put	Class B
1980	Chris Boehmer	Lapeer West	Long Jump	Class B
1980	Melanie Deters	Durand	400 Dash	Class B
1982	Chris Boehmer	Lapeer West	Long Jump	Class A
1987	Amy Warner	Linden	High Jump	Class B
1988	Cari Byrd	Oxford	800 Run	Class B
1990	Karri Kuzma	LakeVille	Shot Put	Class B
1990	Laura Bell	LakeVille	3200 Run	Class B
1991	Karri Kuzma	LakeVille	Shot Put	Class B
1991	Laura Bell	LakeVille	1600 Run	Class B
1994	Kari Karhoff	Durand	400 Dash	Class B
1996	Kari Karhoff	Durand	300 Hurdles	Class B
1996	Terresha Derossett	LakeVille	High Jump	Class B
1997	Dru Bishop	Fenton	800 Run	Class B
1997	Terresha Derossett	LakeVille	110 Hurdles	Class B
1997	Kari Karhoff	Durand	300 Hurdles	Class B
1998	Dru Bishop	Fenton	800 Run	Class B
2000	Morgan Acre	LakeVille	Discus	Div. 2
2006	Amy Morrison	Fenton	Pole Vault	Div. 1
2007	Amy Morrison	Fenton	Pole Vault	Div. 2
2017	Breanna Perry	Flushing	High Jump	Div. 1

FLINT METRO LEAGUE GIRLS TRACK AND FIELD RECORDS

Event	Name	School	Mark	Year
100 Meter Dash	Krysten Sylva	Oxford	12.0	2005
200 Meter Dash	Mary Brown	Ainsworth	25.2	1982
400 Meter Dash	Kelli Hammond	LakeVille	59.1	1991
800 Meter Run	Laura Bell	LakeVille	2:20.0	1991
1600 Meter Run	Alexa Keiser	Fenton	4:59.61	2018
3200 Meter Run	Jessi Lindstrom	Flushing	11:37.59	2017
110 Meter Hurdles	Shae Batten	Kearsley	15.28 FAT	2010
	Teressha DeRosset	LakeVille	15.3	1997
300 Meter Int. Hurdles	Kari Karhoff	Durand	45.2	1997
Discus	Morgan Acre	LakeVille	140' 10"	2002
High Jump	Amy Warner	Linden	5' 6"	1988

Long Jump	Kari Karhoff	Durand	17' 7 ½"	1997
Pole Vault	Amy Morrison	Fenton	12' 1"	2007
Shot Put	Niki Sargent	Linden	41' 0"	2013
400 Meter Relay		Brandon	49.66	2012
	Tiffani Owens, Jayona Dent, Madee Pierce, Kierra Johnson			
800 Meter Relay		Brandon	1:46.7	2013
	Jayona Dent, Kierra Johnson, Cyonna Rush, Ashlee Roussey			
1600 Meter Relay		Oxford	4:06.7	2010
	Megan Seeley, Shannon Seeley, Brittany Johnson, Kate Wolanin			
3200 Meter Relay		Fenton	9:35.17	2017
Brenna Bleicher, Cambria Tiemann, Jenna Keiser, Alexa Keiser				

GIRLS RETIRED RECORDS   (events or distances no longer used)

100 Yard Dash	Mary Brown	Ainsworth	11.1	1984
220 Yard Dash	Ramona Wirostek	Carman	26.2	1975
440 Yard Dash	Melanie Deters	Durand	58.2	1980
880 Yard Run	Lynn Walters	Fenton	2:23.6	1980
Mile Run	Lynn Walters	Fenton	5:18.0	1980
Two Mile Run	Rhonda Prime	Ainsworth	11:55.5	1983
70 Yard Hurdles	Glenda Lowell	Swartz Creek	10.3	1969
80 Yard Hurdles	Nola Pettus	Ainsworth	11.8	1972
110 Yard Low Hurdles	Kelly Sparks	Lapeer East	14.3	1979
100 Meter Low Hurdles	Evie Landrum	Holly	15.5	1981
110 Yard Int. Hurdles	Verlynda Wilson	Mt. Morris	15.4	1984
220 Yard Low Hurdles	Jill Sutton	Lapeer West	30.6	1979
200 Meter Low Hurdles	Evie Landrum	Holly	29.9	1981
330 Yard Low Hurdles	Mary Brown	Ainsworth	47.2	1985
300 Yard Relay		Fenton	37.2	1969
440 Yard Relay		Fenton	51.6	1975
	Catherine Anderson, Margaret Aldrich, Michelle Henderson, Marie Pushman			
880 Medley Relay		Fenton	1:53	1972
880 Yard Relay		Fenton	1:47.5	1977
	Marie Pushman, Stanette Aldrich, Angie Pittman, Sandi Johnson			
Mile Relay		Fenton	4:11.5	1978
	Sue Hintz, Sue Ambler, Kim Beatty, Peggy Edwards			
Two Mile Relay		Holly	9:59.2	1985
	Laura Merewether, Heidi Wright, Stacey Zerbaz, Chris Wilson			
Standing Long Jump	Nancy Josef	Swartz Creek	8' 8 ½"	1969
Softball Throw	Kathy Schetler	Swartz Creek	192' 11"	1971

Nancy Josef, Swartz Creek

Won seven individual league titles in
sprints and jumps 1969-71

Mary Brown, Ainsworth

Won eight league titles and broke
five league records in three events,
1982-85; four-time league champ at
100 yards or meters; still holds league
record for 200m dash at 25.2 seconds
(1982)

Chris Boehmer, Lapeer West

Four-time league long jump
champion 1979-82; state long jump
champion 1980 (Class B) and 1982
(Class A)

Amy Warner, Linden

Won five league titles in the high
jump, long jump and high hurdles
1986-88; her 1988 high jump league
record of 5' 6" still stands; 1987 state
championship in high jump came
with cast on her arm (pictured)

Laura Bell, LakeVille

Won ten league titles in 800m, 1600m and 3200m runs 1988-91; doubled in 1600m and 3200m all four years; her league records in 800m and 1600m still stand; state champion in 1990 (3200m) and 1991 (1600m)

Kelli Hammond, LakeVille

Won ten league titles in 100m, 200m and 400m dashes, 1988-91; won all three dash titles three times

Karri Kuzma, LakeVille

Won six league titles in the shot put and discus 1989-91; back-to-back state Class B shot put champion 1990-91

Kari Karhoff, Durand

Thirteen individual league titles in five events, 1994-97; Three-time state champion, 1994 (400m dash), 1996 and 1997 (300m hurdles); her 1997 records in 300m hurdles and long jump still stand

Teressha DeRossett, LakeVille

Four-time league champion in high jump 1994-97, and 100m hurdles 1996-97; state Class B champion in high jump 1996 and 100m hurdles 1997

Dru Bishop, Fenton

Three-time league champion in 800m run 1996-98; also won league title at 400m (1998) and four winning relays (1997-99); back-to-back state 800m champion 1997-98

Amy Morrison, Fenton

Four-time league champion in pole vault and 100m hurdles 2004-07; won state titles in pole vault back-to-back 2006 (Div. 1) and 2007 (Div. 2)

FLINT METRO LEAGUE VOLLEYBALL CHAMPIONS

1976-77	Fenton and Lapeer East	1997-98	Fenton
1977-78	Ainsworth	1998-99	Fenton
1978-79	Fenton	1999-2000	Fenton and Lapeer East
1979-80	Mt. Morris	2000-01	Lapeer East
1980-81	Lapeer East	2001-02	Oxford
1981-82	Fenton and Lapeer East	2002-03	Oxford
1982-83	Fenton and Mt. Morris	2003-04	Lapeer East
1983-84	Fenton	2004-05	Lapeer East
1984-85	Fenton	2005-06	Lapeer East & Lapeer West
1985-86	Fenton	2006-07	Fenton
1986-87	Fenton	2007-08	Oxford
1987-88	LakeVille	2008-09	Fenton
1988-89	LakeVille	2009-10	Fenton
1989-90	Fenton	2010-11	Fenton
1990-91	Fenton	2011-12	Fenton
1991-92	Fenton	2012-13	Fenton
1992-93	Fenton	2013-14	Fenton
1993-94	Holly and LakeVille	2014-15	Flushing
1994-95	LakeVille	2015-16	Fenton
1995-96	Lapeer East	2016-17	Fenton
1996-97	Lapeer East and Oxford	2017-18	Fenton

MHSAA State Runners-up: Ainsworth (Class B) 1978   Fenton (Class B) 1983, 1990, 1992

Three-time First Team All League

Sandi Johnson, Fenton	1977-79	Nikki Cranick, Lapeer East	2004-06
Lisa Sanford, LakeVille	1993-95	Katie Nelson, Lapeer West	2005-07
Cori Hopkins, Linden	1994-96	Savannah Stedman, Brandon	2005-07
Stephanie McKeachie, Lapeer East	1995-97	Emily Idoni, Fenton	2007 winter to 2008 fall
Carol Price, Fenton	1998-2000	Lauren Zepeda, Fenton	2008-10
Rebecca Moller, LakeVille	1999-2001	Megan Klavitter, Linden	2013-15
Ashley Purvis, Lapeer East	2003-05		

Tracey Jones, Fenton

Leader of Fenton's state runner-up team in 1983; first team all-league 1982-83 with league championships both years; Class B All-State second team 1982, first team 1983

Natalie Koan, Fenton

Lone setter on Fenton's 1990 state runner-up team; Set single season record with 837 assists, named first team Class B All-State in 1990 as well as first team All-League in 1988 and 1990

Lisa Sanford, LakeVille

Three-time 1st team All-League in 1993-95, as LakeVille won league titles in her junior and senior years; first team Class B All-State in 1995

Stephanie McKeachie, Lapeer East

Led Lapeer East to two league titles while garnering three 1st team All-League selections 1995-97; honorable mention Class A All-State in 1997

Carol Price, Fenton

Three years as 1st team All-League selection coincided with Fenton three-peat for Metro League championships, 1998-2000; first team Class B All-State in 2000

Ashley Purvis, Lapeer East

First team All-League in 2003-05, Class A All-State honorable mention in 2005, as Lapeer East won Metro League titles in 2004 and 2005

Nikki Cranick, Lapeer East

Lapeer East won Metro League championships in 2004-06, the three years she was named first team All-league; honorable mention Class A All-State in 2006

Lauren Zepeda, Fenton

Libero named first team All-League in 2008, 2009 and 2010, as Fenton won league titles all three years. The libero position, a defensive specialist, had been adopted by the MHSAA for the 2006 season.

FLINT METRO LEAGUE WRESTLING CHAMPIONS

1969	Carman	1994	Durand and LakeVille
1970	Swartz Creek	1995	Durand
1971	Fenton	1996	Mt. Morris
1972	Fenton	1997	Mt. Morris
1973	Fenton	1998	Fenton
1974	Swartz Creek	1999	Oxford
1975	Fenton	2000	Lapeer West
1976	Swartz Creek	2001	Lapeer West
1977	Fenton	2002	Lapeer West
1978	Fenton	2003	Lapeer West
1979	Fenton	2004	Lapeer West
1980	Fenton	2005	Holly
1981	Fenton	2006	Linden
1982	Durand	2007	Holly and Oxford
1983	Holly	2008	Oxford
1984	Ainsworth and Fenton	2009	Oxford
1985	Fenton	2010	Oxford
1986	Fenton	2011	Holly
1987	Durand and Mt. Morris	2012	Holly
1988	Fenton and LakeVille	2013	Holly
1989	Fenton	2014	Brandon
1990	Fenton	2015	Brandon and Clio
1991	Mt. Morris	2016	Kearsley
1992	Holly	2017	Kearsley
1993	LakeVille	2018	Holly

MHSAA State Champions: Fenton (Class B) 1972, 1973, 1990 Lapeer West (Div. 2) 2000, 2001

MHSAA State Runners-up:
Fenton (Class B) 1971		Swartz Creek (Class A) 1972
Durand (Class B) 1982		Lapeer West (Div. 2) 2003
Oxford (Div. 2) 2009		

Four-time League Individual Champions:

Terry Nicholson, Carman	1970-73	Tony Holifield, Mt. Morris	1995-98
Greg Tucker, Swartz Creek	1971-74	Harold Eastman, Mt. Morris	1996-99
Stan Marshall, LakeVile	1994-97	Scott Pushman, Fenton	1997-2000

Roger Kish, Lapeer West   2000-03
David Schlaud, Lapeer West   2000-03
Justin Chrznowski, Lap. West 2002-05
Josh Houldsworth, Holly   2007-10

Anthony Gonzales, Holly   2010-13
Mason Smith, Clio   2012-15
Bryan LaVearn, Brandon   2013-16

MHSAA Individual State Champions

Marv Pushman	Fenton	1969	Scott Pushman	Fenton	1998
Brad Tucker	Swartz Creek	1972	Tony Holifield	Mt. Morris	1998
Mark Wiesen	Fenton	1972	Scott Pushman	Fenton	1999
Joseph Varney	Fenton	1972	Justin Torres	Holly	1999
Mark Whaley	Swartz Creek	1973	Lambros Kottalis	Fenton	2000
Randall Chene	Fenton	1973	Rory Medina	Lapeer West	2000
Mike Pickhover	Fenton	1974	James Kish	Lapeer West	2000
Steve Powers	Ainsworth	1975	Roger Kish	Lapeer West	2000
Robin Sweetman	Fenton	1975	Eric Ghiaciuc	Oxford	2000
Dennis Schumaker	Fenton	1976	Jason Fellows	Lapeer West	2001
Jeff Merrill	Fenton	1978	James Kish	Lapeer West	2001
Greg Sargis	Durand	1979	Roger Kish	Lapeer West	2001
Jeff Ellis	Durand	1980	Willie Breyer	Oxford	2001
Brian Hittle	LakeVille	1980	Jon Herstein	Fenton	2001
Rex Hart	Ainsworth	1981	Mike Pickhover	Fenton	2002
Scott Savoie	Ainsworth	1981	Roger Kish	Lapeer West	2002
Mark Clough	Durand	1982	Justin Chrzanowski	Lapeer West	2003
Rick Walt	Ainsworth	1983	Tim Breyer	Oxford	2003
Dave Ketter	Ainsworth	1983	Tony Lyssiotis	Oxford	2003
Dave Walt	Ainsworth	1984	Roger Kish	Lapeer West	2003
Rick Walt	Ainsworth	1984	Justin Chrzanowski	Lapeer West	2004
Walt Pannick	Ainsworth	1984	Justin Joseph	Lapeer East	2006
Craig Sheeran	Ainsworth	1985	Dave Priest	Swartz Creek	2007
Jim Bailey	LakeVille	1986	Vince Lahar	Clio	2007
Mike Anderson	Mt. Morris	1986	Josh Houldsworth	Holly	2009
Steve Yobuck	Holly	1987	Jake Hyde	Holly	2009
Mike Anderson	Mt. Morris	1987	Phillip Joseph	Lapeer East	2009
Stan Boyd	Holly	1989	Dylan Smith	Oxford	2009
Alan Tyler	Durand	1989	Anthony Gonzales	Holly	2010
Dave Caslmon	Fenton	1990	Josh Houldsworth	Holly	2010
Jeff Nichols	Fenton	1990	Anthony Gonzales	Holly	2012
Corey Kalo	Linden	1994	Shawn Scott	Holly	2012
Stan Marshall	LakeVille	1995	Mason Smith	Clio	2013
Stan Marshall	LakeVille	1996	Mason Smith	Clio	2014
Tony Holifield	Mt. Morris	1997	Ben Cushman	Flushing	2017
Stan Marshall	LakeVille	1997	Ben Cushman	Flushing	2018

Stan Marshall, LakeVille
League Champion 1994-97
State Champion 1995-97

Tony Holifield, Mt. Morris
League Champion 1995-98
State Champion 1997-98

Scott Pushman, Fenton
League Champion 1997-2000
State Champion 1998-99

Roger Kish, Lapeer West
League Champion 2000-03
State Champion 2000-03

Justin Chrznowski, Lap. West
League Champion 2002-05
State Champion 2003-04

Josh Houldsworth, Holly
League Champion 2007-10
State Champion 2009-10

Anthony Gonzales, Holly
League Champion 2010-13
State Champion 2010, 2012

Mason Smith, Clio
League Champion 2012-15
State Champion 2013-14

ATHLETES

FLINT METRO LEAGUE WINNERS OF THE DONALD B. SARK FLINT AREA ATHLETE OF THE YEAR AWARD

1980	Jeff Crace, LakeVille
1987	Michael Anderson, Mt. Morris
1988	Amy Warner, Linden
1989	Robert Oginsky, Mt. Morris
1991	Laura Bell, LakeVille
1992	Emily Kaiser, LakeVille
1993	David Dodge, Mt. Morris
1995	Molly Hugan, Holly
1995	Stephen Burdis, Mt. Morris
1999	Jessica Hoppe, Lapeer East
2007	Amy Morrison, Fenton
2010	Tori Bailey, Fenton
2010	Josh Houldsworth, Holly
2016	Hannah Ploof, Kearsley

**Tori Bailey and Josh Houldsworth
2010 Sark Award Winners**

First Team All-Metro League in Three or More Sports

The pinnacle of athletic accomplishment for an athlete in the Flint Metro League is being named first-team all-league, either by the selection of league coaches or by being the individual champion in a league championship meet event. To do so in multiple sports over an athlete's career exemplifies the highest caliber of athletic achievement, especially while maintaining a high degree of excellence in the classroom and with great character.

Only 56 student-athletes from Flint Metro League schools have been named first team All-League in three or more different sports over the league's first fifty years. They are pictured on the following pages in chronological order with their sports and years of first team all-league status listed.

Swartz Creek's Jackson Maxwell exemplified the qualities of a multi-sport athlete. The only male athlete in Metro League history to be named first team all-league in four sports, Jackson excelled in soccer, football, swim/dive and track & field. He was the MHSAA state diving champion in 2014, and kicked a 48-yard field goal, tied for fourth best all time, in 2012.

Jayce Smith

Fenton
Football 75
Basketball 75
Baseball 76

Julie Roberts

Fenton
Track 74, 75, 76
Basketball 75, 76
Volleyball 77

Gale Valley

Lapeer West
Basketball 75, 76
Volleyball 77
Softball 77

Chris Gilbert

Fenton
Cross Country 76, 77
Basketball 77
Track 76, 77

Sue Williams

Ainsworth
Basketball 76, 77, 78
Volleyball 78, 79
Softball 77, 78

Sandi Johnson

Fenton
Volleyball 77, 78, 79
Track 77
Softball 78, 79

Jeff Crace

LakeVille
Football 78, 79
Basketball 80
Baseball 80

Polly Edwards

Fenton
Basketball 80
Volleyball 81
Track 79, 80

Matt Dunlop

Fenton
Golf 82
Wrestling 83
Tennis 83

Dave Hintz

Fenton
Football 83
Basketball 84, 85
Track 85

Steve Buerkel

Linden
Football 87
Basketball 88
Baseball 87

Jeff Nichols

Fenton
Football 89
Wrestling 89, 90
Track 88, 89, 90

Bruce Bretzke

Linden
Football 86
Basketball 87
Track 87

Colleen Curcio

Oxford
Basketball 88
Track 87
Soccer 89

Angie Griffin

Fenton
Basketball 89
Volleyball 90
Softball 89, 90

Ron Buff

LakeVille
Football 86, 87
Basketball 87
Baseball 88

Scott Winterlee

Mt. Morris
Football 88
Basketball 89
Baseball 88, 89

Patti Earnheart

Oxford
Basketball 89
Track 88
Softball 90

Alex Lukshaitis

Holly
Football 89
Basketball 90
Baseball 90

Jeff O'Neill

Lapeer West
Football 89, 90
Basketball 91
Baseball 90

Chris Laidlaw

Oxford
Football 90
Basketball 91
Baseball 90

Ryan Buckler

Linden
Football 91
Basketball 93
Track 92, 93

Kelly Spencer

Holly
Basketball 92
Volleyball 92, 93
Track 91

Amanda Behrenbrinker

Lapeer East
Basketball 92, 93
Softball 92, 93, 94
Track 92

Molly Hugan

Holly
Basketball 93, 94
Volleyball 95
Softball 95

Jaimie Kelly

Holly
Basketball 93
Volleyball 94
Soccer 94

Becki Wheatley

Fenton
Basketball 94, 95
Volleyball 95, 96
Softball 96

147

Josh Clymer

Durand
Football 95
Wrestling 94, 95
Track 94

Dru Bishop

Fenton
Basketball 96, 97, 98
Volleyball 98, 99
Track 96, 97, 98, 99

Kyle Hopkins

Linden
Football 97
Basketball 98
Baseball 97

Shelley Slater

Lapeer East
Basketball 96
Volleyball 97
Soccer 95
Track 96

Jessica Hoppe

Lapeer East
Basketball 97, 98
Volleyball 98, 99
Soccer 96, 97, 98, 99

Kyle Korpalski

Lapeer East
Golf 97, 98, 99
Cross Country 98, 99
Track 98, 99

Sarah Courtwright

Oxford
Basketball 96, 97
Volleyball 98
Soccer 95, 96, 97, 98

Lindsay Hourtienne

Lapeer East
Volleyball 97
Soccer 95, 96, 97
Track 96

Rebecca Moller

LakeVille
Basketball 99, 00
Volleyball 99, 00, 01
Track 99

Eric Ghiaciauc

Oxford
Football 99
Wrestling 98, 99, 00
Track 99, 00

Caryn Inman

Oxford
Basketball 02
Volleyball 02, 03
Track 00, 01, 02, 03

Taylor Erwin

Fenton
Basketball 03
Volleyball 03, 04
Softball 04

Bert DesJardins

Lapeer East
Football 99
Basketball 00
Tennis 98

Luis Gomez

Oxford
Football 02
Wrestling 03
Track 03

Chris Francis

Lapeer East
Football 03, 04
Basketball 05
Track 02, 05

Breanne Hulette

Lapeer East
Basketball 00
Volleyball 01
Soccer 99, 00, 01

Desi Mayner

Linden
Football 02, 03
Basketball 04
Baseball 03

Savannah Stedman

Brandon
Basketball 04, 05, 06
Volleyball 05, 06, 07
Track 05, 06, 07

Amy Morrison

Fenton
Swim/Dive 04, 05, 06
Volleyball 07
Track 04, 05, 06, 07

Kyle Fisher

Linden
Football 09, 10
Wrestling 10, 11
Track 11

Alia Frederick

Linden
Cross Country 15, 16
Track 15, 16, 17
Soccer 15, 16, 17

Josh Williams

Brandon
Golf 05
Football 07
Track 07

Payton Maxheimer

Fenton
Volleyball 11, 12
Basketball 12, 13
Soccer 11, 12, 13

Nick Morrison

Flushing
Soccer 16
Football 17
Track 16, 17, 18

Kelsey Erwin

Fenton
Tennis 06
Volleyball 06, 07
Soccer 05

Jackson Maxwell

Swartz Creek
Soccer 12, 13
Football 12
Swim/Dive 12, 13, 14
Track 13, 14

Cal Endicott

Flushing
Football 17
Basketball 18
Track 17, 18

David Pietryga

Fenton
Football 17
Basketball 18
Baseball 17, 18

Thailyia Christensen

Flushing
Cross Country 17
Basketball 18
Track 18

COACHES

Duane Raffin

Holly

Boys Track State Champs 1971, League Champions 14 times,
Boys CC State Champs 1977 1978, League Champions 15 times,
Girls CC State Champs 1990, League Champions 6 times

The following pages highlight the 98 other Flint Metro League coaches who have coached at least three league championship teams and/or a state championship team.

Ray Ladd

Fenton
Coached the league's first 3
Cross Country champions
1968-1970

Larry Gall

Carman
Baseball
League Champions 1969 71
73 74 76

Duane Wohlfert

Fenton
Wrestling
State Champions 1972 73 90
League Champions 16 times

Ann Maginity

Ainsworth
Girls Basketball
6 time League Champions
Winter 1969 to 73, Fall 1974

Gary Cole

Carman / Ainsworth
Football League Champions
Carman 1969; Ainsworth
1975 76 77

Pat Fields

Carman
League Champions
Football 1971 72 73
Basketball 1971 73

Jane Cook

Swartz Creek
Girls Track
League Champions
1969 to 1972

LeRoy Decker

Fenton
Basketball League Champs
Boys 1970 75 76 77 78
Girls 1978-82, 84

Rod McEachern

Lapeer
Tennis
Boys State Champions 1971
1st 2 League boys' titles 1973
& 74; Girls League Champs
1979 80

Ken Clemens

Swartz Creek
Boys Basketball
League Champions
1972 74 75

Mark Covert

Fenton
League Champions
Football 1972 77 83-85 87 89
Boys Track 1988-89

Bill Jenkins

Fenton
Boys Golf
League Champions
1972 73 74 75

Nancy Clark

Carman
League Champions
Softball 1973 74
Girls Basketball 73 to 75

Roger Lehmann

Swartz Creek
Boys Track
League Champions
1974 to 76

Dave Lazar

Fenton
Softball
State Champions 1978 79 80
League Champions 18 times
1976 to 2003

Ray Campbell

Fenton
Girls Track
League Champions
1976-79

Kenn Domerese

Ainsworth
League Champions
Cross Country 1976 79 81 82
Boys Track 1982
State Champions 1982

Bill Hajec

Fenton
League Champions
Baseball 1975 78 79
Boys Golf 14 times
1976-06

Kirk Louis

Fenton
League Champions
Boys Tennis 1977-83, 85-87
Girls Tennis 1985

Dave Gleason

Lapeer East
League Champions
Boys Basketball 1979-82 84
Boys Track 1999-2000

Conlin Smith

Durand
Boys Basketball
League Champions
1979 83 86

Bob Bruder

Fenton
Boys Basketball
League Champions
1979 83 88-90 99

Rich Burdis

Mt. Morris
Baseball
League Champions
1979 80 88 94 95

Jim Fuller

Durand
League Champions
Football 81 82 83
Baseball 79 83 89

Tim Stone

Ainsworth/ Brandon
Hockey
League Champs
Ainsworth: 1981-86
Brandon: 2006 07

**Linda
Cheseboro/Rusaw**

Fenton
Volleyball
League Champions
1982-87, 1990-93,
2007 (winter), 2008-13
3 times State Runner-up

Brad Gerlach

Lapeer East
Baseball
League Champions
1981 82 84 85

Tom Stasik

Mt. Morris
Softball
State Champions 1984
League Champions
1981 83-85

Don Pluta

Holly
Wrestling
League Champions
1983 92 2005 11-13 18

Jerry Nakoneczny

Lapeer West / East
Boys Basketball
League Champions
West: 1985 87
East: 1995 98 00 02 03 05

Joe Guyski

Durand
Wrestling
League Champions
1982 87 94

Ray Sutherland

Oxford
League Champions
Girls CC 1983 84 88 2000 09
Boys CC 1992 1997-2003
Girls Track 1984 87 88
Boys Track 1993

Darrell Morton

LakeVille
Track
Girls State Champions 1991
League Champions: Girls 85
89-97; Boys 80 92 94-97

Bill McDaniel

Holly
Tennis
League Champions
Boys 15 times 1984-2005
Girls 1982-2004

Elmer Ball

Oxford
Boys Track State Champions
1991
League Champions
1984 87 88 91

Dennis Hopkins

Linden
League Champions
Baseball 1986 87
Basketball 1992 94-96
Football 2002 05 06 08-10 12

156

Bud Rowley

Oxford
Football
State Champions 1992
League Champions 1986 89-
94 98-00 2007 08

Ian Smith

Oxford
Girls Basketball
League Champions
1986-89 91 97 99-01

Bob Vanitvelt

Mt. Morris
Wrestling
League Champions 1987 91
96 97; 3rd in State 1987

Clark Barnes

Fenton
Hockey
League Champions
1987 88 99 2002

Brad Walker

Lapeer West
Softball
League Champions
1987-91 2003-05 08-09 11

Eric Pfeifer

Oxford
Soccer
League Champions
Boys 1987-93 95 96
Girls 1996

Fred McDowell

LakeVille
Volleyball
League Champions
1988 89 94 95

Bill Sawer

Fenton
League Champions
Soccer 1988 to
1993 (5 times)

Tim Bradley

Lapeer West
League Champions
Boys Golf 1988 96 2000 03
Baseball 1991-93 96 01 03-05

157

Dave DiPietro

Linden
Hockey
League Champions
1989 1992-1996

Jeff Putnam

Lapeer West
Football
State Champions 1995
League Champions 89 95-97

Mike Halstead

Lapeer East
Girls Basketball
League Champions
1990 to 97

Bill Kinzer

Lapeer East
League Champions
Girls Soccer 15 times
1990 to 2009
Girls Basketball 2012

Bill Landrem

Linden
Boys Golf
League Champions
1993 97-99

Dan Purvis

Lapeer East
Volleyball
League Champions
1996-97, 2000-01, 04-06

Lori Campbell

Oxford
Volleyball
League Champions
1997 2002 03

Don Delabbio

Linden
Hockey
League Champions
1997 98 99

Paul Harasti

Lapeer West
Boys Soccer
League Champions
1997 98 99

158

Matt Weisdorfer

Holly
Girls Cross Country
League Champions
1998 99 2001 02 06 08 09 11

Todd Mills

Fenton
League Champions
Girls Cross Country 2002
Girls Track 98 99 02 04 14 16

Kevin Fiebernitz

Linden
Soccer League Champions
Boys 2000 04-06 14-15
Girls 2001-04 10 14-15

Brad DeWitt

Fenton
Girls Basketball
League Champions
1998, 2004 05 07-09
Most BB Coaching Wins (261)

John Virnich

Lapeer West
Wrestling
State Champions 2000 01
League Champions 2000-02

Mike Smith

Lapeer West
Football
League Champions
2000 01 03 07 14

Natalie (Koan) Cook

Fenton
Volleyball
League Champions
1998 99 00

Chad Logan

Fenton
Baseball
League Champions
2000 01 05

Clint Lawhorne

Linden
Boys CC
State Champions 2008
League Champions
Boys CC: 2008-13
Boys Track: 2001 04

Matt Sullivan

Fenton
League Champions
Boys Soccer 2001-03 09 16
Girls Soccer 2005 08 11 13 16
18

Cathy North

Linden
Girls Golf
League Champions
7 times 2002 to 08

Kurt Nuss

Oxford
Baseball
League Champions
2002 07 08

Rick Cradit

Fenton
Boys Track
League Champions
2002-06

Becky Harryman

Linden
League Champions
Girls Track 2003
Girls CC 2007 09 10

Brad Jones

Fenton
League Champions
Girls Swim/Dive 2005 to 17
Boys Swim/Dive 2012 to 18

Kevin McGlashen

Holly
Boys Swim/Dive
League Champions
2005 to 2009

Erin Lane

Lapeer West
Competitive Cheer
League Champions
2005 06 07

Greg Hyde

Brandon
Girls Track
League Champions
2005-07 12-13

Brennan Brown

Holly
League Champions
Boys Tennis 2006-11
Girls Tennis 2005-11

Chad Kenny

Lapeer East
League Champions
Boys Soccer 2007 11
Girls Soccer 2011

Jeff Setzke

Fenton
Football
League Champions 2008
2011-17

Wes Hull

Swartz Creek
Boys Golf
State Champions 2014
League Champions 2006 11
12 14

Scott Couch

Oxford
Wrestling
League Champions
2008 09 10

Will Sophiea

Holly
Tennis
League Champions
Boys 2008-11, 13-17
Girls 2009-11, 13, 15-18

Ron Wiens

Swartz Creek
Boys Track
League Champions
2007 2010 2012

Jamie Slot

Brandon
Competitive Cheer
League Champions
2008-13

Rob Basydlo

Holly
Track
League Champions
Boys: 2008 09 11
Girls: 09 12

Tim Olszewski

Fenton
Boys Basketball
League Champions
2009-13

Lance Baylis

Holly
Boys Basketball
League Champions
2009 14 15

Rob Ploof

Kearsley
Girls Bowling
State Champions 2012 14-18
State Runner-up 2010
League Champions 2010-18

Troy Stamm

Kearsley / Swartz Creek
Boys Bowling
League Champions
Kearsley 2010 11
Sw Ck 2012 13 15 16

Larry Grumley

Lapeer East
Baseball
League Champions
2010 11 12

Kurt Herbstreit

Fenton
League Champions
Girls Golf 2012 13 15-17
Boys Golf 2017 18

Rick Clolinger

Swartz Creek
Softball
League Champions
2012 13 18

Teresa Wright

Linden
Girls Cross Country
League Champions
2012 13 15

Rich Brinker

Holly
League Champions
Boys CC 13 14
Boys Track 2013 14 15
Girls Track 2013

Bart Rutledge

Kearsley
Boys Bowling
State Champions 2014 15
State Runner-up 2016
League Champions 14 15 17

Jerry Eisinger

Fenton
Volleyball
League Champions
2015 16 17

Adam Smith

Flushing
Boys Basketball
League Champions
2016 17 18

Brooke Sharrard

Brandon/Kearsley
Competitive Cheer
League Champions
Brandon: 2014 15 16
Kearsley: 2018

Larry Ford

Flushing
Girls Basketball
State Champions 2017
League Champions 2015-18

Roger Ellis

Fenton / Linden
Girls Lacrosse
League Champions
2016 17 18

Shawn Lovelace

Brandon
Boys Soccer
League Champions
2015 16 17

Marcus Endicott

Flushing
League Champions
Girls Track 2015 18
Boys Track 2016 18

LEADERS

FOUNDERS

The six men who served as principals of the high schools that formed the original membership of the Flint Metro League:

Herbert Palmer,

Ainsworth

Richard Knoop,

Carman

Josef Horak,

Fenton

Norm Jones,

Holly

Henry Smith,

Lapeer

Richard Johnson,

Swartz Creek

These high school principals, as the educational leaders of their buildings, were responsible for drafting the league's constitution. They established the precedents that would allow future change as progress in interscholastic athletics occurred (for example, the growth of girls' athletics) without deviating from the core values of *fair and safe competition* while viewing athletics as an *extension of the classroom*.

LEAGUE LEADERSHIP

Fred Briggs

First Commissioner of the
Flint Metro League
1968-1992; received
MHSAA's Vern Norris
Award in 1993

Gary Oyster

Executive Director
2005-2016

Cathy North

Executive Director
2016 to present

STATE-WIDE LEADERSHIP

**Robert Doctor,
Durand**

Served on the MHSAA
Representative Council
after becoming Principal of
Durand HS in 1993; had
been MHSAA president
from 1976 to 1978 while
principal at Petoskey HS

**Nancy Clark,
Carman**

Pioneering girls' coach at
Carman HS; one of the
state's first female athletic
directors, she served on
the MHSAA
Representative Council
and received the MHSAA's
Women in Sports
Leadership Award in 2003

**Dave Durkin,
Lapeer**

Commissioner of the
Genesee County HS
Hockey League;
managed the MHSAA state
hockey tournament for the
years it was held in Flint.
He received the MHSAA's
Norris Award in 2001.

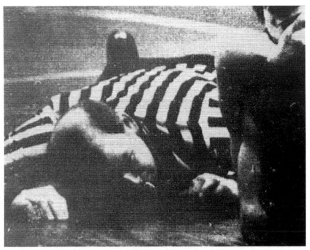

Joe Piwowarczyk, Linden

Linden's long-time athletic director was also
a highly respected wrestling official, shown
here officiating at the MHSAA finals

Caycee Turczyn, Lapeer West

Member of MHSAA Student Advisory
Council 2013-15
Helped develop and hosted MHSAA's online
Captains Course

**Deb VanKuiken,
Holly**

President of the state
Athletic Directors
association (**MIAAA**) 2008;
MIAAA Athletic Director of
the Year 2015;
Recipient of the MHSAA's
2009 Women in Sports
Leadership Award and
2016 Allen W. Bush Award

**Mike Bakker,
Fenton**

President of the **MIAAA**
2015
Long-time President of the
Greater Flint Athletic
Administrators Association

**Dr. Dallas Lintner,
Owosso**

President of the **MIAAA**
2018

INDEX OF FIRST TEAM ALL-LEAGUE 1968 – 2018

What would a "starting lineup" look like if all of a league's schools formed a single team in a given year? In essence that lineup would look like the first team All-League athletes selected for or earning that status for that season.

Beginning in the Flint Metro League's first year, league coaches selected All-League Teams for football, boys' basketball, and baseball. League champions were determined for each weight class in the league wrestling tournament and each event in the league track and field championship meet; the top finishers in the league cross country championship meet were recognized and earned medals. Within four years Metro League principals and athletic directors standardized All-League honors by purchasing identical league medals and certificates to be presented to athletes chosen by coaches or earning individual championships in their sports.

The following is an alphabetical listing of every athlete known to have earned first team All-Metro League status starting in 1968. Please note that because the standardization of All-League status did not occur until

1972, years prior to that in this list include the first seven finishers in the league cross country meets and the top five finishers in the league golf tournaments. Golf coaches began selecting All-League boys' golf teams at post-season meetings in 1978, then resumed using combined tournament finish to determine all league in 2009.

Key to abbreviations used for sports:

BSB	Baseball	LAX	Lacrosse
BSK	Basketball	SB	Softball
BWL	Bowling	SCR	Soccer
CC	Cross Country	SW	Swim/Dive
CHR	Competitive Cheer	TEN	Tennis
FB	Football	TR	Track & Field
GLF	Golf	VB	Volleyball
HKY	Hockey	WR	Wrestling

Key to abbreviations used for schools:

AIN	Ainsworth	LAP	Lapeer (HS or Co-op)
BRAN	Brandon	LAP E	Lapeer East
CAR	Carman	LAP W	Lapeer West
CLIO	Clio	LIN	Linden
DUR	Durand	LKV	LakeVille
FEN	Fenton	MT M	Mt. Morris
FLU	Flushing	OWO	Owosso
HOL	Holly	OXF	Oxford
KEAR	Kearsley	SW CK	Swartz Creek

NOTE: While every effort has been made to correctly spell the names on this listing, the data is based on records found in newspaper files.

The list of first team all-league selections for the following teams is incomplete as no record was found in Flint Journal archives, and what is listed was gathered from local newspapers or high school yearbooks: 1976 softball; 1984 boys' golf; 1986 boys' soccer; and 1989 boys' soccer.

Name	Team	Sport	Yr				
Aaron, Jeff	AIN	**FB**	80				
Abood, Greg	LAP W	**FB**	92				
Accardo, Greg	AIN	**TEN**	84				
Achtabowski, Jack	LAP	**FB**	73				
Acken, Gayle	AIN	**VB**	83				
Acker, Chelsea	LIN	**BSK**	03	**SCR**	04		
Acox, Taylor	LIN	**SCR**	18				
Acre, Morgan	LKV	**TR**	00	01	02		
Acton, Jeff	LAP W	**BWL**	10	12			
Acton, Matt	FEN	**BSB**	15				
Adado, Mackenzie	CLIO	**CHR**	17	18			
Adam, Jake	LAP W	**FB**	04	05			
Adams, Amy	FEN	**BSK**	78	**SB**	78		
Adams, Andrew	HOL	**TEN**	90	92			
Adams, Brendan	FLU	**BWL**	15				
Adams, Bridget	LIN	**VB**	15				
Adams, Clarke	LAP	**BSK**	69	70			
Adams, Corey	CLIO	**BSB**	15				
Adams, Corey	HOL	**TEN**	01				
Adams, Dave	HOL	**WR**	96	97			
Adams, Greg	FEN	**FB**	79	**TR**	80	81	
Adams, Jennifer	LAP W	**BSK**	03	04	05		
Adams, Jerry	LKV	**GLF**	76				
Adams, Jim	FEN	**SCR**	02				
Adams, Jim	FEN	**TR**	77				
Adams, Liam	FEN	**SCR**	15	16			
Adams, Peter	FLU	**SW**	18				
Adams, Rick	FEN	**BSK**	69				
Adams, Scott	LKV	**CC**	76				
Adams, Thomas	FEN	**WR**	18				
Adamson, Dan	AIN	**FB**	68				
Adas, Lauren	SW CK	**BSK**	13	**SB**	12	13	
Adas, Paul	KEAR	**BSK**	11	12	**BSB**	12	
Addis, Keith	HOL	**TR**	77	79			
Aderholdt, Jessica	HOL	**TEN**	11				
Adkins, Greg	LAP E	**BSK**	94				
Aguirre, Alex	LKV	**SCR**	02				
Aiken, Ray	LIN	**HKY**	87				
Aikens, John	HOL	**WR**	05				
Aikins, Bryan	HOL	**BSK**	79				
Alban, Kevin	OXF	**FB**	00				
Albert, Darryl	LAP W	**SCR**	94				
Albert, Mitch	FLU	**FB**	14	**BSB**	15		
Albertson, Tory	OXF	**CC**	00	01			
Albrecht, Madeliene	FEN	**LAX**	16				
Alburtus, Kaitlyn	KEAR	**CHR**	15	17			
Alderman, Lea	KEAR	**SB**	14				

Alderman, Tom	DUR	**WR**	87	88			
Alderson, Julie	LKV	**BSK**	87				
Alderson, Shane	LKV	**BSK**	85	86			
Aldred, Kiley	FEN	**TR**	17				
Aldrich, Jan	FEN	**TR**	70	71			
Aldrich, Margaret	FEN	**TR**	72	75			
Aldrich, Stanette	FEN	**TR**	77				
Aleman, Toni	CLIO	**SCR**	17				
Alexander, Ashley	LIN	**SB**	00				
Alexander, Melina	CLIO	**SCR**	11				
Alexander, Nikki	LKV	**CC**	93	94	**TR**	93	94
Alexander, Sean	FEN	**BSB**	07				
Allen, Chad	MT M	**WR**	90				
Allen, Cliff	FEN	**WR**	73	74			
Allen, Corey	FEN	**BSB**	89				
Allen, Heather	HOL	**TR**	80	81			
Allen, Heidi	HOL	**TR**	80	81			
Allen, Jimmy	FEN	**FB**	09				
Allen, Karen	DUR	**VB**	81				
Allen, Kenny	FEN	**FB**	10	11			
Allen, Kenny	OXF	**FB**	97	**BSB**	97	98	
Allen, Libbie	AIN	**CC**	81				
Allen, Luke	MT M	**BSK**	02	**BSB**	01	02	
Allen, Mike	BRAN	**TR**	17				
Allen, Tim	CAR	**TR**	72				
Allessie, Casey	SW CK	**SCR**	15	16	17		
Allie, Aaron	FEN	**BSB**	03				
Allie, Amber	FEN	**SB**	98	00			
Allison, Cash	HOL	**WR**	83				
Allison, Conn	FEN	**WR**	85	86			
Allmand, Wes	LAP W	**BSB**	83				
Allmond, Melissa	LAP W	**TEN**	86				
Almassy, Andrea	SW CK	**BSK**	09				
Almasy, Ben	MT M	**BSB**	92				
Almeranti, Shawn	OXF	**SCR**	92				
Almquist, Dave	CAR	**SW**	71				
Altheide, Tracy	LAP E	**CC**	79				
Alvaredo, Emily	HOL	**TR**	14	15			
Alvord, Brad	MT M	**FB**	92				
Alvord, Brendan	FEN	**BSB**	18				
Amatucci, Jamie	LIN	**SCR**	03				
Amatucci, Kyle	LIN	**SCR**	04				
Ambler, Pam	FEN	**TR**	70	71	72		
Ambler, Sue	FEN	**TR**	75	76	77	78	
Amell, Todd	HOL	**TEN**	81				
Amerson, Terry	HOL	**TR**	85				
Amman, Jack	DUR	**FB**	78				
Ammon, Dale	FEN	**TEN**	79	80			

Name	School	Sport						
Anderson, Andrew	HOL	**BWL**	11					
Anderson, Brian	LAP W	**GLF**	93					
Anderson, Clyde	CLIO	**CC**	13					
Anderson, Craig	FEN	**FB**	68					
Anderson, Erik	OXF	**SCR**	06					
Anderson, Jane	FEN	**SB**	77					
Anderson, Jennifer	LAP E	**VB**	86					
Anderson, Jerry	FEN	**BSB**	77					
Anderson, Jesse	FEN	**CC**	05	06	07	**TR**	06	07	08
Anderson, Joel	DUR	**TR**	95	96				
Anderson, John	FEN	**CC**	68					
Anderson, Katie	FEN	**BSK**	76	**TR**	75	76	77	
Anderson, Matt	OXF	**CC**	99					
Anderson, Mike	MT M	**WR**	86	87				
Anderson, Rachell	FEN	**TEN**	14					
Anderson, Ray	AIN	**BSB**	80	81				
Anderson, Russell	HOL	**SCR**	99	**TEN**	99	00		
Anderson, Sam	SW CK	**BSB**	17					
Anderson, Taylor	LIN	**TR**	11	12				
Anderson, Wanda	FEN	**TR**	73					
Andre, Patrice	BRAN	**BSK**	02					
Andreski, Adam	FEN	**SW**	12	13				
Andreski, Austin	FEN	**SW**	10					
Andrews, Hunter	LAP W	**FB**	13					
Andrews, Tyler	LAP W	**FB**	09					
Andrykovich, Dick	SW CK	**TR**	75					
Anetrini, Anthony	HOL	**TEN**	06					
Angell, Gethin	OXF	**SCR**	07					
Anibal, Dan	FEN	**TEN**	82					
Anschutz, Kevin	FEN	**BSB**	84					
Antcliff, Allan	CLIO	**BSB**	12					
Antcliff, Dylan	CLIO	**BSK**	17					
Antior, Mike	AIN	**FB**	81					
Antonides, Adam	LAP W	**FB**	03	04	**WR**	04	05	
Applin, Laurie	FEN	**SB**	99	00				
Arajuuri, Niila	LAP E	**SCR**	05					
Arasim, Maria	LIN	**TR**	86					
Archambeault, Dan	FEN	**SW**	76					
Archibald, Tariq	BRAN	**BSK**	15	16				
Ardelan, Julie	LAP W	**CHR**	08					
Ardelan, Libby	OXF	**CHR**	06	07				
Aris, Paul	FEN	**TEN**	86	88	89			
Aris, Tammy	FEN	**TEN**	88					
Arkwright, Jaylon	CLIO	**BSK**	14					
Armour, Bryce	LIN	**SCR**	94	95	96			
Armour, Mark	LIN	**SCR**	00					
Arms, Emily	LAP W	**TR**	04	05				
Armstrong, Ben	LIN	**FB**	11	12				

Armstrong, Nate	LIN	**FB**	08	09			
Arney, Paige	BRAN	**CC**	11	12	13		
Arnold, Jenny	OXF	**SCR**	96				
Arnold, Todd	HOL	**TEN**	92				
Arnott, Paul	HOL	**TEN**	03				
Arnott, Rachelle	HOL	**TEN**	00	01			
Arnott, Rick	SW CK	**BSK**	72				
Aro, Cassie	LIN	**SCR**	08				
Ashford, Danielle	BRAN	**CC**	04				
Ashley, Jerad	HOL	**SCR**	07				
Ashley, Jim	HOL	**FB**	78	**TR**	79		
Atalos, Mike	HOL	**CC**	89				
Atherton, Drew	SW CK	**BSB**	17				
Atwood, Josh	LAP W	**SCR**	00				
Atwood, Katie	LAP W	**SCR**	09	10			
August, Cheri	AIN	**SB**	75				
Aumiller, Joe	FEN	**SW**	74	75			
Auquier, Heather	LAP E	**SCR**	90				
Austin, Alex	OXF	**SCR**	05				
Austin, Chad	OXF	**FB**	95				
Austin, D'Anthony	HOL	**TR**	16				
Austin, Jon	FEN	**SW**	10				
Austin, Mark	OXF	**FB**	99	01			
Avery, Ken	FEN	**FB**	71	**WR**	72		
Avery, Mark	DUR	**FB**	78				
Avis, Brad	LAP	**CC**	72	73			
Ayan, Laura	LAP W	**CHR**	09				
Ayan, Laura	OXF	**CHR**	08				
Ayanian, John	FEN	**TEN**	83				
Ayotte, Kirk	FEN	**BSK**	88				
Ayres, Kate	LAP E	**SB**	08	09			
Azelton, Matt	LKV	**FB**	85				
Bachand, Melissa	LAP E	**SCR**	93				
Back, Jackie	BRAN	**CC**	02	**SCR**	03	04	05
Backhus, Brad	FEN	**FB**	90				
Backhus, Greg	FEN	**FB**	88				
Badgley, Mark	SW CK	**CC**	72	**TR**	72	73	
Baeckeroot, Katherine	LAP	**SW**	07				
Baguley, Laura	LAP E	**SB**	78				
Bailey, Amanda	FEN	**SCR**	06	07			
Bailey, Jason	OXF	**FB**	95				
Bailey, Jeff	LKV	**BSB**	87				
Bailey, Jeremy	LKV	**WR**	88				
Bailey, Jim	LKV	**WR**	85	86			
Bailey, Kelly	FEN	**SB**	94	95	96		
Bailey, Megan	LAP E	**TR**	03				
Bailey, Mike	FEN	**TEN**	83				
Bailey, Nick	HOL	**WR**	06				

Bailey, Tori	FEN	**SCR**	07	08	09	10	
Baird, Brandy	HOL	**TEN**	99	00			
Baird, Heather	HOL	**TEN**	99	00	01		
Baker, Dave	AIN	**TEN**	79				
Baker, Jamie	FEN	**TEN**	97				
Baker, Kevin	LIN	**FB**	10	11	**TR**	12	
Baker, Malinda	AIN	**TR**	83				
Baker, Matt	FEN	**GLF**	91	92			
Bakos, Zach	LIN	**SCR**	10	11	12	13	
Baldwin, Brad	LIN	**BSB**	88				
Baldwin, Tom	LAP	**TEN**	74				
Balhorn, Dawn	HOL	**TEN**	84	85			
Balizkat, Zach	HOL	**SW**	08	09			
Balk, Stephan	LAP E	**HKY**	93				
Balkevitch, Dave	LAP E	**TR**	86				
Ballard, Bill	HOL	**CC**	76				
Ballard, Jason	LKV	**TR**	94				
Ballard, Madison	FEN	**TEN**	12	13	14	15	
Ballard, Randy	AIN	**WR**	71				
Ballard, Ray	LIN	**TR**	16				
Ballenberger, Emily	OXF	**SCR**	97				
Ballenberger, Jessica	OXF	**SCR**	96	97			
Baltizkat, Brittany	HOL	**SW**	07				
Baltosser, Hailey	KEAR	**CHR**	15	16	17		
Baltosser, Isabella	KEAR	**CHR**	18				
Bancroft, Andy	FEN	**SW**	76				
Bancroft, Bob	FEN	**CC**	75	**TR**	76		
Bancroft, Dan	FEN	**TR**	74				
Bancroft, Evan	FEN	**CC**	07	08	**TR**	06	08	09
Banes, Colin	HOL	**TR**	12				
Banks, Kathy	LKV	**TR**	93				
Banner, Kyle	FEN	**SW**	15	16	17		
Banner, Mike	FEN	**SW**	13	14			
Bannister, Jason	LAP E	**TR**	96	97	99		
Bannister, Kyle	LAP W	**FB**	09				
Banyas, Brad	LKV	**TR**	77				
Banyas, Derrick	LKV	**SCR**	01				
Banyas, Jason	LKV	**SCR**	96				
Barabour, Ian	FLU	**SW**	18				
Baran, Jon	FEN	**CC**	02	03	**TR**	03	
Barber, Adam	HOL	**WR**	04	**TR**	05		
Barber, Blake	HOL	**TEN**	07f	08	**SW**	09	
Barber, Brittany	BRAN	**TEN**	05	08			
Barber, Eddie	LAP E	**TR**	04				
Barber, Jamie	LAP W	**FB**	93				
Barclay, Barb	FEN	**SB**	78	79			
Barcome, Jeff	FEN	**FB**	83	84			
Barden, David	LKV	**TR**	95	96			

Barisch, Blake	FEN	FB	97	98				
Barish, Blake	FEN	TR	99					
Barker, Chris	LAP E	BSB	78					
Barker, Geoff	LAP E	HKY	79	80				
Barker, Jason	LAP E	FB	03					
Barker, Scott	OXF	TR	87					
Barletta, Jason	FEN	SCR	95					
Barnes, Gordie	FEN	HKY	88					
Barnes, John	FEN	HKY	85					
Barr, Javon	HOL	FB	15	TR	13	14		
Barr, Rick	LKV	SCR	94	97				
Barr, Ross	LKV	SCR	90					
Barr, Sean	HOL	TR	12	13				
Barraco, Todd	LAP W	FB	94	95				
Barrett, Isabella	CLIO	SW	12	13	14			
Barrett, Robin	LAP E	CHR	07					
Barrett, Ruby	HOL	TEN	17	18				
Barrett, Taylor	HOL	TEN	16	17	18			
Barron, Doug	SW CK	SW	73	76				
Barrows, Brent	FEN	TEN	08					
Bartholomew, Devon	CLIO	TR	14					
Barton, Debbie	HOL	CC	90	91	92	TR	93	
Barton, Emily	HOL	TEN	92	93	94	95	SB	95	96
Barton, George	HOL	CC	97					
Bartow, Evan	FEN	SW	17	18				
Baryo, Brad	MT M	CC	86	87	WR	86	88	
Bascom, Donna	LAP W	TR	76					
Bashore, Kelli	FEN	SCR	00					
Bashore, Mark	LAP E	WR	05					
Bashore, Mike	LAP E	WR	05					
Bashore, Tim	LAP E	WR	04	05				
Basinger, Andrew	FLU	SW	15					
Bates, Brian	SW CK	TR	75					
Bates, Curtis	HOL	TR	74	75				
Bates, Dave	FEN	TEN	82	83				
Bates, Julie	LAP E	TEN	85					
Battaglia, Emily	FEN	TR	14					
Batten, Shae	KEAR	TR	10	11				
Batterbee, John	MT M	FB	81	82				
Batterbee, Lauren	MT M	FB	78					
Battles, Jessica	LIN	TR	03					
Bauer, Steve	HOL	CC	71					
Bauserman, Justin	SW CK	BSB	15					
Baxter, Chris	MT M	BSK	97					
Baylis, Morgan	HOL	TEN	11	12	13	14		
Baylis, Noah	HOL	BSK	18					
Beadlescomb, Mickey	BRAN	BWL	14					
Beam, Katie	OXF	VB	97					

Bean, Katrina	SW CK	**CC**	09						
Bean, Mike	LAP W	**HKY**	98						
Beard, D'Asia	SW CK	**CHR**	16	17					
Bearden, Ashley	FEN	**VB**	12	13	**TEN**	13			
Beardon, Bob	LAP W	**TR**	88						
Beardsley, Rachel	FEN	**TR**	02						
Bearss, Rich	LAP E	**FB**	86						
Beatty, Eileen	AIN	**TR**	73						
Beatty, Kim	FEN	**TR**	78						
Beauchamp, Ryan	BRAN	**FB**	17						
Beauregard, Katelyn	HOL	**TEN**	15						
Beck, Elizabeth	FEN	**TR**	97	98	99				
Beck, Sarah	HOL	**TR**	00	01					
Beckemeyer, Bob	FEN	**BSB**	83						
Becker, Scott	FEN	**FB**	14						
Beckman, Jaxson	SW CK	**BSB**	17						
Beckner, Matt	HOL	**SCR**	10	**BSB**	11				
Beckwith, Cameron	SW CK	**GLF**	18						
Bectal, Nick	OXF	**TR**	98						
Bedore, Fred	DUR	**CC**	90	91					
Beebe, Brian	LAP W	**FB**	08						
Beecher, Chase	CLIO	**SCR**	16	**WR**	16				
Beeler, Jonathon	HOL	**TR**	09	10					
Beemer, Justin	FEN	**SW**	16	17					
Beesley, Madisen	HOL	**SB**	17	18					
Begley, Jessie	BRAN	**TEN**	10						
Behme, Sebastian	CLIO	**TR**	15	16					
Behrenbrinker, Amanda	LAP E	**BSK**	92	93	**SB**	92	93	94	**TR**	92
Behrend, Brad	HOL	**BSK**	04						
Behrens, Chelsea	LIN	**GLF**	07f	08					
Belill, Liam	CLIO	**SCR**	13	**TR**	14				
Belitsos, George	OXF	**FB**	01	**TR**	01	02			
Belitsos, Vince	OXF	**TR**	04	05					
Bell, Emily	LAP E	**SB**	99	01					
Bell, Laura	LKV	**CC**	88	89	90	**TR**	88	89	90	91
Bell, Mark	HOL	**BSK**	89						
Bell, Pat	OXF	**FB**	97						
Bellairs, Molly	LIN	**SCR**	09	10					
Bellinger, Heather	FEN	**TR**	90	91					
Belmore, Lucas	LIN	**TR**	11						
Beltz, Katie	LAP E	**VB**	02						
Beltz, Wendy	OXF	**TR**	85						
Bemis, Cory	DUR	**TR**	94						
Bemis, Emily	FEN	**TR**	11	13	14				
Benedict, Jamie	FEN	**SW**	06	07	08				
Benedict, Tyler	LIN	**BSB**	12						
Benge, Sawyer	LIN	**FB**	15	16					
Benjamin, Alena	SW CK	**TR**	16						

Name	School	Sport				
Benner, Devon	LAP E	**VB**	08	**SCR**	10	
Benner, Hannan	CLIO	**SB**	16	17		
Bennett, Lesa	OXF	**BSK**	89			
Bennett, Rich	KEAR	**BSB**	15			
Bennett, Stephanie	FEN	**TR**	86			
Benscoter, Catherine	LAP W	**GLF**	07f	08	09	
Benscoter, Jaquee	LAP W	**GLF**	05	06	07	
Bensett, Amy	HOL	**TEN**	84	85		
Benson, Logan	FEN	**BSB**	17			
Bentley, Beth	HOL	**SB**	77			
Bentoski, Casey	LKV	**WR**	98	99		
Bentowski, Celena	LKV	**SB**	97			
Berent, Terese	FEN	**TEN**	96	97		
Berger, Grant	HOL	**TEN**	05			
Berish, Jon	LAP W	**GLF**	00			
Berkley, Teresa	LAP W	**TEN**	80	**SB**	81	
Berlanga, Lorenzo	AIN	**CC**	85	**TR**	85	
Berlin, Lauren	LIN	**TR**	10			
Berlinger, Dave	OXF	**FB**	91	**BSB**	91	92
Berman, Emily	LAP W	**BSK**	94	95		
Bernard, Dave	LAP W	**FB**	89			
Berney, Dave	OXF	**FB**	90	**TR**	91	92
Berra, Steve	FEN	**GLF**	96			
Berry, Chris	LIN	**TR**	06			
Berry, Jordan	LAP W	**FB**	03			
Berry, Kevin	LIN	**FB**	03			
Berry, Margaret	FEN	**GLF**	16	17	**SCR**	16	18
Berry, Patrick	FEN	**HKY**	10			
Berry, Sam	HOL	**BSB**	82			
Berth, Larry	MT M	**FB**	78			
Bertolini, Dave	OXF	**FB**	93			
Beshears, Dennis	FEN	**TR**	71			
Besko, Jake	FLU	**TEN**	16			
Best, Matt	LAP W	**HKY**	03	04		
Betley, Stephanie	FEN	**SCR**	94			
Betz, Chris	LKV	**CC**	98			
Betz, Dean	LAP W	**WR**	84			
Beukema, Mike	HOL	**TR**	86	87		
Bidelman, Ralph	FEN	**WR**	89			
Biebuyck, Brenda	OXF	**CC**	83	**TR**	84	
Bien, Chris	OXF	**CC**	96	97		
Bigelow, Jeff	MT M	**FB**	83			
Bigelow, Megan	FLU	**SCR**	15	16		
Bilbia, Makayla	HOL	**TEN**	18			
Bilkos, Ryan	BRAN	**GLF**	05	06		
Bilkos, Ryan	HOL	**GLF**	08			
Billings, Jeff	FEN	**BSB**	91			
Billups, Eric	FEN	**HKY**	90			

Binkowski, Sam	FLU	**TR**	15									
Birchmeier, Carson	LIN	**SCR**	16	17								
Bisbee, Lainie	HOL	**CC**	01									
Bishop, Darlene	LKV	**SB**	90									
Bishop, Dru	FEN	**BSK**	96	97	98	**VB**	98	99	**TR**	96	97	98	99
Bishop, Jeremy	LAP E	**HKY**	02									
Bison, Joe	AIN	**FB**	75									
Bissonette, Vickie	LAP E	**SCR**	89									
Bittle, Chris	OXF	**FB**	98									
Black, Derek	FLU	**GLF**	15	16								
Black, Lauren	BRAN	**SB**	14									
Black, Lauren	SW CK	**SB**	13									
Blackmer, Blake	FEN	**HKY**	99	00	01							
Blackwell, Debbie	LAP E	**TR**	79									
Blackwell, Paul	LKV	**CC**	78									
Blackwell, Rob	LAP E	**CC**	76	**TR**	78	79						
Blade, Derrick	MT M	**BSK**	93									
Blaine, Josh	LAP E	**FB**	02									
Blake, Christy	MT M	**SB**	85	87								
Blake, Ryan	OXF	**FB**	99									
Blakeley, Joe	BRAN	**SCR**	08									
Blakely, Ginny	HOL	**TEN**	03	04	05	06						
Blakely, Mike	FEN	**TEN**	94									
Blakely, Sarah	FEN	**VB**	91	92	**SB**	92						
Blaney, Tanner	LIN	**CC**	17	**TR**	18							
Blank, Bella	LIN	**TR**	14	15								
Blank, Dallas	LIN	**WR**	10	11								
Blank, Dawson	LIN	**WR**	16	17								
Blasie, Scott	FEN	**GLF**	73	74	**TEN**	75						
Blaszczyk, Thad	LAP W	**BSB**	00									
Blazo, Brett	LAP E	**FB**	99									
Blazo, Howard	LAP W	**GLF**	77									
Bleicher, Brenna	FEN	**TR**	17									
Blewett, Josh	LAP W	**FB**	92									
Bliss, Kyle	FEN	**LAX**	17	18								
Blissett, Frank	FEN	**CC**	68	69	70							
Blond, Imari	KEAR	**BWL**	17	18								
Blondin, Bill	OXF	**FB**	87									
Bloomfield, Mike	MT M	**BSB**	82									
Blough, Jake	FEN	**TR**	04									
Blugerman, Dana	HOL	**SB**	00	01	02	03						
Boatwright, Karen	FEN	**SB**	75									
Bochard, Linda	AIN	**VB**	78									
Bodette, Shannon	CLIO	**CHR**	12									
Bodnar, Hannah	CLIO	**CHR**	14	15								
Bodnar, Mackenzie	CLIO	**CHR**	10	13								
Boehmer, Chris	LAP W	**BSK**	81	**TR**	79	80	81	82				
Boeneman, Aleasha	LAP E	**SB**	05									

Boggs, Ashley	LIN	**CHR**	12				
Bogie, Ayla	CLIO	**GLF**	11	12			
Bogie, Jim	MT M	**BSB**	77				
Bogie, Steve	MT M	**BSB**	79				
Bogusky, Greg	LIN	**HKY**	88	89			
Bohl, Darren	LAP W	**TR**	97	98			
Boike, Connor	FLU	**WR**	16				
Bonbrisco, Dana	FEN	**TEN**	89				
Bond, Alec	LIN	**GLF**	14				
Bond, Andrew	FEN	**CC**	15	16	**TR**	17	
Bond, Bill	OXF	**TR**	84				
Bond, Chris	LIN	**FB**	11				
Bond, Sarah	BRAN	**TR**	04	05	06		
Bond, Stacey	SW CK	**TR**	76				
Bonfiglio, Marco	OXF	**SCR**	09				
Bonfiglio, Molly	OXF	**CHR**	10				
Bono, Sam	OXF	**SCR**	05	06	07		
Book, Tony	FEN	**FB**	88				
Book, Tony	FEN	**TR**	88	89			
Boose, Jason	OXF	**FB**	91				
Boots, Pam	OXF	**CC**	83	84	85	**TR**	84	86
Borck, Todd	LAP W	**FB**	82	**BSB**	82		
Borck, Trisha	LAP W	**SB**	89	90	91		
Borella, Holly	HOL	**TR**	90				
Borror, Beth	AIN	**SB**	77				
Borror, Laura	AIN	**TR**	74	75			
Borrow, Doug	DUR	**FB**	85				
Borwder, Shari	FEN	**TEN**	81				
Bosak, Lisa	FEN	**TEN**	82				
Bosard, Cathy	HOL	**TR**	08				
Bosetti, Katherine	OXF	**TR**	09				
Bosway, Nick	FEN	**TEN**	78				
Bothwell, Alex	HOL	**TR**	85	86	87		
Bott, Melissa	HOL	**TR**	11	12			
Bouchard, Josh	SW CK	**GLF**	16				
Bouchard, Linda	AIN	**SB**	77	79			
Bouck, Jeff	HOL	**FB**	70				
Bourassa, Mark	LKV	**FB**	78	79			
Bourassa, Tyler	LIN	**HKY**	16				
Bourdeau, Trevor	BRAN	**WR**	14				
Bourke, Frank	CAR	**FB**	71				
Bourne, Kyle	KEAR	**BSB**	11				
Bourne, Tom	FEN	**FB**	84				
Bowden, Alex	FLU	**BSB**	17	18			
Bowden, Greg	LKV	**FB**	95	**TR**	94	95	
Bowden, Jeff	OXF	**CC**	97	**TR**	98		
Bowden, Katie	OXF	**TR**	97				
Bowdish, Grant	CLIO	**TR**	14				

Name	School	Sport	Yr1	Yr2	Sport2	Yr3	Yr4	Sport3	Yr5
Bowen, Dave	LKV	**HKY**	80						
Bowers, Natalie	LAP E	**BSK**	95	96					
Bowers, Nick	DUR	**WR**	93	96					
Bowles, Chaz	HOL	**GLF**	11						
Bowles, Nancy	CAR	**TR**	74	75					
Bowman, Caleb	LAP W	**TR**	99						
Bowman, Taylor	SW CK	**SCR**	14						
Boyd, Jamie	HOL	**TEN**	98						
Boyd, Mike	AIN	**HKY**	80						
Boyd, Stan	HOL	**FB**	88		**WR**	87	88	89	
Boyer, Danielle	HOL	**TEN**	06						
Boyer, Scott	SW CK	**SW**	76						
Bozy, Steve	HOL	**FB**	06						
Brabon, Rachel	FEN	**VB**	82						
Brabon, Scott	FEN	**BSB**	74						
Bracciano, Dan	FEN	**TEN**	95						
Bracciano, Mary	FEN	**CC**	98	99	**TR**	99			
Brace, Marie	LAP E	**BSK**	92		**SCR**	92	94		
Brackney, Tina	LIN	**TR**	99						
Braden, Theresa	LAP W	**TR**	81	82	83				
Bradford, Greg	MT M	**BSB**	98						
Bradford, John	MT M	**FB**	77	78	**BSB**	79			
Bradford, Monica	MT M	**SB**	73						
Bradley, Darren	DUR	**GLF**	83		**BSB**	84			
Bradley, Kyle	FEN	**TEN**	07						
Bradley, Nick	LAP W	**GLF**	00	01	02	**BSB**	03		
Bradley, Sue	MT M	**TR**	77	78					
Bradley, Tim	FEN	**BSK**	86						
Bradshaw, Dorothy	SW CK	**TR**	18						
Bradshaw, Scott	LAP W	**BSB**	91	92					
Bradshaw, Steve	LAP W	**BSB**	02	03					
Bradsher, Amy	HOL	**TR**	87						
Bradsher, Mark	FEN	**FB**	83						
Brady, Ashley	BRAN	**SB**	06						
Brady, Derek	BRAN	**SCR**	08	09					
Brady, Matt	LAP E	**WR**	06						
Brady, Ryan	LIN	**WR**	96	97					
Brady, Wayne	SW CK	**FB**	68						
Brammer, Kyle	OXF	**WR**	07						
Brancheau, Connor	FEN	**WR**	10						
Brancheau, Dan	FEN	**BSB**	00						
Brandon, Kim	OXF	**CC**	84	85					
Brandt, Ken	FEN	**BSB**	86						
Braniecki, Amanda	LAP E	**SB**	05						
Brant, Cailey	LIN	**LAX**	16						
Brant, Emma	FEN	**SB**	14	15					
Brant, Ken	FEN	**FB**	85		**WR**	85	86		
Brantley, John	AIN	**TR**	81						

Brauer, Chuck	LAP W	**BSB**	99					
Brault, Dave	DUR	**BSB**	89					
Braunschneider, Brian	OXF	**FB**	86	87				
Brauze, Matt	FEN	**HKY**	90					
Bravomalo, Andrew	LAP E	**TEN**	98					
Brayton, Shelby	FEN	**SB**	00	01				
Braziel, Raydoffa	KEAR	**TR**	18					
Brecht, Cory	LIN	**HKY**	06					
Brecht, Kelsey	LIN	**VB**	12					
Brecht, Todd	LAP E	**HKY**	83	84	**BSB**	84		
Breier, Lisa	LIN	**SB**	88					
Breitling, Erica	LIN	**SCR**	18					
Brendel, Colleen	BRAN	**CHR**	09	10	**TR**	07	08	10
Brendel, Jill	BRAN	**CHR**	08	09	10	**TR**	07	08
Brennan, Adam	LAP W	**FB**	01	**BSK**	02			
Bretzke, Bruce	LIN	**FB**	86	**BSK**	87	**TR**	87	
Brewer, Jill	LAP E	**TR**	79					
Breyer, Tim	OXF	**WR**	02	03				
Breyer, Willie	OXF	**FB**	00	**WR**	00	01		
Bridges, Brian	SW CK	**TR**	16	17				
Briggs, Patrick	SW CK	**TR**	07					
Brigham, Brandon	FEN	**HKY**	94	**BSB**	94			
Brilhart, Molly	LIN	**SB**	98					
Brilhart, Sam	LIN	**TR**	03					
Brimley, Roger	SW CK	**CC**	72					
Brinley, Walt	SW CK	**BSB**	75					
Briscoe, Kayla	LIN	**TR**	13					
Brittain, Julie	DUR	**SB**	87					
Brittain, Scott	DUR	**BSB**	83					
Brittain, Spenser	LAP E	**SCR**	87	88				
Brochu, Dave	HOL	**GLF**	77	78				
Brody, Derek	LIN	**GLF**	97	98	99			
Brody, Don	LIN	**GLF**	87					
Broecker, Tom	LAP W	**GLF**	75					
Brohn, Jim	CAR	**SW**	71					
Brohn, John	CAR	**BSB**	73					
Bronson, Bradly	CLIO	**SCR**	15					
Brookman, Allie	SW CK	**SB**	13					
Brooks, Angie	BRAN	**TR**	07	08				
Brooks, Chris	HOL	**TR**	76					
Brooks, Craig	HOL	**TR**	76					
Brooks, Janice	DUR	**SB**	87					
Brooks, Jeff	LAP E	**FB**	79					
Brooks, Julie	HOL	**CC**	81	**TR**	79	80	81	82
Brooks, Ross	FEN	**TR**	12					
Brotherton, Easton	FLU	**FB**	16					
Brotzke, Jesse	LAP W	**SCR**	94					
Browder, Shari	FEN	**VB**	82					

Brown, Abby	HOL	TR	13				
Brown, Andy	FEN	SCR	90				
Brown, Barry	CAR	SW	71				
Brown, Brandon	LAP E	TR	99	00			
Brown, Brennan	HOL	TEN	92	93	94		
Brown, Chris	AIN	SB	81				
Brown, Dennis	OXF	FB	08				
Brown, Ed	LKV	TR	79				
Brown, Eldon	CAR	FB	75				
Brown, Hayden	FEN	TR	09				
Brown, Jada	KEAR	CHR	17	18			
Brown, Ken	FEN	FB	77				
Brown, Kevin	OXF	CC	02	03			
Brown, Kim	LAP W	GLF	08	09			
Brown, Kristi	LAP E	CC	95	97			
Brown, Leonard	HOL	GLF	78	BSB	78	79	
Brown, Mackenzie	CLIO	SB	12				
Brown, Mary	AIN	TR	82	83	84	85	
Brown, McKenzie	SW CK	TR	18				
Brown, Melissa	LAP E	CC	98	00			
Brown, Meredith	FEN	TR	11				
Brown, Michelle	LAP W	SCR	00	01	02		
Brown, Nick	FLU	GLF	17	18			
Brown, Rick	LKV	TR	80				
Brown, Ryan	FEN	TR	07	08			
Brown, Shannon	LAP W	BSK	13	SCR	12	13	
Brown, Sharon	AIN	BSK	74	SB	73	74	75
Brown, Shaye	LIN	FB	12				
Brown, Wess	DUR	BSK	86				
Brown, Zach	LIN	FB	17				
Browne, Randy	HOL	BSB	93				
Browne, Stephanie	HOL	TEN	89	90	91		
Brownell, Larry	AIN	BSB	84				
Brownlee, Cashay	KEAR	CHR	15				
Bruce, Aaron	OXF	GLF	03				
Bruder, Chad	FEN	BSK	89	90	TR	90	
Bruder, Dave	FEN	CC	79				
Bruder, Todd	FEN	TR	87	88			
Brunan, Jeremy	FEN	SCR	96				
Brundage, Michelle	LAP E	TR	91				
Brushaber, Bill	CAR	TEN	75	76			
Bryant, Chauncey	CLIO	BSK	14				
Bryant, Jessica	LAP W	SB	11				
Bryant, Joshua	FEN	SW	12				
Bryant, Steve	HOL	WR	73				
Bryl, Mike	LIN	TR	92				
Bryl, Robin	LIN	CC	82				
Bryson, Scott	CAR	BSK	76	BSB	76		

Bublitz, Bill	LAP	**TEN**	74						
Bubnar, PJ	FEN	**HKY**	80	81					
Bucci, Mike	OXF	**SCR**	00						
Bucci, Ron	OXF	**SCR**	92	93					
Buchanan, Michelle	LAP W	**SB**	87						
Buchanan, Tyler	LIN	**CC**	17	**TR**	18				
Bucherie, Woody	CAR	**FB**	69	70					
Bucholz, Jackie	HOL	**CC**	93	94	95	96	**TR**	95	96	97
Bucholz, Jackie	HOL	**TR**	94						
Buck, Andy	FEN	**BSB**	96						
Buckel, Kortnee	FEN	**SW**	07						
Buckel, Mike	LKV	**WR**	77						
Buckham, Jerry	MT M	**TR**	79						
Buckler, Ryan	LIN	**FB**	91	**BSK**	93	**TR**	92	93	
Buda, Sarah	BRAN	**SCR**	16	17					
Budd, Joe	HOL	**SCR**	11						
Buerkel, Austin	LIN	**BSB**	13	14	15	**TR**	12		
Buerkel, Brendan	LIN	**BSB**	16	17					
Buerkel, Lauren	LIN	**SB**	18						
Buerkel, Steve	LIN	**FB**	87	**BSK**	88	**BSB**	87	88	
Buff, Ron	LKV	**FB**	86	87	**BSK**	87	**BSB**	88	
Bukoski, Andrew	OXF	**BSB**	03						
Bukoski, Jeremy	OXF	**BSB**	05	06	07				
Bukovchik, Mike	DUR	**BSK**	97						
Bukowski, Randy	LAP E	**FB**	90	**BSB**	90				
Bulzan, Gary	LAP E	**FB**	11	**BSB**	11	12			
Bulzan, Joe	LAP	**CC**	74	75					
Bunce, Hal	FEN	**TEN**	75						
Bundy, Jenny	FEN	**SCR**	91						
Burch, Kevin	SW CK	**GLF**	70	71	71f				
Burdick, Scott	FEN	**SW**	73	74					
Burdis, Stephen	MT M	**BSB**	94	95					
Burger, Brenden	CLIO	**BWL**	17						
Burger, Carley	LIN	**CC**	02	**TR**	05				
Burgess, Tim	LAP E	**WR**	84						
Burk, Tiffany	HOL	**TR**	99						
Burke, Connor	BRAN	**SCR**	17						
Burke, Del	FEN	**TEN**	82						
Burke, Dick	CAR	**WR**	76						
Burke, Jamie	LIN	**TR**	98						
Burke, Matt	CAR	**WR**	75						
Burke, Paige	CLIO	**SCR**	06						
Burke, Tom	HOL	**TEN**	80						
Burkhardt, Daniel	FLU	**SW**	17	18					
Burkhardt, David	FLU	**SW**	15	16					
Burkhardt, Fred	LAP W	**FB**	77						
Burks, Bob	CAR	**TR**	73						
Burns, Andrew	LIN	**TR**	18						

Burns, Bob	LKV	**TR**	99	00		
Burns, Charlene	AIN	**VB**	85	86		
Burns, Jim	SW CK	**CC**	69	70	**TR**	71
Burns, Megan	OXF	**SCR**	92	93	94	95
Burns, Pat	OXF	**GLF**	00			
Burns, Tim	HOL	**FB**	68			
Burns, Vern	SW CK	**FB**	74			
Burr, Ashley	OXF	**TR**	10			
Burr, Kendall	OXF	**CHR**	10			
Burrough, Josh	LAP E	**BSK**	01	**TR**	00	
Burrough, Myles	LAP W	**GLF**	12			
Burrough, Rick	LAP E	**BSB**	82			
Burt, Lisa	HOL	**TEN**	87			
Burt, Nick	FEN	**SCR**	97			
Burt, Tiffany	HOL	**TR**	00			
Burton, James	HOL	**SW**	06	07		
Burton, Lorraine	LAP W	**VB**	88			
Burwell, DeNise	LAP W	**SCR**	88			
Burwell, Mike	LAP W	**FB**	81			
Butchar, Randy	FEN	**HKY**	79			
Butcher, Sharna	OWO	**CHR**	18			
Butler, Bryn	FLU	**SCR**	18			
Butterfield, Dave	LAP E	**FB**	86	**TR**	87	
Butterfield, Duane	LKV	**FB**	92	93		
Butterfield, Kevin	LKV	**FB**	95			
Butts, Mike	FEN	**BSK**	78			
Butts, Mike	FEN	**TEN**	77	78		
Butzier, Colleen	LAP W	**SB**	95			
Butzier, Maureen	LAP W	**SB**	02			
Buzzell, Bethany	LIN	**TR**	98			
Buzzell, Krista	LIN	**CC**	96	97	**TR**	98
Byam, Becky	AIN	**SB**	72			
Byrd, Cari	OXF	**TR**	87	88		
Byrd, Cass	CAR	**FB**	73			
Byrne, Pat	HOL	**SCR**	94			
Byrnes, Bryan	LAP W	**SCR**	94			
Bysko, Ted	CAR	**BSK**	71			
Cabic, Kim	OXF	**TR**	94			
Cage, Matt	OXF	**FB**	98			
Cage, Valerie	OXF	**CC**	88			
Cagle, Emma	FEN	**SW**	15			
Cairnduff, Joe	FEN	**BSK**	82			
Cairnduff, Katey	FEN	**SB**	14	15		
Cairns, Tiffany	FEN	**SCR**	13			
Caldwell, Connor	HOL	**TEN**	14			
Caldwell, John	HOL	**TEN**	07f	08		
Caldwell, Laura	HOL	**TEN**	05	06	08	
Caldwell, Sam	HOL	**TEN**	09	10	11	

Caldwell, Wyatt	HOL	**TEN**	16	17						
Caldwell, Zac	BRAN	**HKY**	07							
Calkins, Liz	LAP E	**CC**	97	**TR**	96					
Call, Kristin	HOL	**TEN**	90	91						
Cameron, Aaron	FEN	**WR**	96							
Cameron, Dana	FEN	**TEN**	79							
Caminiti, Melissa	LAP E	**SCR**	01							
Campbell, Andy	FEN	**FB**	99							
Campbell, Casey	SW CK	**CC**	08	10	11	**TR**	09	11		
Campbell, Cassandra	FEN	**TR**	16	17	18					
Campbell, Cody	SW CK	**BSK**	10							
Campbell, Don	LAP E	**TR**	93							
Campbell, Lauren	FEN	**SW**	04	05	06	07	**GLF**	06	07	07f
Campbell, Laurie	MT M	**VB**	80							
Campbell, Mitch	FEN	**TEN**	11	13						
Campbell, Morgan	FEN	**GLF**	08	09						
Campbell, Nick	FEN	**GLF**	16							
Campbell, Travis	SW CK	**TR**	11							
Candela, Vinnie	LKV	**TR**	94	95	96	97				
Cantara, Keegan	OXF	**WR**	10							
Canterbury, Chloe	CLIO	**CHR**	14							
Cantu, Vincent	HOL	**CC**	12	13						
Carbary, Kaitlyn	FEN	**CC**	02	03	05					
Cardona, Jeff	OXF	**FB**	96							
Carey, Devon	LAP E	**FB**	10							
Cargill, Chris	LKV	**WR**	88	89	90					
Caris, Mary	CAR	**TR**	74							
Caris, Nancy	CAR	**TR**	73							
Carlson, Ben	LIN	**FB**	00	**BSB**	00					
Carlson, Madison	SW CK	**GLF**	14							
Carlson, Marvin	SW CK	**FB**	75							
Carlson, Nick	LIN	**FB**	12							
Carlson, Zach	HOL	**TR**	00							
Carlyon, Izzy	FLU	**TR**	17	18						
Carmean, Kelsey	BRAN	**CC**	03	04	05	06				
Carne, Shane	HOL	**TEN**	07							
Carnell, Dane	FEN	**HKY**	89							
Carnell, Kay	FEN	**SB**	85							
Carnell, Rob	MT M	**HKY**	88							
Carnes, Brad	FEN	**GLF**	84							
Carol, Dave	AIN	**CC**	82	83						
Carol, Ken	AIN	**HKY**	76	77						
Carpenter, Adam	LAP E	**HKY**	89							
Carpenter, Alanna	BRAN	**CHR**	11	13						
Carpenter, Bill	CAR	**TEN**	74	75						
Carpenter, Casey	HOL	**TEN**	92							
Carpenter, Dori	FEN	**SB**	14							
Carpenter, Gary	AIN	**BSB**	70							

Carpenter, Jeff	MT M	**FB**	95				
Carpenter, Joel	LIN	**HKY**	95				
Carpenter, Karla	FEN	**BSK**	80	**SB**	80		
Carpenter, Kim	FEN	**SCR**	89				
Carpenter, Kim	LKV	**VB**	02				
Carpenter, Kyle	FLU	**HKY**	16				
Carpenter, Pat	LIN	**HKY**	88	89			
Carpenter, Steve	LIN	**HKY**	87				
Carpenter, Trevor	CLIO	**SW**	06				
Carr, Griffin	FEN	**TEN**	15				
Carr, Ron	SW CK	**FB**	70				
Carr, Timberly	LAP W	**SB**	87	88			
Carr, Tracy	LAP W	**VB**	92	**SB**	89	90	91	92
Carrette, Suzie	HOL	**SCR**	91	92			
Carrithers, Shaun	LAP E	**TEN**	97	98			
Carriveau, Jacob	CLIO	**SCR**	14	15			
Carriveau, Jamie	MT M	**SB**	91	92			
Carroll, Charlie	HOL	**SW**	07	08			
Carsey, Bobby	LIN	**WR**	05	07			
Carsey, Sam	LIN	**WR**	05	06			
Carson, Chad	LAP E	**BSB**	10	11	12		
Carson, Mike	LAP E	**BSB**	06	07	08	09	
Carter, Brice	SW CK	**WR**	08				
Carter, Chad	LIN	**HKY**	94	95			
Carter, Char	LIN	**BSK**	90	**VB**	90	91	
Carter, Clyde	LKV	**FB**	76	**TR**	77		
Carter, Dante	KEAR	**TR**	12				
Carter, Erin	FEN	**SB**	16	18			
Carter, Gary	FEN	**WR**	91				
Carter, Logan	FEN	**SB**	16	17			
Carter, McKenzie	LAP W	**CHR**	12	13			
Carter, Rachel	FEN	**TR**	02	04			
Cartner, Kelly	OXF	**BWL**	09	10	**SB**	09	10
Cartwright, Beau	FEN	**FB**	98	99			
Casacelli, Teresa	HOL	**TR**	90				
Case, Emma	FLU	**LAX**	17				
Case, Maureen	LAP W	**CHR**	07				
Casey, Maura	HOL	**TR**	09				
Caslmon, Dave	FEN	**WR**	90				
Caslmon, Tim	FEN	**BSB**	92				
Cason, Leda	OXF	**TR**	87				
Cassar, Dave	HOL	**TR**	85				
Cassar, Kevin	HOL	**TR**	93	94			
Cassar, Steve	HOL	**CC**	86	**TR**	85	86	87
Cassar, Todd	HOL	**CC**	89				
Cassidy, Brant	FEN	**SW**	13	14			
Cassidy, Elise	FEN	**SW**	13	14	15	16	
Cassner, Meagan	FEN	**SW**	11	12			

Casteel, Krystal	LKV	TR	92						
Caster, Paul	HOL	WR	93						
Castigilione, Jamie	FEN	BSB	13	14					
Cates, Ginny	FEN	VB	04	SCR	03	04			
Cathey, Kyle	HOL	TR	81						
Caudill, Brian	HOL	TEN	99	00					
Cavanaugh, Robert	LAP E	HKY	06						
Cavendar, Jake	HOL	TEN	15						
Cavender, Tanner	HOL	TEN	16	17					
Ceccacci, Katelynn	BRAN	SB	18						
Celini, Julie	FEN	CHR	18						
Celli, Dominic	OXF	SCR	00						
Cerato, Kim	OXF	SCR	01	02					
Chabot, Luke	FEN	TR	16						
Chabot, Mitchell	FEN	CC	17	TR	16	17			
Chadwell, Laura	FEN	TEN	88						
Chamberlain, Bryce	BRAN	FB	16	TR	17				
Chamberlain, Tony	DUR	FB	78						
Chambers, Don	HOL	FB	77	TR	78				
Chambers, Jeff	HOL	GLF	98						
Chambers, Kim	FEN	TR	86						
Chambers, Melissa	DUR	TEN	88						
Chambers, Michaele	AIN	SB	83						
Champagne, Dan	LIN	FB	95	BSK	96				
Champagne, Jon	LIN	FB	95	BSK	95	96			
Champagne, Liz	LIN	TR	92	93					
Champion, Heather	LAP E	CHR	09						
Chang, Judia	FEN	SW	04	05					
Chapel, Jeff	LIN	GLF	97						
Chapel, Jon	LIN	GLF	95						
Chapin, Debbie	FEN	VB	05						
Chapin, Hannah	FEN	TR	17	18					
Chapin, Matt	LKV	BSB	96						
Chapman, Angie	DUR	SB	95	96					
Chapman, Becky	HOL	TR	81						
Chapman, Jakob	KEAR	WR	13	15					
Chappell, Hunter	FEN	FB	17						
Chappell, Julie	LAP E	TR	87						
Chappell, Kamryn	FLU	SCR	17						
Chappell, Kevin	HOL	TR	69	70	71				
Chappell, Mackenzie	KEAR	GLF	13						
Chappell, Matt	FEN	TR	90						
Chappell, Nick	FEN	FB	12						
Charder, Marc	LIN	TR	92	93					
Chargo, Nick	SW CK	TR	14						
Charles, Kara	OXF	TR	08						
Charlick, Ben	HOL	TEN	07f	08	09	BWL	09	10	
Charlton, Brent	LAP W	BSB	01						

Name	Team	Sport	Year						
Charnley, Adam	LAP E	**SCR**	95						
Charnley, Jason	LAP E	**FB**	97	**BSK**	98				
Chase, Alex	FEN	**SW**	12	13					
Chase, Lindsay	FEN	**SW**	08						
Chatfield, Abby	HOL	**TEN**	12						
Chatters, Rob	AIN	**HKY**	81						
Chatterton, Lee	HOL	**SW**	05						
Chedister, Tom	CAR	**FB**	71						
Cheladyn, Todd	LIN	**FB**	87						
Chenault, James	LAP E	**TR**	01						
Chene, Randy	FEN	**WR**	71						
Chene, Wayne	FEN	**WR**	70	71					
Chenoweth, Korey	HOL	**FB**	05	06					
Cherry, Mike	CAR	**BSB**	69						
Cherubim, Jay	CAR	**TEN**	73						
Chewning, Becca	BRAN	**TEN**	10						
Chiatalas, Andrew	LIN	**BSB**	04	05					
Chiatalas, Eleni	LIN	**CHR**	09						
Chiatalas, Lee	LIN	**TR**	09	10					
Childress, Les	HOL	**TR**	83						
Childress, Mike	HOL	**FB**	84	**TR**	85				
Childs, Paul	DUR	**FB**	88						
Childs, Terry	DUR	**BSB**	79						
Chilson, Mikayla	CLIO	**SB**	17						
Chimento, Tony	LKV	**TR**	88						
Chipman, Ashlynn	FLU	**TR**	16						
Chisholm, Zac	LKV	**TR**	94						
Chmura, Austin	HOL	**FB**	14	**TR**	13				
Chmura, Nina	HOL	**LAX**	18						
Chojnacki, Caitlin	LAP W	**SCR**	06	07					
Cholewka, Alex	LAP E	**SCR**	05						
Chopp, Mitchell	FEN	**GLF**	18						
Chouinard, Marc	HOL	**WR**	82						
Chouinard, Sam	LAP W	**SCR**	14						
Christensen, Mary	AIN	**BSK**	76	77					
Christensen, Roger	CLIO	**BSB**	09						
Christensen, Thailyia	FLU	**CC**	16	17	**BSK**	18	**TR**	18	
Christian, Jim	AIN	**WR**	70						
Christopher, Torrey	FEN	**CC**	13	**TR**	14				
Chrznowski, Justin	LAP W	**WR**	02	03	04	05			
Churches, Molly	LIN	**SB**	16						
Cianek, Claire	BRAN	**SB**	03						
Ciaravino, Angela	LAP E	**VB**	13	**TR**	12	13	14		
Ciaravino, Cassie	LAP E	**TR**	09						
Cichoracki, Kelly	LAP W	**TR**	00	01	**SB**	03			
Ciesielski, John	LIN	**BSB**	97						
Cieslak, Natalie	HOL	**SCR**	10						
Cinader, Jacob	BRAN	**BSB**	04						

Cinader, Luke	BRAN	**FB**	10					
Cinader, Matt	BRAN	**HKY**	06	07				
Cipa, Lisa	OXF	**TR**	83	85				
Cislo, Jeff	FEN	**TR**	83	84				
Claborn, James	FEN	**FB**	13					
Clapp, Lance	SW CK	**WR**	18					
Clark, Adam	LKV	**SCR**	98					
Clark, Becky	FEN	**TR**	70					
Clark, Dan	OXF	**SCR**	92					
Clark, Jamie	MT M	**BSK**	85	**TR**	85			
Clark, John	HOL	**FB**	89					
Clark, Kyle	CLIO	**SCR**	09					
Clark, Michael	SW CK	**GLF**	11					
Clark, Mike	HOL	**TEN**	04	05				
Clark, Ryan	CLIO	**BSB**	08					
Clark, Sally	OXF	**SCR**	89					
Clay, Chris	LAP W	**FB**	99	00	**TR**	98	99	00
Clay, Scott	LAP W	**FB**	01					
Cleaver, Mason	HOL	**WR**	11	12	13			
Cleis, Marina	FEN	**SB**	11	12				
Clements, Blake	LAP W	**TEN**	13					
Clements, Garrett	LAP W	**SCR**	12					
Clements, Kevin	LAP W	**GLF**	89					
Clements, Macey	SW CK	**VB**	14					
Clements, Zach	BRAN	**FB**	16					
Clink, Ian	HOL	**TEN**	14					
Clink, Natalie	HOL	**TEN**	11	12				
Clinton, Pete	LAP E	**GLF**	92					
Clontz, Baylie	CLIO	**CHR**	17	18				
Clontz, Dale	MT M	**BSB**	85					
Clontz, Larry	MT M	**FB**	72					
Clontz, Mackenzie	CLIO	**CHR**	13	14	15			
Clough, Mark	DUR	**FB**	81	**WR**	81	82		
Clymer, Josh	DUR	**FB**	95	**WR**	94	95	**TR**	94
Cobe, Gary	MT M	**BSB**	88	89				
Cockin, Megan	FEN	**VB**	12					
Coe, Josh	LIN	**TR**	01	02				
Coenen, Jason	MT M	**GLF**	88	89	90			
Coffey, Sam	FEN	**SW**	13					
Coffey, Stuart	CLIO	**BSB**	13	14				
Coffman, Peyton	FEN	**FB**	14	15				
Cohoon, Gillian	HOL	**SB**	17					
Colden, Tonia	MT M	**SB**	82	83	84			
Cole, Daniel	SW CK	**BWL**	16					
Cole, Debbie	DUR	**SB**	88					
Cole, Gary	AIN	**FB**	76	77	**BSB**	78		
Cole, Lindsay	LAP E	**SCR**	03					
Cole, Tom	LIN	**SCR**	94					

Coleman, Darrell	HOL	CC	73				
Coleman, Dave	HOL	TR	69	70	71		
Coleman, Jack	HOL	SW	05	06	07	TR	07
Collett, Vern	OXF	FB	87				
Collier, Josh	BRAN	SW	06				
Collier, Josh	FEN	SCR	08				
Collier, Nick	OXF	TR	05	06			
Collier, Sarah	FEN	VB	11	SB	11		
Collier, Stephanie	HOL	TEN	09	10	11		
Collins, Anthony	CLIO	SCR	06				
Collins, Jim	LAP W	FB	02	03			
Collins, Marc	LIN	SCR	93	BSK	94		
Collins, Rob	CAR	FB	74				
Colson, Keera	HOL	TR	09				
Combs, Jim	DUR	BSB	89				
Combs, Julius	BRAN	FB	10				
Compeau, Mike	AIN	FB	71				
Conder, Floyd	FEN	TR	96				
Condon, Ray	AIN	TEN	83	84			
Congdon, Beth	FEN	TEN	08				
Congdon, David	FEN	SW	12				
Congdon, Stephen	FEN	SW	07				
Conger, Amy	LAP E	SB	00				
Conger, Dan	LAP E	CC	95				
Conlen, Katie	OXF	CC	85				
Conly, Allison	LIN	VB	16	17			
Conn, Greg	LIN	BSB	87				
Conn, Jason	HOL	BSB	94				
Connell, Brent	LAP W	HKY	85				
Connell, Dixie	MT M	SB	91				
Conrad, Curt	LAP E	WR	84				
Conte, Dylan	FEN	GLF	17	18			
Conway, Patrick	FEN	GLF	17				
Conyer, Phil	LIN	FB	03				
Conzelmann, Hunter	LAP W	SB	14				
Cook, Amy	HOL	TEN	89	90	91	92	
Cook, Cameron	LIN	FB	13				
Cook, Tony	MT M	GLF	72				
Cook, Will	FEN	TR	06	07			
Cooke, Lindsay	FEN	TEN	95				
Cookingham, Kalyn	OXF	TR	04				
Cooks, Chelsea	BRAN	TR	15	16			
Cooley, Kurtis	HOL	CC	14	TR	15		
Coon, Jackie	LIN	TR	07	08			
Cooney, Shannon	DUR	SB	86				
Cooper, Bob	LAP	HKY	75				
Cooper, Butch	LAP W	HKY	97	99			
Cooper, Julie	AIN	SB	86				

Cope, Trevor	SW CK	**HKY**	07							
Copley, Allyssa	HOL	**BSK**	12	13	14	**TR**	14			
Cordes, John	CAR	**SW**	72							
Cordonnier, Carina	LAP W	**SCR**	91							
Cornack, Kirk	FEN	**BSK**	06							
Corning, Faye	FEN	**TR**	01	02						
Cornwall, Jim	AIN	**FB**	76							
Corrigan, Danielle	OXF	**BSK**	91							
Corrill, Dave	AIN	**GLF**	69							
Corriveau, Ashley	LAP	**SW**	06	07	08					
Coselman, Chase	FEN	**BSB**	15	16	17					
Costigan, Bri	FEN	**SW**	13	14	15	**SCR**	14	15	16	
Costigan, Kyle	FEN	**SCR**	12							
Cottrell, Racquel	CLIO	**CHR**	16	17						
Cottrell, Sharon	FEN	**TR**	73	74						
Cottrell, Sherry	AIN	**SB**	75							
Coughlin, Ali	FEN	**VB**	89							
Coughlin, Ben	LIN	**FB**	98	**TR**	99					
Coughlin, Sarah	LIN	**VB**	03							
Coughlin, Sierra	BRAN	**CHR**	13	14	15	16				
Coulter, Pat	LAP E	**BSK**	99	00						
Coulter, Randy	LKV	**TR**	77							
Coulter, Roxanne	LAP E	**SCR**	94							
Coulter, Sheilah	LAP E	**BSK**	94							
Coulter, Stephanie	LAP E	**TEN**	89							
Courser, Roseanne	LAP E	**TR**	92							
Courtright, Sarah	OXF	**BSK**	96	97	**VB**	98	**SCR**	95	96	97	98
Coutcher, Scott	SW CK	**TR**	74	75						
Couture, Laura	LAP W	**SB**	87							
Couzens, Betsy	LAP E	**SB**	91							
Couzens, Courtney	LAP E	**SCR**	99							
Covert, Brett	FEN	**FB**	81							
Covert, Kim	FEN	**TEN**	78							
Cowan, Bill	FEN	**GLF**	71f							
Cowan, John	FEN	**GLF**	70							
Cowger, Ellie	FEN	**SB**	12	13	14					
Cowger, Kate	FEN	**SB**	05							
Cowger, Samantha	FEN	**SB**	10	11	12					
Cox, Cory	FEN	**BSK**	12	13						
Cox, Jacob	LIN	**TR**	15	16						
Cox, Mark	LAP W	**FB**	13							
Cox, Mike	LAP W	**BSK**	04							
Cox, Peter	FEN	**FB**	11							
Coxen, Zach	HOL	**FB**	10							
Coy, Mike	CAR	**TR**	73							
Crace, Jeff	LKV	**FB**	78	79	**BSK**	80	**BSB**	80		
Craft, Justin	OXF	**WR**	00							
Craig, Cameron	BRAN	**SCR**	09	10	11					

Cramer, Rob	LAP E	**BSB**	81						
Crandall, Dallas	HOL	**TR**	11						
Crandall, James	LIN	**BSK**	03						
Crandell, John	FEN	**BSK**	83	**TEN**	82	83			
Crane, Robin	HOL	**TR**	72						
Cranick, Michelle	LAP W	**SB**	84						
Cranick, Mike	LAP W	**FB**	82						
Cranick, Nikki	LAP E	**VB**	04	05	06	**TR**	03	05	06
Crankshaw, Dylan	FEN	**FB**	15	16					
Craves, Bryan	OXF	**CC**	92						
Crawford, Ben	BRAN	**BSB**	11	12					
Crawford, Blake	BRAN	**SCR**	13	14					
Crawford, Rodger	LAP E	**FB**	94						
Cregar, George	LAP E	**TR**	81						
Creger, George	LKV	**TR**	80						
Crelley, Colleen	FEN	**BSK**	92	**SB**	93				
Crelley, Stephanie	FEN	**BSK**	90	**TR**	90	91			
Crenshaw, Laura	FEN	**TEN**	78						
Creque, Ed	CAR	**GLF**	73						
Crimmins, Audrey	HOL	**TEN**	11	12					
Crimmins, Austin	BRAN	**SW**	15						
Crimmins, Haley	HOL	**TEN**	16						
Crissan, Terry	OXF	**FB**	85						
Crockett, Bob	CAR	**FB**	68						
Crockett, Megan	HOL	**TEN**	02						
Croft, Dan	SW CK	**FB**	15						
Cronin, Katie	LAP W	**GLF**	07f						
Crosby, Amber	HOL	**TEN**	02	04					
Crosby, Barb	FEN	**TR**	77	78					
Crosby, Justin	HOL	**TEN**	01	02	03				
Cross, Darren	LIN	**HKY**	08	09					
Cross, Jeff	LIN	**CC**	92	93	94				
Cross, John	LIN	**BSK**	92						
Crossman, Kevin	FEN	**BSB**	89						
Crowe, April	LAP W	**SCR**	13						
Crowe, Julie	OXF	**SCR**	88						
Crowell, Scout	BRAN	**CC**	15						
Crum, Jordan	FLU	**TR**	15	16					
Cruthers, Hayley	SW CK	**SB**	11	12	13				
Cruthers, Vicki	MT M	**SB**	88						
Cryderman, John	FEN	**BWL**	15						
Cucksey, Scot	FEN	**GLF**	86	**TEN**	87				
Culver, Kaileigh	SW CK	**SCR**	18						
Culver, Katie	SW CK	**SCR**	17						
Cummings, Autumn	LAP W	**VB**	95	**SB**	94				
Cummings, Dan	OXF	**FB**	07						
Cummings, Max	SW CK	**FB**	11	12	**BSK**	12	13		
Cummings, Mike	CAR	**FB**	72	**TR**	72				

Cummings, Rob	CAR	**TR**	75	76				
Cummings, Sarah	FEN	**GLF**	12	14	15	**BSK**	15	16
Cunningham, Cathryn	BRAN	**CHR**	09	10	12			
Cupal, Ellen	FEN	**SB**	84					
Curcio, Colleen	OXF	**BSK**	88	**TR**	87	88	**SCR**	89
Curis, Lexi	HOL	**SCR**	18					
Curlett, John	LAP E	**HKY**	13					
Curran, Rachael	LAP E	**TR**	91	92	93			
Currey, Kelley	LAP W	**TR**	96					
Currie, Chris	LAP W	**FB**	84					
Currie, Mike	LAP W	**FB**	89	90				
Curtis, Andrew	LKV	**FB**	00					
Curtis, Ben	LKV	**TR**	94					
Curtis, Bob	LIN	**FB**	99	**TR**	00			
Curtis, Julie	LKV	**SB**	97					
Curtis, Lauren	OXF	**TR**	05	06				
Curtis, Quincy	HOL	**FB**	16					
Cushaway, Travis	LAP E	**WR**	09					
Cushman, Ben	FLU	**WR**	16	17	18			
Cushman, Larry	CAR	**WR**	69	**BSB**	69			
Cuthbert, Carsen	HOL	**TEN**	15	16	17			
Cuthbert, Parker	HOL	**TEN**	10	12	13			
Cuttitta, Stevie	CLIO	**SB**	08	09				
Cybulski, Mike	BRAN	**HKY**	05					
Cygnar, Justin	LIN	**WR**	18					
Cynowa, Mike	OXF	**TR**	10					
Czarnota, Josh	FEN	**FB**	15	16	17			
Czarnota, Mike	FEN	**FB**	12					
Dabbs, Rick	FEN	**WR**	87	88				
Dabney, Lamonte	FLU	**TR**	16					
Dabrowski, Wayne	LAP W	**FB**	00	01				
Dada, Jafar	LAP E	**GLF**	08					
Dafoe, Paul	OXF	**FB**	92					
Dagley, Shelly	LAP W	**TR**	79	80	81			
Dagley, Wendy	LAP W	**VB**	87					
Dahl, Luci	AIN	**CC**	83					
Dahlberg, Tim	MT M	**GLF**	94	95	96			
Dailey, Caitlyn	FEN	**SW**	15	16	17			
Dake, Kaitlyn	FLU	**SCR**	18					
Daley, Erin	LAP W	**VB**	98					
Daley, Mike	LAP E	**HKY**	00					
Dalgren, Bob	AIN	**TEN**	77					
Dallwitz, Cade	HOL	**WR**	17	18				
Dallwitz, Collin	HOL	**WR**	16	17				
Danek, Frank	LIN	**CC**	82	83				
Daniels, Chris	OXF	**TR**	00					
Daniels, Jake	HOL	**BSK**	14	15				
Daniels, Joe	LAP	**HKY**	14					

Daniels, Joe	LAP W	**HKY**	13					
Dant, Todd	LAP W	**HKY**	08					
Darling, Dennis	SW CK	**GLF**	71					
Darrow, Bob	FEN	**BSB**	76					
Darrow, Dawn	LKV	**BSK**	88					
Davenport, Missy	LKV	**TR**	96					
David, Jim	DUR	**FB**	83					
David, Tony	OXF	**TR**	86					
Davidson, Ciera	CLIO	**CHR**	12					
Davidson, Conor	FEN	**FB**	12					
Davidson, Kelli	OXF	**SCR**	99					
Davidson, Larry	HOL	**CC**	76	77				
Davis, Bailey	LIN	**FB**	15					
Davis, Brandon	CLIO	**BSK**	15	**TR**	13	14	15	
Davis, Brian	LAP W	**BSK**	85	86				
Davis, Bryce	LIN	**WR**	16					
Davis, Chris	HOL	**TEN**	84					
Davis, Dylan	CLIO	**TR**	17					
Davis, Elizabeth	FEN	**SCR**	10					
Davis, Jacob	FEN	**SCR**	13					
Davis, James	KEAR	**WR**	14	15				
Davis, Jeff	LAP E	**SCR**	87					
Davis, Josh	OXF	**FB**	93					
Davis, Lauren	FEN	**SW**	12	**TR**	11			
Davis, Malik	KEAR	**WR**	17					
Davis, Nathan	CLIO	**BSB**	13					
Dawes, Jessica	KEAR	**BWL**	12					
Dawson, Andrew	OXF	**SCR**	02					
Dawson, Brian	LIN	**GLF**	92	93				
Day, Jeff	LAP E	**FB**	81	**BSB**	81	82		
Day, Nolan	FEN	**CC**	16	17	**TR**	17		
Dean, Dan	CAR	**CC**	73					
Dean, Miles	FEN	**WR**	90	91				
Dean, Paige	FEN	**SB**	14	15				
Deardorff, Samuel	FEN	**TR**	16	17				
Deaton, Roger	OXF	**TR**	84	86				
Deaver, Bruce	AIN	**TR**	83					
DeBeaubien, Lisa	LAP W	**TR**	79					
Debo, Shawn	FEN	**TR**	04					
DeBoar, Chris	OXF	**SCR**	86	87				
DeBono, Bria	LAP W	**SB**	10	11				
DeBono, Daegan	LAP W	**SCR**	11					
DeBose, Cathy	HOL	**CC**	86					
Debus, Pat	LAP E	**GLF**	97	98	99			
DeButts, Josh	LKV	**CC**	96					
Decker, Darby	FEN	**BSK**	75	76	77	**BSB**	76	77
Decker, Debbie	FEN	**SB**	72	73				
Decker, Drew	FEN	**BSB**	77					

Decker, Sarah	OXF	**BWL**	10				
Deckrow, John	LKV	**TR**	85				
DeCurval, Dave	CAR	**SW**	71				
Dedivanaj, Valbon	FEN	**CHR**	07				
Deehl, Josh	FEN	**WR**	02	03			
Deering, Gabby	SW CK	**GLF**	10	11	**SB**	11	12
Deese, Barry	LIN	**CC**	89	90	91	**TR**	92
Deese, Helen	LIN	**CC**	83				
Deese, Jason	LIN	**CC**	90	**TR**	90	91	
DeFauw, Dave	OXF	**FB**	94				
DeFoe, John	FEN	**WR**	92				
DeGayner, Seeger	LIN	**FB**	17				
DeGayner, Sterling	LIN	**BSK**	16	17	**SB**	17	
DeGayner, Troy	FEN	**FB**	14				
DeHaven, Aaron	HOL	**SW**	11	12	13		
DeHaven, Kris	LAP E	**WR**	92	93	94		
Dehmel, Jim	CAR	**WR**	69				
Dekalita, Silas	CLIO	**CC**	11				
DeKlerk, Bill	LAP E	**FB**	81	**BSK**	82		
Delandsheer, Tyson	BRAN	**SW**	06				
DeLange, Todd	LAP W	**SCR**	07				
DeLavergne, Joe	FEN	**FB**	11				
Delecki, Ryan	FEN	**HKY**	11				
Delecki, Tony	FEN	**TR**	74				
Delisle, Erin	LAP W	**CHR**	08	09			
Dellameter, Jason	LKV	**HKY**	96				
Dellameter, Jeff	LKV	**HKY**	86				
Delley, Fred	FEN	**TEN**	91				
Dellinger, Bob	CAR	**BSB**	70				
DeLoney, Cathy	MT M	**SB**	81				
Delong, Tyler	FEN	**HKY**	12				
DeMaggio, Dawn	FEN	**TR**	86				
Demarr, Molly	KEAR	**SCR**	09				
Dembny, Myron	FEN	**TR**	84				
Demo, Rick	DUR	**BSB**	79				
Dempsey, John	LAP	**TEN**	74				
Deneau, Stephanie	HOL	**TEN**	03	04	05		
Deng, David	FEN	**CC**	04	05	06		
Dennis, Jeff	MT M	**FB**	79				
Dennis, Sierra	KEAR	**SW**	13				
Dennis, Terri	LAP E	**BSK**	79				
Dennis, Toby	AIN	**TEN**	83	84			
Densmore, Mike	LAP	**FB**	74	75			
Denstedt, Sydney	SW CK	**LAX**	17				
Dent, Jayona	BRAN	**TR**	11	12	13		
Depro, Wes	LKV	**TR**	94	95			
Deputy, MacKenzie	FEN	**SW**	12	13			
DePuy, Matt	LAP E	**WR**	09				

Name	School	Sport	Year			
Derno, Dave	HOL	**FB**	89			
Derocher, Rachel	HOL	**TR**	09	11		
DeRoeck, Rachel	FEN	**VB**	03			
DeRosset, Teressha	LKV	**TR**	94	95	96	97
DeShais, Dustin	BRAN	**BSK**	09			
DeShaw, Pat	LAP W	**TR**	80			
DesJardins, Bert	LAP E	**FB**	99	**BSK** 00	**TEN** 98	
DesJardins, Vic	LAP W	**HKY**	89			
Desjarlais, Justin	LKV	**GLF**	99			
Desotell, Jason	LAP W	**FB**	98			
Determan, John	AIN	**CC**	77	78		
Determan, Mark	AIN	**FB**	75			
Deters, Melanie	DUR	**TR**	80			
Detter, Justin	HOL	**SCR**	97	98		
Deuel, Jenny	FEN	**SCR**	91	93		
Devine, Rachel	BRAN	**SCR**	17			
Devore, Brittany	SW CK	**TR**	18			
DeWaelsche, Jenna	HOL	**CC**	88	89	90	91
Dewaelsche, Sarah	HOL	**TR**	12			
DeWeese, Jason	HOL	**CC**	90	91	92	**TR** 92 93
Dewey, Taylor	OXF	**CC**	07			
DeWitt, Barry	HOL	**TR**	85			
DeWitt, Cole	LAP E	**TR**	93			
DeWitt, Kara	FEN	**BSK**	01			
DeWitt, Keith	HOL	**WR**	82	83		
DeWitt, Logan	FEN	**BSK**	99			
Dewyer, Matt	CLIO	**WR**	15			
Diamond, Bill	LIN	**TR**	00			
Diamond, Marty	FEN	**HKY**	88			
Diamond, Nick	LAP W	**FB**	96			
Diaz, Cassie	LAP E	**BSK**	11			
Diaz, Cristian	HOL	**FB**	15			
Diccion, Joel	FEN	**SW**	18			
Dickie, Alexis	BRAN	**TEN**	08			
Dickie, Jeremy	SW CK	**CC**	08	09	10	**TR** 09 10 11
Dicks, Julie	FEN	**VB**	93			
Dickson, Cade	LIN	**FB**	15	16	17	**TR** 15
Dickson, Phoenix	LIN	**FB**	17			
Dieck, Jordan	SW CK	**BSK**	09			
Diehl, Aaron	HOL	**TEN**	03	04		
Diehl, Kian	HOL	**TEN**	98	99		
Diehl, Zach	HOL	**TR**	11	13		
Diener, Brandon	FEN	**GLF**	17			
Diener, Isaac	KEAR	**SCR**	11	**TR** 11		
Dieterling, Paige	FLU	**CC**	14	15		
Dietz, Randy	MT M	**FB**	88			
DiFalco, Gage	BRAN	**FB**	17			
DiGiamberdine, Candi	HOL	**TEN**	86	87		

Dikos, Gary	SW CK	**FB**	73					
Dikos, Greg	SW CK	**FB**	74	**BSB**	74	75		
Dikos, Jim	SW CK	**BSB**	72					
Dikos, Joe	SW CK	**BSB**	76					
Diller, Brian	DUR	**BSK**	79					
Dillion, Jeff	LAP W	**FB**	04					
Dillon, Anne	LAP E	**TEN**	81	83				
Dillon, Liam	MT M	**WR**	94	95				
Dilts, Matt	LIN	**FB**	09					
Dimambro, Angeline	FEN	**CC**	07					
Dimambro, Dominic	FEN	**CC**	13	15	16	**TR**	16	17
Dimambro, Joe	FEN	**CC**	05	06	**TR**	05	06	07
Dimmer, Matt	LAP E	**SCR**	90					
Dinse, Darcy	LIN	**SB**	98					
Disessa, Will	HOL	**TEN**	09					
Dissmore, Matt	OXF	**FB**	92					
Dixon, Bruce	SW CK	**BSK**	72					
Dmoch, Nicolle	FEN	**VB**	87					
Doan, Kayla	BRAN	**CC**	03	04				
Dobbs, Brian	SW CK	**BSB**	74					
Dobbs, Harry	FEN	**WR**	90					
Dobson, Billy	LIN	**FB**	02					
Dodge, Chris	HOL	**TEN**	88	89				
Dodge, David	MT M	**FB**	91	92	**BSB**	91	92	93
Dodson, Cathie	OXF	**TR**	89					
Doerlich, Bjoern	FEN	**TEN**	06					
Doherty, Pat	LAP E	**BSB**	80					
Dolan, Jason	MT M	**BSK**	91					
Dolata, Dave	LIN	**SCR**	00	01				
Dolata, Kate	LIN	**SCR**	01	02	03	**TR**	01	02	03
Dolliver, Abigail	FEN	**SW**	17					
Dolloff, Mike	MT M	**FB**	80					
Dolsen, Scott	OXF	**FB**	97					
Domagalski, Rachel	HOL	**TR**	11	12				
Domako, Billy	FEN	**WR**	99					
Dombrowski, Summer	HOL	**TR**	02					
Donahue, Ariana	LAP E	**SCR**	09	10	11			
Donahue, Jake	CLIO	**GLF**	09					
Donley, Nick	FLU	**TEN**	14	**BSB**	15			
Donnelly, John	FLU	**SW**	16					
Donnert, Skip	FEN	**WR**	70					
Donoho, Alex	SW CK	**WR**	10					
Donovan, Casey	LAP E	**VB**	08	09				
Doolan, Dani	KEAR	**BWL**	14					
Doolin, Felicia	HOL	**TEN**	12					
Dormire, Brianna	KEAR	**SB**	13					
Dormire, Kaitlin	KEAR	**SB**	13	14	15			
Dorr, Diane	LAP E	**VB**	83	**SB**	82	83		

Name	School	Sport					
Dorsey, Tracy	OXF	TR	83	85	86		
Dort, Dave	FEN	TR	83	84			
Dotson, Joel	CLIO	TEN	15				
Dotson, Kevin	FEN	BSB	90				
Dotson, Madison	FEN	CHR	18				
Dougherty, Nate	LAP E	BSB	09				
Dougherty, Savannah	SW CK	BWL	12				
Dougovito, Andy	LAP W	FB	03	BSB	04		
Dovre, Eric	HOL	GLF	01				
Dowdy, Leanne	LIN	TR	92				
Dowling, Cyle	FEN	TR	05				
Down, Mark	FEN	FB	01				
Downes, Ethan	LIN	TR	09				
Downing, Roger	HOL	TR	69	70			
Doyle, Dave	LIN	CC	13				
Doyon, Kyle	BRAN	SCR	12	13	TR	13	14
Drabek, Lorie	LIN	CC	88				
Draheim, Lexi	FLU	TR	15	16			
Draper, Scott	LIN	FB	86				
Dreese, Helen	LIN	CC	82				
Dreyer, Dan	LAP W	FB	96	97	BSB	96	98
Dreyer, Katie	LAP W	VB	06	SB	03	04	05	06
Driskell, Nikki	LAP W	SB	90				
Drlik, Dwain	DUR	FB	81				
Drost, Austin	LAP E	FB	99				
Dryer, Greg	HOL	TEN	04				
Dubay, Anthony	BRAN	TR	07				
DuBois, Matt	LIN	FB	02	04			
DuBois, Nick	LIN	FB	06				
DuCharme, Kaitlin	OXF	VB	07				
Duckwall, Debbie	LAP W	TEN	82				
Duffy, Riley	KEAR	CC	10	12			
DuFresne, Dan	FEN	WR	84				
Dufty, Pete	LAP	SW	05				
Dugan, Brad	OXF	BSB	05	06			
Dugan, Brandon	OXF	BSB	06	07			
Dugas, Alyssa	SW CK	LAX	18				
Duke, Danielle	HOL	TEN	98	99	00		
Duke, Fred	HOL	WR	84	85			
Duke, Kayla	LIN	CC	06	TR	04	05	07
Dunavant, Ray	DUR	FB	82				
Dunbar, Curt	LAP E	TR	99	00			
Dunbar, Pat	LAP E	TR	96	97			
Duncan, Aaron	KEAR	GLF	12				
Duncan, Eugene	SW CK	SW	71				
Duncan, James	LIN	SCR	93				
Duncan, Rick	SW CK	SW	71	72	73		
Duncan, Scott	LAP W	FB	84				

Dundas, Mack	CLIO	BSB	16				
Dunklee, MacKenzie	CLIO	SB	15				
Dunlap, Jordan	FEN	SCR	04				
Dunlap, Taylor	FEN	SCR	07	08	09		
Dunleavy, Kaitlyn	LIN	VB	11				
Dunlop, Matt	FEN	GLF	82	WR	83	TEN	83
Dunmire, Kelly	LAP E	BSK	78				
Dunmire, Kim	LAP E	SB	83	TR	83		
Dunn, Jeff	LAP W	BSB	82				
Dunn, Kris	LAP W	SB	86				
Dunn, Mike	OXF	CC	92	93			
Dura, Meredith	BRAN	SB	04				
Durgan, Kevin	FEN	FB	85				
Durso, Jim	HOL	TR	92	93			
Durso, Rich	HOL	CC	88	89	TR	90	
Dusseau, Allison	SW CK	SB	18				
Duval, Steve	FEN	FB	73				
Duval, Theresa	HOL	TR	87				
Duvall, Trace	FEN	WR	77				
Dwyer, Mike	OXF	FB	93	94			
Dye, Luke	LAP W	FB	96				
Dymowski, Butch	CAR	SW	76				
Dymowski, Harold	CAR	SW	75				
Dymowski, Mike	CAR	SW	72				
Dymytryzyn, Dawn	OXF	SCR	91				
Eads, Mike	FEN	WR	89	BSB	88		
Early, Travis	LAP E	BSB	10	11			
Earnheart, Patti	OXF	BSK	89	TR	88	SB	90
Earp, Perry	OXF	FB	93				
Easler, Brandon	FEN	BSB	95				
Easler, Bryan	LIN	GLF	99				
Easley, Lucas	FLU	SW	16	17			
Eastman, Bobbie	FEN	VB	13				
Eastman, Harold	MT M	WR	96	97	98	99	
Eastman, Jamie	MT M	SB	98				
Eastman, Jessie	FEN	VB	15				
Eastman, Tim	LAP E	HKY	01				
Easton, Isabelle	KEAR	SB	18				
Easton, Kim	FEN	BSK	78				
Eaton, Heather	HOL	TEN	87	88			
Eaton, Pam	FEN	TR	87	88	89		
Eaton, Trent	FEN	SW	17				
Ebeling, Eric	OXF	FB	90				
Ebert, Kurt	HOL	BSK	77	TR	76	77	
Ebert, Ross	FEN	FB	14				
Eckel, Jessica	LAP W	VB	10				
Eckel, Kaitlin	LAP W	VB	11	12			
Eckert, Skylar	CLIO	SCR	15	16			

Eckert, Spencer	CLIO	**BSB**	10	12				
Ecklesdafer, Missy	AIN	**VB**	86	**SB**	86			
Ecklund, Jim	CAR	**TEN**	73					
Eddy, Joe	FEN	**FB**	10					
Eddy, Kody	KEAR	**HKY**	12					
Edgar, Chuck	SW CK	**SW**	76					
Edgar, Trevor	FEN	**FB**	17					
Edgemon, Cassie	OXF	**SB**	10					
Edmonds, Blake	LAP W	**FB**	99	00				
Edwards, Cindy	LAP W	**TEN**	81					
Edwards, Donna	AIN	**SB**	73	75				
Edwards, Jason	LIN	**FB**	00	01	02			
Edwards, Kelsey	BRAN	**GLF**	13	14				
Edwards, Kent	DUR	**WR**	94					
Edwards, Mike	LAP E	**HKY**	87					
Edwards, Peggy	FEN	**TR**	77	78				
Edwards, Polly	FEN	**BSK**	80	**VB**	81	**TR**	79	80
Edwards-House, Jakara	FLU	**TR**	17					
Eggleston, Drew	HOL	**BSB**	13					
Ehle, Dan	LAP W	**TR**	04					
Eible, Tyler	CLIO	**WR**	12	13				
Eickholt, Scott	MT M	**BSB**	95					
Eisinger, Ashlee	LAP E	**TR**	09					
Ekhardt, Marian	AIN	**SB**	84					
Ekleberry, Helen	DUR	**TR**	91	92				
Elberg, Andreas	LIN	**SCR**	09					
Elder, Brian	LKV	**WR**	91					
Eldon, Sarah	BRAN	**TR**	07					
Eldred, Evan	SW CK	**SW**	15	16				
Eldridge, Jason	OXF	**WR**	02					
Eldridge, Katelyn	OXF	**CHR**	08					
Eldrige, Jason	OXF	**FB**	01					
Eleza, Rob	OXF	**FB**	00					
Elizondo, Ed	LIN	**FB**	86					
Elizondo, Zachery	KEAR	**WR**	17					
Eller, Ashlee	OXF	**TR**	04	05	06			
Ellinger, Chad	LKV	**TR**	96	97				
Ellinger, Reid	LKV	**SCR**	00					
Elliott, Dan	LAP E	**SCR**	06	07				
Elliott, Gareth	LIN	**FB**	11					
Elliott, Graham	LIN	**CC**	11	12	**TR**	13		
Elliott, Matt	LAP E	**SCR**	03					
Elliott, Shannon	BRAN	**TEN**	05					
Ellis, Jeff	DUR	**WR**	79	80				
Ellis, Nick	FEN	**SCR**	95					
Ellison, Keon	HOL	**TR**	10	11				
Ellsworth, Brook	LAP W	**CHR**	11					
Ellsworth, Cody	LAP W	**FB**	09					

Name	School	Sport					Sport				
Ellsworth, Dillon	LAP E	WR	13	14							
Elmer, Dave	HOL	CC	85				TR	86			
Elmer, Jeff	HOL	TR	84								
Elmer, Sydney	LIN	CC	10	11	12	13	TR	11	12	13	14
Elston, Jessica	FEN	SW	04								
Elston, Louis	HOL	TEN	03	04	05						
Elston, Trisha	HOL	TEN	98	99							
Eltringham, Brian	LIN	FB	95	96							
Elwood, Danielle	LAP W	CC	01				TR	01			
Elzarelli, Tom	OXF	TR	02								
Emch, Mike	OXF	BSB	02								
Emenaker, Tiffany	OXF	BSK	86	87							
Emerton, Anne	LIN	SB	98								
Emerton, Dan	LIN	FB	99								
Emery, Nick	BRAN	BSK	03								
Emmendorfer, Colin	FLU	FB	15								
Emmendorfer, Kayla	KEAR	BWL	13	15							
Emmitt, Tim	HOL	WR	95								
Emmons, Joe	DUR	TR	90								
Endicott, Cal	FLU	FB	17	BSK	18		TR	17	18		
Engel, Brad	HOL	FB	89	WR	89	90					
England, Debbie	LAP W	SB	07	08							
Ensign, Michelle	FEN	BSK	82	SB	82						
Epperson, Ryan	LAP W	TR	94								
Erickson, Jay	LAP W	SCR	87								
Erickson, Mark	CAR	SW	72								
Ernst, Eric	LAP E	SCR	99								
Erwin, Bill	MT M	WR	91	92							
Erwin, Kelsey	FEN	TEN	06	VB	06	07	SCR	05			
Erwin, Taylor	FEN	BSK	03	VB	03	04	SB	04			
Esparsa, Anthony	OXF	FB	08								
Essenmacher, Kevin	LAP W	FB	13								
Essman, Matt	FEN	TEN	95								
Essmann, Matt	FEN	GLF	95	TEN	96						
Estelle, John	LAP E	SCR	04								
Estes, Mike	CAR	TR	70								
Evans, Mallory	BRAN	CHR	12								
Evans, Mark	FEN	CC	68	69			TR	69			
Evans, Tammy	LIN	SB	88	91							
Evart, Stuart	CAR	BSB	71								
Evo, Emma	FEN	BSK	15								
Evo, Hannah	FEN	BSK	14	SCR	12						
Ewing, Anne	LAP E	TEN	83								
Ewing, Mike	LAP E	TEN	84								
Ewles, Bev	AIN	SB	81								
Ewles, Bev	HOL	BSK	80								
Ezell, Korey	KEAR	GLF	10								
Fabatz, Michael	FEN	SW	15	16							

Faber, Nick	HOL	**TEN**	07f			
Fahle, Mindy	LAP W	**TEN**	82			
Fahr, Janessa	BRAN	**CHR**	07	08	09	
Fahr, Jason	MT M	**FB**	94	95		
Fahy, Ethan	OXF	**FB**	99			
Fahy, Stephanie	OXF	**TR**	94			
Falkner, Travis	HOL	**SCR**	07			
Faris, Scott	FEN	**TEN**	85	86	87	
Faris, Steve	FEN	**TEN**	81	82		
Farnsworth, Todd	MT M	**FB**	87			
Farrand, Rob	LAP E	**SCR**	99			
Farrell, Mike	FEN	**FB**	80			
Farthing, Brad	LIN	**BSK**	11			
Farver, Orman	CAR	**BSB**	69			
Farver, Tim	LAP W	**BSB**	79			
Farwell, Alexis	HOL	**LAX**	17			
Farwell, Tania	HOL	**TEN**	90			
Fayling, Jeff	FEN	**HKY**	81			
Fearson, Mike	LAP W	**BSB**	12			
Featherston, Jim	AIN	**TR**	80	81	82	
Fechik, Katie	AIN	**VB**	80	**SB**	78	
Fedorinchik, Mike	OXF	**FB**	90	**BSB**	91	
Feetham, Courtney	LIN	**CHR**	09			
Feetham, Kelli	LIN	**TR**	85	86		
Felix, Beth	OXF	**SCR**	90			
Felix, Jeff	OXF	**FB**	93	**TR**	92	
Felix, Ryan	OXF	**SCR**	89			
Felix, Zac	HOL	**CC**	14	**TR**	15	
Fell, Greg	LAP E	**GLF**	85			
Fell, Heath	LAP E	**GLF**	85	86	87	88
Fellows, Jason	LAP W	**WR**	00	01	02	
Fellows, Jeremy	LAP W	**FB**	96			
Fellows, Tim	AIN	**TR**	81	82	83	
Feltner, Casey	HOL	**VB**	04			
Feltner, Cathi	HOL	**SB**	07			
Felts, Aaron	FEN	**TR**	09			
Felts, Ryan	FEN	**TR**	06	07		
Feltz, Jim	OXF	**TR**	84	85		
Fenslau, Jake	LAP W	**FB**	09			
Fenton, Angie	HOL	**TEN**	90	91	92	
Ferguson, Aron	FEN	**SCR**	12	13		
Ferguson, Kara	OXF	**TR**	88	90		
Ferguson, Kim	OXF	**TR**	90			
Ferguson, Marc	HOL	**TEN**	84			
Ferguson, Norm	OXF	**FB**	86			
Fern, Dustin	DUR	**FB**	92			
Ferranti, Breanne	FEN	**SW**	16			
Ferrara, Brad	LIN	**CC**	06	07	08	

Name	School	Sport	Yr	Yr	Sport	Yr	Yr	Yr
Ferrara, Savannah	LIN	CC	13	14	TR	14		
Ferrier, Tiffani	LKV	SB	02					
Fettig, Kim	HOL	TEN	91	92	93	SCR	92	93	94
Fettig, Kristen	HOL	TEN	96	98	99	SCR	00		
Fettig, Mamie	LAP W	VB	11					
Fetzer, Ann	HOL	SCR	15					
Fetzer, Roy	CAR	SW	75	76				
Fetzer, Sue	CAR	TR	71					
Feurstein, Kelly	FEN	TR	97					
Fex, Richard	HOL	TEN	01					
Fick, Nicole	LAP W	SB	02	03	04	05		
Fick, Terisa	LAP W	TEN	79	80				
Fiebernitz, Jeanette	LIN	SCR	06					
Fiebernitz, Mary-Kathryn	LIN	SCR	08	09	10	11		
Fiebernitz, Phil	LIN	FB	09					
Fiedler, John	LKV	BSB	77	78				
Fiedor, Josh	HOL	TR	09	10				
Fiedor, Justin	HOL	TR	08					
Field, Gary	SW CK	FB	73					
Fields, Mike	CAR	FB	70	BSK	71			
Fife, Jake	HOL	TR	13					
Filipiak, Ryan	LAP W	BSK	01					
Fillmore, Brett	LKV	WR	97	99	00			
Findley, Jim	MT M	CC	97	TR	97	98		
Finger, Kali	FEN	SW	09	11				
Finnegan, Brian	LAP W	GLF	79					
Finout, Janet	FEN	TR	69					
Fiorello, Rob	HOL	TR	02	03	04			
Fischer, Kelsie	FEN	VB	14					
Fischer, Tracy	LAP E	TR	92	93				
Fishback, Randy	HOL	FB	72					
Fisher, Aaron	LAP E	BSK	91					
Fisher, Brandon	LAP E	BSK	92	93				
Fisher, Bryan	LAP W	HKY	02	03				
Fisher, Dave	DUR	FB	81					
Fisher, Kyle	LIN	FB	09	10	WR	10	11	TR	11
Fisher, Parker	LAP E	BSB	14					
Fisher, Steve	CAR	FB	68					
Fisher, Tom	LIN	FB	08					
Fitzko, Ryan	SW CK	BSB	14					
Fitzpatrick, Chad	LKV	HKY	92					
Fizette, Nick	FEN	SCR	93					
Flannery, Alex	FEN	SCR	17					
Flannery, Pat	OXF	FB	02					
Fleming, Chase	FLU	BWL	17					
Fleming, Rick	LAP E	GLF	93	94				
Fletcher, Rhonda	HOL	TEN	82					
Fletcher, Ryan	MT M	BSB	97					

Flewelling, Tim	AIN	**FB**	76		
Fliam, Tim	FEN	**TR**	02		
Flones, Holly	LAP W	**CHR**	06	07	
Flood, Alexxa	KEAR	**BWL**	15	16	
Flood, Alicia	KEAR	**GLF**	09	10	11
Flood, Evan	KEAR	**GLF**	15		
Flores, Steve	OXF	**BSB**	03	04	
Florine, Linda	CAR	**TR**	76		
Floyd, Scott	MT M	**BSB**	80		
Fluty, Jake	LKV	**BSB**	99		
Fluty, Joe	LKV	**FB**	94		
Flynn, Linda	FEN	**TR**	73		
Flynn, Pat	FEN	**TR**	72		
Fochesato, Anna	BRAN	**TR**	12		
Foco, Kaitlyn	KEAR	**SB**	15	17	18
Foether, Hanna	CLIO	**SCR**	18		
Foguth, Carly	FEN	**SCR**	04	05	
Foguth, Carter	FEN	**HKY**	09		
Foguth, Jake	FEN	**HKY**	12	**GLF**	11
Foguth, Joe	FEN	**HKY**	12		
Foguth, Keith	FEN	**WR**	82	83	84
Foguth, Mike	FEN	**WR**	78		
Foley, Grady	FEN	**GLF**	09		
Foley, Mike	FEN	**FB**	74		
Foley, Scott	FEN	**FB**	69		
Foor, Chloee	FEN	**SCR**	15	16	
Forbush, Chloe	SW CK	**CHR**	18		
Forbush, Margaret	LAP E	**SCR**	88		
Ford, Ray	MT M	**BSB**	75		
Foren, Casey	BRAN	**VB**	10		
Forfar, Parri	LAP E	**VB**	85		
Forsten, Jan	LAP	**TR**	74		
Forsten, Mary	LAP	**TR**	74		
Fortier, Christine	OXF	**SCR**	03		
Fortier, Denise	LAP E	**SB**	77		
Fortney, Hillary	CLIO	**BWL**	11		
Foss, Brian	LAP W	**BSB**	04		
Foster, Bob	DUR	**BSB**	79		
Foster, Hanna	BRAN	**CHR**	11	12	
Fouracre, Luke	OXF	**SCR**	96	97	
Fouracre, Scott	OXF	**SCR**	90	91	92
Fowler, David	LIN	**SCR**	17		
Fowler, Jordan	HOL	**BSK**	09		
Fowler, Justin	HOL	**BSK**	10		
Fowler, Tahea	HOL	**TR**	80	81	
Fox, Danielle	HOL	**TEN**	05	06	
Fox, Doug	FEN	**CC**	96		
Fox, Hailey	SW CK	**SB**	13		

Name	School	Sport	Year	Year	Year	Sport	Year	Year	Year	Sport	Year	Year	Year
Fox, Jennifer	LAP E	BSK	91			TR	92						
Fox, Richard	HOL	TEN	99										
Fox, Tony	HOL	TEN	03	04	05								
Fox, Tracy	FEN	TR	91	92	93								
Foyt, Derek	BRAN	BSB	04	05		FB	04						
Fragoso, Lee	OXF	FB	90			TR	89	90	91				
Fraidenburg, Dana	LIN	SCR	04										
Francek, Rusty	LAP W	HKY	90										
Francek, Scott	LAP W	SCR	87	88		HKY	88	89					
Francis, Chris	LAP E	FB	03	04		BSK	05			TR	02	05	
Francis, Matt	LAP E	BSK	95										
Franklin, Keaton	FLU	TEN	16										
Franks, Chris	CLIO	CC	16										
Frasier, Nate	HOL	CC	13	14		TR	14	15					
Frawley, Nick	HOL	SW	08	09									
Frederick, Alia	LIN	CC	15	16		SCR	15	16	17	TR	15	16	17
Freeborg, Larry	CAR	FB	71										
Freeborn, Nick	OXF	TR	02										
Freeman, Christine	OXF	CC	93	95	96	TR	95	96	97				
Freeman, Erik	CLIO	WR	07										
Freeman, Jake	LIN	SCR	03										
Freeman, Jared	LIN	SCR	02										
Freeman, Jason	MT M	FB	81										
Freeman, Josh	LIN	WR	01										
Freeman, Krystn	LIN	SCR	98	99	00	01							
Freeman, Vicki	MT M	SB	74										
Freiberg, Scott	HOL	TEN	96										
Freitas, Josh	LIN	WR	08	09									
French, Bruce	OXF	TR	93										
French, Don	HOL	TR	75										
French, James	BRAN	BSB	14										
French, Nick	FEN	CC	09										
Frey, Andrew	FEN	FB	08			TEN	07						
Frey, Bobby	LAP E	BSB	08	09									
Frezza, Chris	LAP E	TEN	07										
Frick, Darrell	LAP E	GLF	00										
Fries, Delaney	FEN	SW	17										
Frisch, Matt	OXF	WR	08	09									
Fritz, Ray	LKV	TR	89										
Fritz, Todd	OXF	FB	84										
Fruner, Darcy	FEN	SCR	96										
Fuerst, Jadyn	FLU	TR	15										
Fuerstein, Kelly	FEN	TR	98										
Fugate, Josh	HOL	BSK	11										
Fugate, Rebecca	HOL	BSK	17	18									
Fugenschuh, Bill	CAR	WR	69	71									
Fulcher, Diane	MT M	SB	85										
Fulgenzi, Dom	LAP W	GLF	03										

Name	School	Sport						
Fuller, Al	LKV	**BSB**	86					
Fuller, Alan	LKV	**WR**	85					
Fuller, Chad	HOL	**WR**	92	93	94			
Fuller, Devin	FEN	**FB**	17					
Fuller, Marva	HOL	**BSK**	82	83				
Fulton, Alyssa	KEAR	**SCR**	09					
Fulton, Kara	FEN	**SW**	05					
Fultz, Jim	HOL	**TR**	76					
Fultz, Payton	LIN	**FB**	07					
Fyvie, Dan	FEN	**FB**	00	**BSB**	00	01		
Gabel, Skye	LIN	**TR**	03	04				
Gable, Kelly	FEN	**SB**	94					
Gabler, Spencer	FEN	**SW**	18					
Gabold, Braxton	FLU	**WR**	18					
Gach, Anita	AIN	**TR**	79	80				
Gach, Mike	AIN	**TEN**	77					
Gach, Rose	AIN	**TR**	82	84				
Gallero, Steve	HOL	**TR**	82	83				
Gamble, Don	MT M	**TR**	73					
Gamble, Ron	MT M	**TR**	73					
Gangi, Catherine	FEN	**SW**	09					
Garafalo, Frank	MT M	**TR**	97	98				
Garcia, Ashleigh	LAP W	**SCR**	14					
Garcia, Dan	LAP W	**TR**	04					
Garcia, Jamie	FEN	**BSB**	10					
Garcia, Julie	LAP W	**SCR**	94					
Garcia, Tony	LAP W	**BSB**	05					
Garcia, Valerie	KEAR	**CHR**	16					
Garcia, Valerie	SW CK	**CHR**	17					
Gardner, David	SW CK	**TR**	07	08				
Gardner, Jim	CAR	**SW**	72	73				
Gardner, Mike	OXF	**FB**	93					
Garner, Kirk	HOL	**WR**	87	88				
Garrett, Dwight	LAP E	**BSK**	83	84				
Garrett, Rich	OXF	**FB**	86					
Garris, Tyler	LAP W	**GLF**	09	10				
Garrison, Amanda	HOL	**TR**	09					
Garrison, Jordan	HOL	**BSK**	99					
Garza, Paul	AIN	**TR**	81	84				
Gaston, Chris	LIN	**BSK**	00					
Gatlin, Tyler	SW CK	**CC**	08					
Gatza, Jim	FEN	**TEN**	78	79	80	81		
Gatza, Margaret	FEN	**TEN**	84	**TR**	86	88		
Gatza, Mike	FEN	**TEN**	80	81				
Gaumer, Justin	HOL	**SW**	08	09	10	**TR**	08	09	10
Gauthier, Garrett	LAP W	**BWL**	09					
Gauthier, Hannah	LAP W	**BWL**	11	**SB**	09	11		
Gauthier, Mike	CAR	**WR**	69					

Name	School	Sport	Yr			Sport	Yr			Sport	Yr	
Gavan, Scott	LKV	FB	91	TR	90	91	92					
Gavel, Jamey	HOL	SCR	06									
Gay, Kevin	LAP W	FB	95	BSB	96							
Gayer, Brad	OXF	FB	89									
Gaylor, Amy	LAP E	TR	12									
Gazetti, Marty	HOL	BSB	96									
Gazetti, Nikki	HOL	TEN	01									
Gazetti, Ricci	HOL	HKY	75									
Gazetti, Tony	HOL	TEN	05	SW	05	06						
Gearig, Dave	HOL	TR	78									
Gehrig, Trevor	KEAR	TR	15									
Geisler, Helge	HOL	TEN	98									
Gelen, Arianna	BRAN	CHR	14	16								
Gelen, Stephanie	BRAN	CHR	10	11								
Genovesi, Renee	SW CK	TR	16									
Genovesi, Toni	SW CK	FB	72									
Genslak, Megan	BRAN	SB	15									
Genslak, Megan	SW CK	SB	14									
Georgakopoulos, Jake	FEN	FB	10									
Georgakopoulos, Jared	FEN	FB	08									
George, Dave	LIN	CC	98	HKY	99							
George, Hannah	OXF	TR	06	07	08	09						
George, Kellie	LIN	SCR	90	91								
George, Laura	OXF	TR	88									
George, Scott	LAP W	GLF	77									
Gepfrey, Marianne	LAP W	SB	87									
Gepfrey, Pam	LAP W	SB	90									
Gerbe, Shannon	OXF	SB	03	04								
Gerbig, Rob	FEN	HKY	88									
Geren, Paul	SW CK	TR	14									
Gerhardt, Kayla	FLU	GLF	15	16	SCR	17						
Gerlach, Ann	LAP	TR	74									
Gerlach, Ann	LAP E	VB	77									
Gerlach, Brad	LAP	BSB	69									
Gerlach, Roger	LAP	TR	72									
Gerwold, Jim	LKV	FB	97									
Gettel, Steve	LAP W	GLF	96									
Getz, Stephanie	LAP E	SB	99									
Geyer, Julia	LIN	SB	89									
Gheller, Gary	MT M	FB	79									
Gheriani, Yussef	FEN	TR	08									
Ghiaciuc, Eric	OXF	FB	99	WR	98	99	00	TR	99	00		
Ghiaciuc, Kelly	OXF	TR	98									
Ghilardi, Jessie	LAP E	SCR	04	05	06							
Ghilardi, Katy	LAP E	SCR	04	05	06	07						
Giacomantonio, Easton	LIN	FB	17									
Gibbons, Bill	LAP W	HKY	88	89								
Gibbons, Glen	LAP W	HKY	81	82								

Gibbons, Rick	LAP	**HKY**	75							
Gibbs, Tyree	BRAN	**BSK**	16							
Gibson, Austin	SW CK	**BSB**	13							
Gibson, Tyler	HOL	**WR**	11	12						
Gibson, Zach	LAP E	**FB**	95	**BSK**	96					
Gidcumb, Kallie	MT M	**SB**	00							
Giegler, Ken	HOL	**BSB**	84							
Giesey, Aleisha	FEN	**SB**	06	07	08					
Giesey, Aubre	FEN	**SB**	00							
Giesey, Austin	FEN	**HKY**	10							
Giesly, Wes	FEN	**GLF**	05							
Gilbert, Chris	FEN	**BSK**	16	**GLF**	16					
Gilbert, Chris	FEN	**CC**	75	76	**BSK**	77	**TR**	76	77	
Gilbert, Courtney	LAP W	**CHR**	12							
Gilbert, Jenna	CLIO	**SB**	16	17	18					
Gilbert, John	FEN	**BSK**	84							
Gilbert, Julie	FEN	**VB**	11							
Gilbert, Matt	FEN	**CC**	08	09	11	**TR**	12			
Gilbert, Paul	MT M	**BSB**	97							
Gilbert, Vickie	FEN	**TR**	72	73	74					
Gildner, Tim	OXF	**SCR**	87							
Giles, Stephanie	CLIO	**GLF**	16							
Gilley, Davin	SW CK	**SW**	17							
Gilliam, Scott	FEN	**TR**	88	89	90					
Gillies, Brian	MT M	**BSB**	95							
Gillman, Jacob	FEN	**FB**	13							
Gillum, Hermon III	CLIO	**WR**	07	09						
Gisse, Craig	HOL	**WR**	83							
Glass, Lori	FEN	**SB**	80							
Glass, Xavier	HOL	**TEN**	16							
Glasson, Terri	FEN	**TEN**	78							
Glazier, Rob	AIN	**CC**	82							
Gleason, Erin	LAP E	**SB**	99	00						
Gleason, James	BRAN	**HKY**	11	12						
Gleason, Matt	LAP E	**FB**	80	**BSK**	81					
Glime, Bill	HOL	**TEN**	84							
Gloster, Chianne	SW CK	**TR**	18							
Gloster, Cianna	SW CK	**TR**	18							
Glowaz, Amy	HOL	**TEN**	84	85	86	87				
Glowaz, Kara	HOL	**TEN**	86	87	89	**VB**	90			
Glowaz, Stacie	HOL	**TEN**	82	83	**TR**	84				
Glowniak, Clare	FLU	**BSK**	15	16						
Glozier, Bob	FEN	**TR**	76							
Gocha, Bella	SW CK	**TR**	16							
Godar, Brian	HOL	**CC**	03							
Godfrey, Ray	LAP W	**GLF**	96							
Godwin, Larry	LAP	**FB**	71							
Godwin, Nick	LAP E	**HKY**	00							

Goemaere, Erica	LAP W	SCR	03	04				
Goff, Jerry	MT M	FB	76					
Goff, Steve	MT M	WR	80	81				
Goin, Crystal	FEN	SB	06	07	08			
Goin, Mike	FEN	TR	74					
Gold, Mike	LIN	TR	15					
Golden, Austin	LIN	WR	13					
Golden, Jamie	HOL	SCR	94					
Goldner, Lee	SW CK	FB	72	73				
Goldstein, Tyler	CLIO	BSB	06					
Golson, Nick	LAP W	TEN	01					
Goltz, Kianna	BRAN	SB	14	15				
Gomez, George	OXF	FB	98					
Gomez, Hugo	OXF	FB	04					
Gomez, Luis	OXF	FB	02	WR	03	TR	03	
Gonzales, Anthony	HOL	WR	10	11	12	13		
Gonzales, Esteban	HOL	WR	10	11				
Gonzales, Estenban	BRAN	WR	09					
Good, Jesselyn	LIN	VB	97	98				
Goodearl, Greg	HOL	TR	75					
Goodfellow, Heather	HOL	CC	94					
Goodfellow, Mark	OXF	CC	90	91	92	TR	91	93
Goodfellow, Mike	OXF	CC	86	87	88	TR	87	88	89
Goodrich, Ben	HOL	TR	07	08				
Goodrich, Zac	HOL	TEN	10	11	12	13		
Gordon, Annette	AIN	VB	81					
Gordon, Chris	LAP E	BSB	87					
Gordon, Dakota	HOL	SW	11					
Gordon, Hannah	LAP W	VB	12					
Gordon, Travis	SW CK	SW	07					
Gornowicz, Josh	FEN	SCR	08					
Gorski, Alisa	HOL	TR	02					
Gott, Jaslyn	SW CK	SCR	17					
Gould, Alex	LAP W	GLF	12					
Gould, Craig	FEN	FB	76					
Gould, Dan	FEN	TR	99					
Gould, Dave	FEN	TR	73					
Goulet, Mic	AIN	FB	68					
Gouthier, Andrea	CAR	TR	69					
Goward, Mike	LKV	FB	79					
Goyette, Angie	LKV	TR	98	99				
Grabenhorst, Ted	MT M	FB	74					
Grace, Jacqui	OXF	GLF	02	03				
Graff, Abby	HOL	TEN	15					
Graham, Larry	LKV	HKY	85	86				
Graham, Scott	FEN	WR	81	82				
Graham, Tyler	LAP E	BWL	12					
Grahl, Colin	FEN	FB	78	79				

Grainger, Andrea	FEN	**TR**	79	80	81					
Grainger, Patti	FEN	**TR**	78	79						
Grambush, Jordan	FEN	**GLF**	07							
Granger, Carly	FEN	**VB**	13	14						
Granger, Samantha	FEN	**BSK**	10	11	**VB**	09	10			
Grant, Cody	SW CK	**CC**	09	10	11					
Grasley, Sharon	LIN	**CC**	83							
Grasso, Vince	HOL	**TR**	08							
Graveldinger, Jaclyn	BRAN	**TEN**	10							
Graves, Dylan	LAP E	**TEN**	13							
Graves, Kelly	HOL	**BSK**	81	82						
Gray, Anderius	HOL	**FB**	10	**TR**	11					
Gray, Jimmy	HOL	**FB**	15	**WR**	16					
Gray, Scott	LAP W	**GLF**	82							
Graziano, Sara	SW CK	**LAX**	18							
Green, Bill	CAR	**WR**	74	75						
Green, Brandan	LIN	**FB**	07	08						
Green, Chris	HOL	**BSB**	12							
Green, Clark	LAP E	**TR**	05							
Green, Justin	LKV	**TR**	00							
Green, Matt	OXF	**FB**	94	95	96	**SCR**	93	94	95	96
Green, Mike	HOL	**WR**	08							
Green, Tiffany	FEN	**SCR**	90	91	92	93				
Greene, Miranda	LIN	**TR**	14							
Greene, Samantha	LIN	**TR**	14							
Greenleaf, Austin	LAP E	**FB**	11	**BSB**	10	11				
Greenwald, Julie	FEN	**BSK**	83	**VB**	84					
Gregory, Dan	HOL	**SCR**	07	09	**TR**	09				
Gregory, Doug	FEN	**HKY**	79							
Gregory, Doug	FEN	**HKY**	77							
Gregory, Holly	LAP E	**SB**	93							
Gregory, Ken	FEN	**FB**	68							
Gregware, Brianne	LAP	**SW**	07							
Grenillo, Jesse	HOL	**WR**	99	01						
Greyerbiehl, Laura	LKV	**TR**	91	92						
Gribble, Jeff	HOL	**CC**	99	01						
Gribble, Jessica	HOL	**CC**	01							
Griffin, Angie	FEN	**BSK**	89	**VB**	90	**SB**	89	90		
Griffin, Karlee	KEAR	**BWL**	18							
Griffin, Scott	LAP E	**WR**	86							
Griffin, Tre'Ron	KEAR	**TR**	16							
Griffith, Craig	FEN	**GLF**	87							
Grimm, Brian	LIN	**WR**	94							
Grinenik, Mark	SW CK	**CC**	74	75						
Grizzard, Eric	LAP	**BSB**	73							
Groat, Megan	BRAN	**CHR**	13	14	15					
Grobbel, Rachel	LAP W	**SB**	10	11						
Grode, Eddie	LIN	**FB**	17							

Groll, John	FEN	**FB**	82						
Gromak, Kathy	HOL	**SB**	73						
Grossman, Chelsea	FEN	**SW**	04						
Groulx, Scott	MT M	**FB**	91	**BSB**	92				
Grove, Bill	FEN	**BSK**	73	74					
Grove, Dave	FEN	**FB**	72						
Grove, Stewart	FEN	**FB**	71						
Gruber, Lauren	FEN	**SW**	14	15	16				
Grugel, Chantal	HOL	**CHR**	13						
Grumley, Larry	LAP E	**BSB**	81						
Grunewald, Brad	OXF	**TR**	06						
Gruno, Brian	LKV	**BSB**	88						
Guckian, Julie	LIN	**GLF**	10	11	12				
Gudith, Mike	HOL	**BSK**	77						
Guerra, Ryan	LAP E	**FB**	02	03					
Guerrero, German	OXF	**CC**	04						
Guevara, Mauricio	SW CK	**SCR**	09						
Guglielmello, Gina	HOL	**TR**	83						
Guibault, Diane	FEN	**TEN**	79	81					
Guilbault, John	FEN	**GLF**	70						
Guilbault, Steve	FEN	**FB**	68	**GLF**	69				
Guilbault, Susi	FEN	**SB**	72						
Gundry, Molly	FEN	**GLF**	15	16	17				
Gunnels, Becky	MT M	**SB**	75						
Gunnels, Dan	CAR	**SW**	75	76					
Gunsell, Ed	FEN	**WR**	80						
Gunsell, Rod	DUR	**FB**	83						
Gutierrez, Amie	LIN	**SCR**	89	90	91				
Gutierrez, Damon	LIN	**SCR**	91	92	**TR**	93			
Gutierrez, John	LAP E	**SCR**	87	88					
Gutierrez, Rachel	LIN	**CC**	00	01	02	03	**TR**	01	02 03 04
Guy, McKayla	LIN	**CC**	12	13					
Guyer, Brian	DUR	**BSB**	84						
Guyzik, Thad	LIN	**BSB**	10						
Haack, James	LAP W	**FB**	96						
Haaraoja, Gabrielle	FEN	**SW**	10	11	12	13			
Haase, Tommy	BRAN	**SCR**	15						
Hack, Mike	LIN	**FB**	01	**TR**	00	01			
Hackett, Lauren	HOL	**CC**	14	15					
Hackney, Deron	LAP E	**GLF**	81						
Haddad, Dan	FEN	**TR**	89						
Hadji, Steve	FEN	**HKY**	82						
Hadley, Tim	HOL	**TR**	07						
Hagen, Katie	HOL	**CC**	98	**TR**	02				
Hagen, Tim	HOL	**FB**	74						
Hager, Cody	HOL	**SW**	07						
Hagerman, Jennifer	FEN	**SB**	97						
Haggadone, Matt	LAP W	**TR**	05						

Haggadone, Preston	LAP W	**FB**	07	08	09	
Haggadone, Ryan	LAP W	**FB**	06			
Haggadone, Scott	LAP E	**TR**	01			
Hagstrom, Erin	LIN	**TR**	92	93	94	95
Hagy, Tyler	CLIO	**SCR**	10			
Haicl, Mike	SW CK	**BSB**	70	71		
Haight, Andy	LKV	**FB**	96			
Haines, Monica	LAP E	**SB**	80			
Haines, Tony	LAP E	**GLF**	79	80		
Hajciar, Ben	FEN	**FB**	15			
Hajec, Angie	FEN	**SB**	93			
Hajec, Marlene	FEN	**TEN**	97			
Hajec, Pete	FEN	**TR**	79			
Hajec, Stephanie	FEN	**VB**	00	01	**TR**	99	01
Hajnal, Lisa	LAP E	**SCR**	88			
Hale, Danielle	KEAR	**BWL**	09			
Haley, Rod	LIN	**FB**	86			
Hall, Adam	LIN	**SCR**	95			
Hall, Alec	CLIO	**GLF**	12			
Hall, Bill	LIN	**FB**	96	97		
Hall, Brian	CAR	**FB**	75			
Hall, Carrie	MT M	**TR**	82	83		
Hall, Chuck	LIN	**CC**	84			
Hall, Frank	LKV	**WR**	80			
Hall, Heather	OXF	**BSK**	83	84		
Hall, Lanie	LIN	**TR**	92			
Hall, Madaline	FEN	**SW**	15	**TR**	15	16	17
Hall, Mike	CAR	**TEN**	73			
Hall, Sabrina	FEN	**SW**	15	16	17	
Hall, Savannah	LKV	**CC**	99	00		
Hall, Steve	LIN	**TR**	89			
Hall, Tim	LIN	**FB**	99			
Hall, Tom	LKV	**WR**	87			
Hallandal, Alex	FLU	**TEN**	15			
Hallberg, Corbin	BRAN	**WR**	17			
Hallowell, Richard	HOL	**WR**	06			
Halstead, Sarah	FEN	**SB**	12			
Halverson, Marty	AIN	**FB**	75	76		
Hamblin, Shayla	HOL	**TR**	01			
Hambly, Jason	OXF	**GLF**	01			
Hamell, John	OXF	**FB**	95	**TR**	96	
Hamilton, Abby	FEN	**SW**	04			
Hamilton, Baylor	FEN	**TEN**	17			
Hamilton, Brooke	SW CK	**LAX**	18			
Hamilton, Don	HOL	**TR**	79			
Hamilton, Greg	HOL	**BSB**	03			
Hamilton, Kelly	BRAN	**CHR**	14	15	**TR**	12	
Hamilton, Kyle	FEN	**BSB**	05			

Hamilton, Mac	FEN	**FB**	13					
Hamilton, Tyler	FEN	**FB**	07	08	09	**BSK**	10	
Hamlin, Forrest	OXF	**FB**	00					
Hammond, Kelli	LKV	**TR**	88	89	90	91		
Hanak, Jon	LIN	**GLF**	00	**BSB**	00			
Hanchett, Darin	LAP W	**WR**	89					
Hancock, Chris	LAP E	**FB**	81					
Hand, Gabe	FEN	**TEN**	16	17				
Handgis, Tammy	OXF	**TR**	86					
Hankins, Barry	CAR	**BSK**	74					
Hanna, Ed	FEN	**FB**	97					
Hanna, John	LAP E	**TR**	09					
Hannick, Ashley	LAP W	**CHR**	06	07				
Hansen, Henrick	LKV	**FB**	82					
Hansen, Linsey	BRAN	**TEN**	10					
Hanson, Dale	FEN	**TR**	78					
Hanson, Dan	FEN	**GLF**	75	**TR**	78			
Hanson, Dave	FEN	**GLF**	77					
Hanson, Justine	FEN	**TEN**	12					
Haragos, Cody	BRAN	**TR**	11					
Harbin, Troy	SW CK	**CC**	11					
Harburn, Tadd	CAR	**BSB**	76					
Harden, Amy	HOL	**TEN**	92	93	94			
Harden, Joel	HOL	**TEN**	85					
Hardenbough, Amber	HOL	**TR**	99	00				
Hardenburgh, Chad	HOL	**TEN**	05					
Hardesty, Rob	CLIO	**SW**	07					
Harding, Andy	BRAN	**BSB**	05	06				
Harding, Bethany	BRAN	**CHR**	07					
Harding, Isabel	FEN	**TR**	04					
Harding, Tiffany	BRAN	**CHR**	06					
Hardy, Jake	BRAN	**FB**	07					
Hardy, Tori	CLIO	**CHR**	14					
Hargas, Adrian	BRAN	**BSK**	06	07				
Harlan, Mike	LAP W	**FB**	92					
Harless, Austin	HOL	**BSK**	17					
Harmon, Carly	HOL	**SCR**	07	08	09			
Harmon, Emily	HOL	**TEN**	09	10				
Harmon, Lora	SW CK	**TR**	76					
Harmon, Tatum	HOL	**TR**	11	12	13			
Harms, Joelle	OXF	**BSK**	08					
Harp, Megan	LIN	**SCR**	12					
Harper, Brian	LIN	**FB**	95					
Harrington, Alison	MT M	**GLF**	02					
Harrington, Luke	HOL	**GLF**	17					
Harrington, Paige	BRAN	**TR**	12					
Harris, Brad	FEN	**TEN**	83					
Harris, Brian	FEN	**CC**	70					

Harris, Doug	LAP W	**SCR**	88				
Harris, Frank	HOL	**FB**	88	89			
Harris, Kevin	DUR	**WR**	82				
Harris, Meagan	FEN	**TEN**	08				
Harris, Nick	LAP W	**FB**	13				
Harris, Robin	LAP E	**VB**	91				
Harris, Taveon	KEAR	**TR**	16				
Harris, Tim	HOL	**TEN**	94	96			
Harrison, Aiden	FLU	**FB**	17	**TR**	17	18	
Harrison, Don	AIN	**TEN**	83	84			
Harrison, Logan	FEN	**SW**	17				
Harrison, Matt	HOL	**BWL**	13				
Harrison, Sheena	FEN	**TR**	97				
Harrod, Sara	HOL	**TEN**	86	87	88		
Hart, Alex	LAP	**SW**	07	10			
Hart, Brian	MT M	**BSB**	83				
Hart, Jeff	MT M	**BSB**	78				
Hart, Kevin	FEN	**TEN**	85	86			
Hart, Luke	CLIO	**CC**	16				
Hart, Molly	OWO	**TR**	18				
Hart, Rex	AIN	**WR**	80	81			
Hart, Ron	MT M	**BSB**	81				
Hartell, Don	CAR	**SW**	72				
Hartley, Dave	CAR	**CC**	70	71	**TR**	72	
Hartman, Gary	CAR	**FB**	69				
Hartwell, Jordan	LAP E	**BSB**	06				
Harvey, Adam	LAP E	**BSK**	06				
Harvey, Darrell	LKV	**BSB**	79				
Harwood, Paige	LIN	**GLF**	10				
Haskell, Alex	LAP E	**GLF**	07	07f	**TEN**	06	
Haskins, Doug	SW CK	**FB**	74				
Hatch, Brenna	FEN	**SB**	15	16			
Hatch, Dave	FEN	**WR**	80				
Hatch, Joe	HOL	**WR**	79				
Hatch, John	FEN	**HKY**	83				
Hatfield, Trevor	HOL	**WR**	14	15			
Hathaway, Richard	LAP E	**HKY**	79				
Hatter, Joshua	CLIO	**TR**	17				
Hautala, Jenny	MT M	**TEN**	88	89			
Havercraft, Tina	FEN	**TR**	91				
Havercroft, Tonya	FEN	**SCR**	92	93			
Havrand, Joe	CAR	**SW**	72	74			
Havrilla, Jeff	AIN	**FB**	80				
Hawes, Barbara	KEAR	**BWL**	16	17	18		
Hawkins, Melissa	AIN	**SB**	79				
Hawkins, Steve	DUR	**WR**	79				
Hawks, Melanie	HOL	**TEN**	12				
Hawley, Elizabeth	HOL	**TR**	11	12			

Hawley, Kevin	CLIO	**TR**	06						
Hawley, Rex	FEN	**HKY**	75						
Hay, Duff	FEN	**FB**	69	70	**BSB**	71			
Hayden, Curtis	CLIO	**GLF**	06						
Hayduk, Andrew	BRAN	**FB**	15						
Hayes, Dave	AIN	**HKY**	82	84					
Hayes, Jayme	LAP E	**SCR**	92	93					
Hayes, Jon	DUR	**FB**	81	**WR**	82				
Hayes, Sandy	LAP	**SB**	75						
Haynes, Mark	LAP	**WR**	76	77					
Hayward, Justin	LAP W	**BSK**	05						
Hazelwood, Liz	OXF	**VB**	07						
Heathcoat, NaKaela	SW CK	**CHR**	18						
Heavner, Ken	LKV	**CC**	86						
Hedenbergh, Max	KEAR	**GLF**	09						
Heffeman, Nick	OXF	**FB**	98						
Heffley, Nate	OXF	**GLF**	95						
Heiden, Eric	FEN	**HKY**	94	95					
Heil, Adam	FEN	**FB**	97						
Heil, Paige	FEN	**VB**	07f						
Heines, Sara	BRAN	**SW**	12	13	14				
Helka, Andy	HOL	**WR**	83						
Helkowski, Dan	MT M	**BSB**	01						
Heller, Bill	LAP W	**TEN**	77						
Heller, Willie	HOL	**TR**	71	72					
Hellesfjord, Triene	LIN	**SCR**	89						
Hellow, Andy	HOL	**SCR**	01	02	**TEN**	01	02	03	
Helms, Mark	FEN	**WR**	77	78					
Helms, Mike	FEN	**CC**	74	**TR**	75				
Helms, Mike	SW CK	**TR**	74						
Hemming, Lisa	HOL	**TEN**	87						
Henard, Jacob	FEN	**FB**	16						
Hendershott, Jamie	BRAN	**CC**	04						
Hendershott, Kaitlyn	BRAN	**BSK**	14	**SB**	15				
Henderson, Michelle	FEN	**TR**	75						
Hendricks, Carl	FEN	**FB**	79						
Hendricks, Nick	LAP W	**WR**	03	04					
Hendrickson, Chelsey	KEAR	**SB**	10	11					
Hendry, Al	DUR	**WR**	87						
Henley, Tim	LAP E	**BSK**	79						
Henley, Todd	LAP E	**BSK**	78						
Henn, Dan	HOL	**WR**	92						
Hennig, Katie	FEN	**TR**	04						
Henry, Autumn	SW CK	**BSK**	12						
Henry, Carrie	AIN	**SB**	86						
Henry, Jim	OXF	**SCR**	03						
Henry, Madisen	SW CK	**SB**	16						
Henry, Mike	AIN	**CC**	80	81					

Name	School	Sport	Y1	Y2	Y3	Y4
Henry, Randy	SW CK	**TR**	71			
Henry, Skyler	SW CK	**GLF**	17			
Hensley, Cristina	FEN	**TEN**	97			
Hensley, Kim	FEN	**SCR**	88	89		
Henson, Brock	FEN	**BSB**	18			
Henson, Joel	AIN	**FB**	75			
Henson, Kevin	AIN	**BSK**	81	82		
Henson, Laura	LAP E	**VB**	88			
Hepner, Jesse	HOL	**VB**	17			
Herbstreit, Brook	FEN	**GLF**	17			
Herfert, Jeremy	LAP W	**FB**	91			
Hermanson, Justin	LAP E	**TEN**	98	00		
Hernandez, Christi	HOL	**TEN**	01	02	03	04
Hernandez, Jasmine	BRAN	**CC**	06			
Hernandez, Tony	HOL	**TEN**	97	98	99	00
Herold, Brandon	FLU	**FB**	14			
Heron, Danielle	SW CK	**SB**	15			
Heron, Scott	AIN	**FB**	81			
Herr, Brennen	OWO	**WR**	18			
Herr, Mason	FLU	**TR**	16	17		
Herron, Jackie	FEN	**TEN**	96			
Herronen, Joe	HOL	**TR**	76			
Herstein, Jon	FEN	**FB**	99	00	**WR**	01
Herta, Barbara	AIN	**VB**	77			
Hervey, Jason	LAP E	**BSK**	97	**TR**	97	
Herzog, Kim	OXF	**SB**	91			
Hester, Wayne	LAP E	**HKY**	77			
Heusted, Steve	LAP W	**FB**	94			
Hewitt, Mike	AIN	**BSB**	69			
Hewson, Jim	LAP W	**WR**	03	05		
Hewson, Katllin	LAP W	**CHR**	06			
Hibbard, Josh	FEN	**BSK**	01	02	**BSB**	02
Hibbard, Tim	FEN	**FB**	79			
Hibbeln, Mary	AIN	**VB**	84			
Hibbs, Chyanne	KEAR	**BWL**	12			
Hibbs, Matt	LIN	**GLF**	97	98	99	
Hice, Steve	FEN	**SW**	75			
Hickey, Meghan	OXF	**TR**	03			
Hickmont, Ryan	OXF	**FB**	99			
Hickoff, Dylan	FEN	**BSK**	10	11	12	
Hickoff, Ryan	FEN	**BSK**	11	12		
Hicks, Rich	HOL	**CC**	95	96		
Hicks, Rich	HOL	**TR**	95	96	97	
Hietala, Ilka	LKV	**HKY**	85			
High, Ashlee	OXF	**BWL**	09			
Hild, Sami	HOL	**TEN**	16	17	18	
Hildebrand, Roxanne	MT M	**BSK**	86	87		
Hill, Chaz	LAP E	**BSB**	11			

Name	School	Sport					
Hill, Desiree	LAP	SB	74				
Hill, Jim	AIN	CC	79	80			
Hill, Joe	SW CK	FB	16				
Hill, Kaylee	KEAR	CHR	17	18			
Hill, Matt	BRAN	FB	16				
Hill, Rory	SW CK	HKY	08				
Hill, Ryan	KEAR	BSB	11				
Hill, Scott	HOL	TR	78	79			
Hill, Todd	HOL	CC	87	88	89	TR	90
Hill, Wayne	MT M	FB	83				
Hill, Zach	LAP W	FB	06				
Hillebrand, Sarah	OXF	TR	10				
Hillis, Sarah	FEN	SB	84				
Hillman, Bill	HOL	BSB	73	74			
Hillman, Derek	FEN	BSB	95				
Hillman, Lisa	FEN	SB	91	92	93		
Hillman, Matt	HOL	FB	93	94	BSB	94	
Hillman, Nicki	FEN	SB	95	96			
Hillman, Pat	HOL	FB	74	75			
Hillman, Rick	HOL	FB	70	BSB	70	71	
Hilton, Wilbur	MT M	WR	98				
Himes, Brian	FEN	SCR	03	04	05		
Himes, Chris	FEN	SCR	99	01			
Hiner, Jenny	LAP E	CC	95				
Hines, Aaron	HOL	TEN	01	02			
Hines, Eric	HOL	TEN	01	02			
Hinton, Mike	FEN	FB	78	BSB	78	79	
Hintz, Dave	FEN	FB	83	BSK	84	85	TR	85
Hintz, Greg	FEN	TR	78				
Hintz, Marcie	FEN	TEN	90				
Hintz, Sue	FEN	VB	78	79	TR	77	78	79
Hippensteel, Jeremy	CLIO	WR	09				
Hiscock, Jeff	CAR	TEN	73	74	75		
Hitchcock, Andrea	OXF	TR	02	03			
Hitchcock, Fred	LIN	HKY	91				
Hittle, Brian	LKV	WR	79	80	TR	80	
Hizelberger, Kelsey	LAP E	SCR	07	08	09		
Hnatow, Joe	LIN	FB	09				
Hoard, Nate	OXF	TR	94	95			
Hoard, Tony	LAP E	BSB	82				
Hoard, Tony	LAP W	BSB	81				
Hobbins, Dan	LAP	TR	72	73			
Hobson, Brett	BRAN	GLF	17				
Hocevar, Cody	FEN	FB	11	12			
Hochkins, Jamie	LIN	HKY	97	98			
Hochkins, Jason	LIN	HKY	96				
Hocker, Nick	OXF	GLF	10				
Hodge, Morgan	CLIO	CHR	11				

Name	Team	Sport	Yr	Yr	Sport	Yr	Yr	Yr	Sport	Yr	Yr	Yr	Yr
Hodges, Ian	HOL	**BSK**	16										
Hodges, Meg	LAP E	**SCR**	90	91									
Hoeberling, Collin	LIN	**SCR**	13										
Hoeflein, Andy	OXF	**SCR**	87	88									
Hoff, Matt	FLU	**TEN**	14										
Hoffert, Glenn	LAP	**FB**	69										
Hoffman, Alex	OXF	**HKY**	06										
Hoffman, Brian	FEN	**WR**	75										
Hoffman, Grace	KEAR	**GLF**	15	16	17								
Hoffman, Leslie	DUR	**TR**	94										
Hoffman, Ron	LKV	**TR**	97	98									
Hoffmeyer, Kevin	HOL	**TEN**	90	92									
Hofstetter, Scott	FEN	**FB**	71	72	**TR**	73							
Hogarth, Maika	HOL	**TEN**	17	18									
Hogrefe, Brandon	LIN	**TR**	09										
Hohenthaner, Ryan	LAP E	**WR**	02										
Holbrook, Liz	OXF	**BSK**	98	99									
Holcombe, Doug	LAP E	**BSB**	81	82									
Holec, Dale	SW CK	**SW**	73										
Holek, Conrad	DUR	**FB**	91										
Holek, Ginnie	DUR	**SB**	94										
Holek, Nick	DUR	**WR**	91										
Holek, Tony	DUR	**FB**	89										
Holifield, Tony	MT M	**WR**	95	96	97	98							
Holland, Ariana	SW CK	**TR**	18										
Hollenbeck, Chris	DUR	**TR**	86	87									
Hollis, Sierra	FEN	**SB**	11										
Holmes, Jerry	DUR	**FB**	81	82									
Holmes, Josh	FEN	**FB**	02										
Holmgren, Kevin	FEN	**WR**	79										
Holscher, Jordan	LIN	**CC**	13	14	15								
Holsinger, Jim	LIN	**BSB**	89										
Hook, Nick	LAP W	**FB**	04										
Hooker, Colin	BRAN	**CC**	13	14	**TR**	13	14	15					
Hooks, Tyler	CLIO	**BSB**	08										
Hooper, Deanna	FEN	**SW**	07	08	09	10							
Hooper, Denise	HOL	**SB**	89										
Hooper, Hunter	HOL	**TR**	12										
Hooper, Sharron	HOL	**BSK**	93	**VB**	94								
Hope, Russell	SW CK	**BSK**	08										
Hopkin, Austin	HOL	**FB**	11										
Hopkin, Lance	HOL	**TEN**	08	**BSK**	09	10							
Hopkins, Cori	LIN	**VB**	94	95	96								
Hopkins, Katie	LKV	**VB**	01	**TR**	98	00	01						
Hopkins, Kyle	LIN	**FB**	97	**BSK**	98	**BSB**	97						
Hoppe, Jessica	LAP E	**BSK**	97	98	**VB**	98	99	**SCR**	96	97	98	99	
Hoppe, Nick	LAP E	**SCR**	00										
Hoppe, Sarah	LAP E	**VB**	96	**SCR**	94	95	96						

Name	Team	Sport	Years					
Hopson, Gordon	HOL	**TR**	69	70				
Hopton, J.D.	SW CK	**TEN**	11					
Hord, Jake	LIN	**CC**	07	08	09			
Horgan, Connor	FEN	**SCR**	15	16				
Horner, Natalie	HOL	**TEN**	92	93	94			
Horst, Cara	CLIO	**BSK**	14					
Horton, Hanna	FEN	**TEN**	13					
Horton, Ron	HOL	**TEN**	80					
Hoskey, Jason	LKV	**WR**	96					
Hoskins, Sandy	FEN	**TR**	71					
Hosler, Hugh	LAP W	**HKY**	76	77				
Hosner, Matt	HOL	**CC**	95	96	**TR**	96		
Hotchkiss, Cindy	LAP E	**VB**	78					
Hotchkiss, Mike	LAP	**FB**	74					
Hotchkiss, Randy	LAP E	**WR**	77					
Houldsworth, Josh	HOL	**WR**	07	08	09	10		
Houle, Chris	LAP W	**FB**	01	**WR**	02			
Houle, Connor	SW CK	**HKY**	13	14				
Hourtienne, Lindsay	LAP E	**VB**	97	**SCR**	95	96	97	**TR**	96
Hourtienne, McKensay	LAP E	**BSK**	99					
House, Gary	AIN	**HKY**	79					
House, Guy	LAP E	**CC**	80					
House, Paul	AIN	**HKY**	84					
House, Tom	HOL	**FB**	70					
Householder, Paul	AIN	**FB**	81					
Houston, Dennis	HOL	**BSB**	87					
Hovey, Jeff	FEN	**HKY**	74					
Howard, Andrew	CLIO	**SCR**	11					
Howard, Celine	LIN	**CC**	07					
Howard, Collin	CLIO	**SCR**	14					
Howard, Greg	HOL	**TEN**	01					
Howard, Jeff	SW CK	**TR**	75					
Howard-III, Roy	LKV	**CC**	87	88				
Howell, Jessica	OXF	**TR**	10					
Howell, Tim	LAP W	**FB**	80					
Howland, Aaron	LIN	**FB**	05					
Hoy, Bernie	SW CK	**GLF**	69	70				
Hoy, Gordie	SW CK	**BSK**	69					
Hoyes, Jake	LIN	**CC**	10					
Hradowsky, Justin	LIN	**TR**	09					
Hranec, Jack	BRAN	**BSB**	11	12	13			
Hrava, Jan	LAP E	**HKY**	95					
Hrischuk, Corey	OXF	**HKY**	10					
Hubbard, Beth	OXF	**GLF**	04	05				
Hubbard, Buddy	AIN	**FB**	85	**TR**	86			
Hubbard, Claire	OXF	**GLF**	07					
Hubbard, Hanna	BRAN	**TEN**	08					
Hubbard, Josh	LIN	**CC**	99	00	01	**TR**	02	

Name	School	Sport							
Hubbard, Kate	OXF	**GLF**	02	04					
Huber, Joel	KEAR	**HKY**	10						
Huckabone, Mallory	BRAN	**BWL**	13						
Huddleston, Scott	OXF	**TR**	96						
Huddleston, Tom	HOL	**TEN**	89						
Hudnut, Jud	FEN	**FB**	85	86					
Huestis, Cheryl	LAP E	**TEN**	83						
Huestis, Rick	LAP E	**FB**	83						
Huff, Brian	DUR	**BSB**	92						
Huff, Mary-Beth	FEN	**SB**	72						
Huff, Randy	LIN	**TR**	92						
Huff, Thad	FEN	**FB**	91						
Huffman, Ron	SW CK	**CC**	70						
Hugan, Molly	HOL	**BSK**	93	94	**VB**	95	**SB**	93	94	95
Hugener, Theresa	FEN	**SCR**	89						
Huggler, Laura	LKV	**VB**	91	92					
Hughes, Mitchell	HOL	**TEN**	14	**GLF**	14	15			
Hulbert, Dennis	AIN	**WR**	70						
Hulette, Breanne	LAP E	**BSK**	00	**VB**	01	**SCR**	99	00	01
Hull, Hunter	SW CK	**GLF**	14						
Hull, Logan	SW CK	**BSK**	11	**GLF**	10	11			
Hulse, Laura	OXF	**TR**	86						
Humphries, Taquavius	SW CK	**BSK**	18						
Hundzinski, Delaney	FEN	**TEN**	15	16					
Hunt, Anthony	LAP E	**FB**	09						
Hunt, Ethan	BRAN	**BSK**	17						
Hunt, Jim	CAR	**BSK**	74						
Hunt, Jon	LAP W	**TR**	94						
Hunt, Paul	LAP E	**BSB**	88						
Hunter, Chris	BRAN	**SCR**	03	04					
Huntley, Shannon	CLIO	**SB**	12	13					
Huntley, Zach	SW CK	**TR**	12						
Huot, Eddie	LIN	**GLF**	93	**BSK**	94				
Hupert, Danielle	HOL	**TEN**	00	01	02				
Hupert, Jason	HOL	**SCR**	03	04					
Hurd, Mike	FEN	**GLF**	72						
Hurrish, David	OXF	**TR**	08						
Hurst, Tim	BRAN	**SW**	07	08					
Hussong, Aaron	BRAN	**SW**	08						
Husza, Chad	LIN	**HKY**	96						
Hutchcraft, Stacy	LKV	**TR**	91	93	94				
Hutcheson, Jacob	SW CK	**BWL**	16						
Hutchings, Bob	LIN	**HKY**	87	88					
Hutchings, Tracy	FEN	**TR**	88						
Hutchins, Gary	CAR	**BSB**	75	76					
Hutchinson, Drew	CLIO	**WR**	16						
Hutchinson, Jamey	MT M	**WR**	90	91					
Hutton, Chris	LAP W	**FB**	07	**BSK**	07	08			

Name	School	Sport				Sport			Sport				
Hutton, Shari	OXF	TR	85										
Huyck, Gregg	LIN	GLF	83										
Hyatt, Adam	HOL	TR	95	96									
Hyde, Aaron	BRAN	WR	08										
Hyde, Adam	BRAN	TR	05										
Hyde, Jake	HOL	WR	09										
Hyde, Justin	HOL	WR	04										
Hylen, Tara	FEN	TEN	95										
Hylen, Travis	FEN	TEN	93										
Hyslop, Caroline	FEN	SW	06	07									
Hyslop, Jenny	HOL	TR	87										
Iadipolo, John	FEN	FB	09										
Iceberg, Jacob	BRAN	SW	11	12									
Idoni, Beth	FEN	VB	05										
Idoni, Chloe	FEN	VB	16	17		BSK	16	17	18				
Idoni, Emily	FEN	VB	07	07f	08								
Idoni, Luke	FEN	FB	12	13									
Idoni, Matt	FEN	BSK	90			BSB	90						
Idoni, Paul	FEN	FB	14										
Ihrke, Kevin	OXF	GLF	95										
Illes, Aaron	MT M	WR	95	96	98								
Ingles, Casi	BRAN	TEN	06										
Ingles, Matt	LAP W	FB	01										
Ingman, Al	SW CK	FB	71			BSK	72						
Inman, Caryn	OXF	BSK	02			VB	02	03	TR	00	01	02	03
Inwood, Alison	FEN	SW	04	05	06								
Iordanou, Katae	LIN	GLF	03	04	05	06							
Irelan, Mallory	OWO	SW	17			SB	18						
Irish, Craig	LAP W	HKY	81	82									
Irvin, Mike	LAP W	CC	96			TR	97						
Irwin, Paul	LIN	FB	84			BSK	85						
Isaacson, Eryn	FEN	SCR	17										
Iversen, Becca	KEAR	BWL	14										
Ives, Dave	SW CK	SW	72	73	74								
Ives, Keeona	OXF	TR	07	08	10								
Ives, Vinnie	OXF	FB	05	06		BSB	07						
Ivey, Jenny	HOL	TEN	93	94	95								
Ivey, Mike	HOL	TEN	97	99									
Jackson, Ben	HOL	TEN	07f	08									
Jackson, Bob	AIN	FB	71										
Jackson, Lorie	HOL	CC	86	87									
Jackson, Michelle	LAP W	TR	01										
Jacksy, Shannon	LAP E	SCR	99										
Jacobi, Pat	OXF	BSB	98										
Jacobs, Art	DUR	FB	82										
Jacobs, Bob	HOL	TR	85	86									
Jacobs, Danae	DUR	VB	93										
Jacobs, Jason	LIN	GLF	89	90	91								

Jacobson, Derek	LAP E	**TEN**	92				
Jacobson, Mike	HOL	**SCR**	95				
Jacobson, Wes	HOL	**TEN**	88	89			
Jacopec, Bryce	HOL	**FB**	16				
Jagtoien, Asa	DUR	**BSK**	89				
James, Jeff	AIN	**BSB**	71	**FB**	70		
James, Leah	LIN	**SCR**	02				
James, Nate	LIN	**SCR**	00	**HKY**	01		
James, Tom	AIN	**BSB**	73				
Jamies, Robert	KEAR	**WR**	12	13			
Jamison, Chris	LKV	**BSB**	85				
Jankowski, Meghan	LAP W	**SB**	05				
Jankowski, Mike	LAP W	**BSB**	03				
Jankowski, Noah	KEAR	**BSB**	15				
Jannette, Randi	BRAN	**SCR**	14	15	16	**TR**	16
Jarrad, Audrey	SW CK	**LAX**	16				
Jelinski, Jon	LAP W	**TR**	04	05			
Jelsch, Jackie	FEN	**SB**	79				
Jenkins, Bryce	KEAR	**BSK**	15				
Jenkins, Carrie	LAP E	**VB**	91				
Jenkins, Coi	KEAR	**WR**	16				
Jenkins, John	FEN	**GLF**	81				
Jenkins, Lauren	LAP E	**SB**	04				
Jenkins, Willie	FEN	**BSB**	78				
Jennings, Angela	LIN	**TR**	06				
Jennings, Pam	LKV	**SB**	80				
Jensen, Fred	FEN	**HKY**	94				
Jensen, Jon	LIN	**FB**	99	**BSB**	00		
Jensen, Justin	LIN	**FB**	96				
Jensen, Mike	OXF	**BSB**	91				
Jepsen, Kelly	LAP W	**TEN**	79	80			
Jergler, Charles	OXF	**FB**	90	**SCR**	89	90	
Jerome, Tiffany	MT M	**VB**	93				
Jesse, Adam	FEN	**CC**	17				
Jewell, Frances	CAR	**SB**	72	73	74		
Jewell, Garrett	SW CK	**GLF**	15	16			
Jewell, Nicole	SW CK	**SCR**	11	12			
Jickling, Kevin	OXF	**TR**	08				
Jimenez, Kathy	AIN	**TR**	70				
Jodway, Maegan	OWO	**SB**	18				
Johns, Kim	HOL	**TEN**	86	87			
Johnson, Absalon	FLU	**TR**	15				
Johnson, Adam	BRAN	**SCR**	02				
Johnson, Alex	HOL	**GLF**	12				
Johnson, Alvin	HOL	**GLF**	01	02			
Johnson, Andrew	HOL	**TEN**	05				
Johnson, Ashley	LAP W	**CHR**	14				
Johnson, Bob	HOL	**BSB**	75				

Name	School	Sport							
Johnson, Bob	LAP	**TR**	69						
Johnson, Brittany	OXF	**TR**	10						
Johnson, Carolyn	FEN	**TR**	75	76					
Johnson, Chelsea	OXF	**TR**	10						
Johnson, Chris	FLU	**TR**	15						
Johnson, Connie	FEN	**TR**	87	88	89	90			
Johnson, Dale	LAP	**GLF**	71	71f					
Johnson, David	FEN	**HKY**	11						
Johnson, Drew	LKV	**BSB**	02						
Johnson, Gabrielle	FEN	**SB**	10	11					
Johnson, Gene	AIN	**BSK**	73						
Johnson, Holli	FEN	**VB**	92	**SB**	92				
Johnson, Jarrett	LAP W	**SCR**	02						
Johnson, Jodi	LAP W	**SB**	94	97					
Johnson, Josh	LAP W	**FB**	00						
Johnson, Jules	FEN	**SW**	05						
Johnson, Justen	LAP W	**TR**	05	06					
Johnson, Karen	AIN	**SB**	82	83					
Johnson, Keith	HOL	**TEN**	02	03	04	05			
Johnson, Kierra	BRAN	**TR**	10	12	13				
Johnson, Mallorie	FEN	**SW**	17						
Johnson, Marty	CAR	**FB**	70						
Johnson, Mike	AIN	**CC**	77						
Johnson, Nicole	HOL	**TEN**	16	17					
Johnson, Paige	HOL	**GLF**	13						
Johnson, Ricky	FEN	**HKY**	84						
Johnson, Ron	LAP W	**BSB**	93						
Johnson, Sandi	FEN	**VB**	77	78	79	**TR**	77	**SB**	78	79
Johnson, Scott	HOL	**TEN**	84						
Johnson, Scott	LIN	**BSK**	90						
Johnson, Scott	OXF	**FB**	94						
Johnson, Stephanie	LAP E	**VB**	99	**SCR**	99				
Johnson, Todd	OXF	**TR**	88	89					
Johnson, Todd	HOL	**WR**	88						
Johnson, Winston	FEN	**TR**	88						
Johnston, Amanda	BRAN	**CHR**	12						
Johnston, Andy	LAP W	**FB**	92						
Johnston, Danny	OXF	**FB**	07						
Johnston, Marc	LIN	**HKY**	86						
Jolly, Josh	OXF	**FB**	98						
Jolly, Ronda	LIN	**VB**	84						
Jones, Alvin	SW CK	**FB**	09						
Jones, Andy	OXF	**CC**	91						
Jones, Ben	OXF	**TR**	92						
Jones, Colin	BRAN	**TEN**	09	**BSB**	10				
Jones, Don	LKV	**WR**	92	93					
Jones, Emily	LAP W	**SB**	09						
Jones, Gary	FEN	**TEN**	77	78					

Jones, Jordan	SW CK	**BSK**	10				
Jones, Mark	OXF	**SCR**	06				
Jones, Matt	BRAN	**TEN**	12				
Jones, Matt	FEN	**SCR**	00	01	02		
Jones, Mike	OXF	**FB**	04				
Jones, Nick	FEN	**TR**	12				
Jones, Sarah	BRAN	**TR**	07	08			
Jones, Shana	OXF	**VB**	05	06			
Jones, Tom	AIN	**GLF**	72				
Jones, Tracey	FEN	**BSK**	84	**VB**	84	85	
Jones, Zach	HOL	**WR**	11	12			
Jones-Parker, Zeshawn	LAP W	**FB**	11	12	**BSK**	13	
Jordan, Blake	DUR	**TR**	90				
Jordan, Brian	BRAN	**GLF**	05				
Jordan, Leiann	LAP W	**CHR**	13				
Jory, Al	SW CK	**WR**	69				
Josef, Nancy	SW CK	**TR**	69	70	71		
Joseph, Isaac	LAP E	**FB**	10	**WR**	11		
Joseph, Jenny	LKV	**TR**	00				
Joseph, Justin	LAP E	**WR**	06	07			
Joseph, Philip	LAP E	**WR**	08	09			
Joslin, Hannah	LIN	**GLF**	14				
Jostock, Will	LAP W	**BSB**	02	03	04		
Joswiak, Bill	SW CK	**HKY**	75	**TR**	76		
Juhl, Mitch	LIN	**BSB**	13				
Jump, Jac	FEN	**SW**	18				
June, Adam	LAP E	**CC**	99	**TR**	99	00	
June, Chanda	LAP W	**BSK**	14				
Juntunen, Lasse	AIN	**HKY**	85				
Juratich, Alyssa	SW CK	**CHR**	15	17			
Jurus, Janet	AIN	**SB**	85	86			
Jury, Myles	FEN	**WR**	04	06			
Kaczmarek, Kayla	LIN	**SB**	07				
Kage, Valerie	OXF	**CC**	89	**TR**	87	88	89	90
Kahn, Erik	HOL	**TEN**	08	09	10		
Kahn, Mark	HOL	**TEN**	06	07	07f		
Kahn, Mark	HOL	**TR**	82	83			
Kahn, Matt	HOL	**TEN**	07	07f			
Kaiser, Emily	LKV	**CC**	90	91	**TR**	89	90	91	92
Kalbfleisch, Jason	LAP W	**FB**	90	**TR**	91		
Kalmar, Mike	CLIO	**BSK**	07	08			
Kalo, Corey	LIN	**WR**	93	94	95		
Kalohn, Tim	OXF	**GLF**	94	95			
Kalso, Keane	OXF	**SCR**	02	03			
Kalso, Kellen	OXF	**SCR**	96	97	98		
Kammerer, Billy	OXF	**BSB**	10				
Kanasty, Abby	LAP E	**GLF**	13				
Kane, Jessica	FEN	**SW**	04	05			

Kane, Kathy	HOL	**TEN**	00	01	02		
Kane, Lori	HOL	**TEN**	83				
Kanga, Kylie	BRAN	**TR**	03				
Kantar, Mike	CAR	**FB**	71				
Kapral, Dustin	LAP E	**FB**	04				
Karas, Chuck	LIN	**SCR**	00	01	**TR**	02	
Karas, Kevin	LIN	**SCR**	03				
Karas, Matt	FLU	**TEN**	15				
Karhoff, Kelli	DUR	**CC**	93	94	**TR**	94	95	96	97
Karns, Dave	FEN	**TR**	73				
Karstens, Nick	SW CK	**HKY**	07				
Karwoski, Rachael	HOL	**TEN**	93				
Kasper, Danielle	BRAN	**TR**	10	11			
Kassian, Tom	AIN	**TR**	81				
Kast, Matt	HOL	**TEN**	08				
Kast, Nathan	HOL	**TEN**	05	06	07		
Katanski, Kay	OXF	**TR**	84				
Katich, Sarah	OXF	**SB**	98	99			
Katulic, Dave	CAR	**FB**	68				
Kaufman, Chase	SW CK	**BWL**	14	15	16		
Kaufman, Cole	SW CK	**BWL**	18				
Kaufman, Marc	FEN	**TR**	76				
Kautman, Scott	FEN	**BSB**	01				
Kearney, Andrew	FLU	**TEN**	16				
Keast, Brad	LAP E	**GLF**	94				
Keech, Brian	HOL	**CC**	88	89			
Keefer, Kyle	HOL	**BSB**	94				
Keehn, Damian	SW CK	**BSB**	07	08			
Keeler, Jessica	CLIO	**SB**	11				
Keen, Robert	HOL	**CC**	93	95	**TR**	94	95
Keenan, Dan	HOL	**TEN**	98				
Keenan, Matt	LIN	**TR**	00	01	03		
Keene, Jerika	KEAR	**GLF**	08				
Keene, Mike	LIN	**WR**	84				
Keiser, Alexa	FEN	**CC**	16	17	**TR**	17	18
Keiser, Jenna	FEN	**CC**	14	16	**TR**	14	16	17
Kellar, Kyle	FEN	**SW**	05	06			
Keller, Aaron	HOL	**BSB**	02				
Keller, Allison	BRAN	**SCR**	18				
Keller, Becky	OXF	**CC**	94	95	96	97	**TR**	97	98
Keller, Lauren	HOL	**VB**	06	07			
Keller, Nick	BRAN	**FB**	13	**BSK**	14		
Keller, Nick	HOL	**SW**	07	08	09	**TR**	08
Kelley, Anthony	KEAR	**BWL**	14				
Kelley, Julia	SW CK	**BSK**	06				
Kelley, Ritch	LAP W	**WR**	88				
Kellogg, Bob	FEN	**BSK**	73				
Kellogg, Sara	LAP E	**BSK**	98	**SB**	99		

Kelly, Jaime	HOL	**BSK**	93	**VB**	94	**SCR**	94			
Kelly, Kandy	MT M	**SB**	81	82						
Kelly, Mike	SW CK	**GLF**	13	14						
Kelly, Shana	BRAN	**CHR**	10	11						
Kelly, Stephanie	LAP W	**BSK**	06							
Kelly, Tom	CAR	**SW**	71							
Kelso, Jay	FEN	**SCR**	03	**TR**	02	03				
Kemp, Lara	FEN	**LAX**	18							
Kendall, Shawn	LIN	**SCR**	08							
Kendrick, Jason	FEN	**FB**	87	88	**BSB**	89				
Kennard, Ashley	LAP W	**CHR**	11							
Kennedy, Jason	OXF	**SCR**	93							
Kennedy, Jodi	LKV	**TR**	97							
Kenney, Thad	LIN	**FB**	10							
Kennings, Peter	FEN	**TR**	18							
Kenny, Cody	KEAR	**GLF**	11							
Kenny, Kross	KEAR	**HKY**	15							
Kerhonen, Brian	OXF	**TR**	86	87						
Kern, Amber	CLIO	**SB**	06							
Kernan, Pat	FEN	**SCR**	88	**TEN**	88					
Kernen, Connie	HOL	**TEN**	90							
Kernen, Kevin	HOL	**TEN**	91	**BSB**	94					
Kernen, Matt	HOL	**BSB**	99	00						
Kernen, Tonia	HOL	**TEN**	94	95						
Kerner, Justis	HOL	**BSB**	13							
Kerr, Eric	HOL	**BSB**	99							
Kerr, Patrick	LIN	**WR**	17							
Kersten, Aaron	LIN	**FB**	12							
Kessler, Chelsea	OXF	**SB**	09	10						
Kesteloot, Korlyn	HOL	**TR**	13							
Keswick, Dale	FEN	**TR**	78	79						
Keswick, Don	FEN	**CC**	68	69	70	**TR**	69	70	71	
Kettle, Courtney	HOL	**TR**	13							
Keyandwy, Kaleigh	FEN	**SCR**	13	14						
Kidd, Kelsey	FEN	**SW**	09	10	11					
Kidder, Melissa	FEN	**TR**	70							
Kiefer, Lexi	FLU	**VB**	14							
Kier, Amber	HOL	**TR**	00	01						
Kilyk, Brooke	BRAN	**TR**	18							
Kimball, Paul	FEN	**WR**	70	71						
Kincer, Ben	FEN	**HKY**	01							
King, Cassie	HOL	**LAX**	16							
King, Chuck	LAP E	**BSK**	84							
King, Lucas	LAP W	**BSB**	05	06						
King, Mitch	LAP E	**BSB**	79	80	81					
King, Savannah	LAP W	**SCR**	12	13						
King, Tom	AIN	**BSK**	71							
King, Zak	LIN	**TR**	02							

Kingsbury, Cory	LAP	**HKY**	14							
Kinser, Emily	FEN	**TR**	14	15						
Kinzer, Bill	LAP E	**SCR**	86							
Kinzer, Gary	LAP E	**FB**	87							
Kippe, Brad	AIN	**HKY**	85	86						
Kippe, Josh	FEN	**SW**	18							
Kippe, Rod	AIN	**HKY**	83	84						
Kiran, Sylee	FEN	**TEN**	16							
Kirby, Bob	AIN	**BSK**	69							
Kirk, Steve	FEN	**BSB**	93							
Kirkland, Erin	FEN	**TR**	98	99						
Kirkwood, Tyler	KEAR	**BSB**	15							
Kirn, Katie	HOL	**SCR**	02	04						
Kirsammer, Dan	LAP W	**HKY**	13							
Kirvan, Terry	CAR	**WR**	69	70						
Kish, James	LAP W	**WR**	00	01						
Kish, Justin	LKV	**FB**	91							
Kish, Roger	LAP W	**FB**	00	01	02	**WR**	00	01	02	03
Kitch, Chris	LIN	**BSB**	16							
Kitchen, Allison	CLIO	**BSK**	12	13						
Kitchenmaster, Deanna	LAP W	**SB**	88	89						
Kittles, Amarae	BRAN	**FB**	16	**WR**	17					
Kivari, Hans	HOL	**SW**	05							
Kivari, Lars	HOL	**TEN**	09							
Klaffer, Jim	LKV	**WR**	93							
Klapko, Jordan	OWO	**BSK**	18	**BSB**	18					
Klavitter, Megan	LIN	**VB**	13	14	15	**SB**	16			
Kleinedler, Dennis	SW CK	**FB**	73	74						
Kleinert, Amanda	FEN	**SW**	05	06	07	08				
Kleinschrodt, Brianna	LIN	**CHR**	09	11						
Klempp, Nick	HOL	**TR**	93							
Klimbal, Andrew	OXF	**TR**	06	08						
Kline, Cody	CLIO	**WR**	11							
Kline, Mark	CAR	**SW**	74							
Klingler, Drew	HOL	**BWL**	09	10						
Klocek, Ellie	LIN	**SB**	17							
Klocek, Travis	LIN	**BSB**	18							
Knack, Brian	CLIO	**HKY**	15	16						
Knapp, Jeremy	LAP W	**FB**	06							
Kneller, Kevin	BRAN	**SW**	11							
Knickerbocker, Holly	FEN	**TR**	05							
Knickerbocker, Kevin	LKV	**FB**	77							
Knickerbocker, Sterling	LKV	**TR**	84							
Kniffen, Chuck	OXF	**TR**	90	91						
Knight, Kurt	HOL	**TEN**	09	**SW**	10					
Knisely, Taylor	LAP W	**VB**	10							
Knoerr, Kristi	LAP W	**GLF**	03							
Knolkemper, Ken	FEN	**SW**	73	74	75					

Name	School	Sport								
Knudson, Conner	HOL	**TEN**	11							
Koan, Jason	FEN	**TEN**	86	87	88					
Koan, Natalie	FEN	**VB**	88	90	**SB**	89				
Koan, Nick	LIN	**SCR**	17							
Koblinski, Kyle	FEN	**SW**	05							
Kobylik, Madison	LAP E	**SCR**	11	12						
Kochan, Skyler	BRAN	**GLF**	15	16						
Koderko, Joe	LIN	**CC**	97							
Koepke, Mike	HOL	**TEN**	06	07						
Koeske, Glen	HOL	**GLF**	84	**TEN**	85	86	87			
Koeske, Rhonda	HOL	**TEN**	84							
Koester, Rik	FEN	**SCR**	88							
Kogut, Anestasia	LIN	**TR**	84							
Kohler, Kevin	HOL	**FB**	90							
Kolb, Mike	FEN	**TEN**	79							
Kolbow, Carolyn	FEN	**TR**	76							
Kolch, Alison	LIN	**VB**	85							
Kolehmainen, Aaron	FEN	**WR**	87							
Kolehmainen, Jason	FEN	**TEN**	87	88						
Koncewicz, Sue	LAP	**SB**	73							
Konczal, Paula	OXF	**TR**	88							
Konieczka, Criag	LAP W	**BSK**	92	**TEN**	92					
Konopitski, Breanna	HOL	**SW**	08	09	10	11	**TR**	08	09	
Konschuh, Ethan	LAP E	**SCR**	09							
Konzer, Cason	HOL	**TEN**	15							
Konzer, Chloe	HOL	**TEN**	08	09	10					
Koon, Chris	CLIO	**CC**	12							
Koons, Stephanee	HOL	**BSK**	05							
Korman, Kyle	LIN	**FB**	12	14						
Korpalski, Kari	LAP E	**TR**	91	93						
Korpalski, Kyle	LAP E	**CC**	98	99	**GLF**	97	98	99	**TR**	98 99 00
Koscielski, Brad	OXF	**BSK**	89							
Kossak, Dave	LAP W	**FB**	05	06						
Kossak, Lily	HOL	**TEN**	14							
Kostelic, Chris	FEN	**BSK**	81	82	**SB**	83				
Kostelic, Cindy	FEN	**TEN**	79	81						
Kostka, Zack	FEN	**BSB**	15							
Kotarak, Rob	DUR	**FB**	82							
Kotarsky, Dave	FEN	**GLF**	94							
Koths, Greg	SW CK	**GLF**	69							
Kottalis, Tom	FEN	**WR**	97	98						
Kourtjian, David	OXF	**SCR**	04	05						
Kovach, Danielle	HOL	**CC**	91	92	93					
Kovacic, Brooke	OXF	**CC**	09	**TR**	10					
Kovacs, Connor	FEN	**FB**	13							
Kovacs, Connor	FLU	**FB**	14							
Kovarik, Ann	SW CK	**TR**	76							
Kowalewski, Brian	LAP E	**GLF**	84							

Koyl, Mikel	LAP W	**FB**	97	98			
Koyl, Ron	LAP	**FB**	73				
Koza, Abigailmae	FEN	**CHR**	17				
Koza, Bill	LAP E	**HKY**	78				
Kozlowski, Alessandra	FEN	**TR**	11				
Kramer, Erin	HOL	**FB**	88				
Kraner, Alicia	OXF	**TR**	02				
Krause, Jake	OXF	**FB**	04				
Krause, Jeff	LIN	**TR**	03	04			
Krause, Luke	OXF	**FB**	99				
Krause, Mark	HOL	**BSK**	78				
Krause, Sherri	HOL	**TR**	80				
Kraut, Morgan	FEN	**TEN**	11				
Kraysovic, Jana	SW CK	**TR**	16				
Kraysovisic, Rachel	SW CK	**SCR**	17				
Krebs, Carolyn	HOL	**CC**	02				
Kreiner, Derek	HOL	**FB**	06				
Kreiner, Mark	LKV	**WR**	77				
Kreiner, Mike	LKV	**FB**	77	78	**WR**	78	
Krejcik, Jeff	HOL	**BSB**	94				
Krepp, Crystal	HOL	**SCR**	99	00			
Kress, Doug	LAP W	**FB**	99	00	01		
Kress, Steve	LAP W	**FB**	97	98	**HKY**	99	
Krings, Cory	LAP W	**WR**	06				
Krist, Kassidy	KEAR	**CHR**	16	17			
Kromer, Lillie	FEN	**SW**	17				
Krowlewski, Sandra	SW CK	**VB**	17				
Krupp, Earl	SW CK	**WR**	73				
Krusina, Michaela	SW CK	**SB**	12				
Kryder, Brent	LIN	**FB**	06	07			
Kryza, Joey	FEN	**CC**	07	**TR**	08		
Kryza, Max	FEN	**CC**	11	12	**TR**	12	13
Kryza, Thomas	FEN	**CC**	10				
Kubica, Chase	OXF	**SCR**	01				
Kuchek, Krista	LKV	**VB**	98				
Kudera, Jeff	LAP E	**FB**	88				
Kuehl, Bryce	BRAN	**SW**	15				
Kujat, Joe	FLU	**BSK**	16	17			
Kujawa, Darci	OXF	**TR**	03				
Kujawa, Deann	OXF	**TR**	04	05			
Kukla, Dave	OXF	**FB**	93	94			
Kumpar, Steve	BRAN	**SCR**	04				
Kundinger, Greg	HOL	**TR**	69	71			
Kundinger, Keith	HOL	**TR**	70				
Kupres, Cheryl	AIN	**SB**	72				
Kupres, Cindy	AIN	**SB**	78				
Kurnz, Katy	FEN	**TEN**	16				
Kurschat, Sean	OXF	**CC**	83	**TR**	84		

Kursick, Rick	CAR	**SW**	72					
Kursik, Emily	LIN	**VB**	09					
Kursik, Nancy	CAR	**BSK**	75	**SB**	74	75		
Kursik, Rick	CAR	**CC**	74	**SW**	74			
Kurtz, Dan	FEN	**FB**	68	**WR**	69			
Kurzer, Jason	LAP W	**TR**	96					
Kuyk, Christine	HOL	**TEN**	94	95				
Kuzma, Karri	LKV	**TR**	89	90	91			
Kuzmich, Keith	LIN	**HKY**	84	85	86			
Kwasiborski, Danielle	BRAN	**VB**	08	**BSK**	09			
Kwasiborski, Janelle	BRAN	**TR**	16	**VB**	17			
Kwasiborski, Nick	BRAN	**BSB**	09	10				
Kwasneski, Jill	DUR	**BSK**	84	85	**TR**	86		
Kwiatkowski, Laura	BRAN	**GLF**	03	04	05	06		
Lab, TJ	DUR	**BSB**	88					
LaBelle, Mark	FEN	**TEN**	95					
LaBelle, Mark	FEN	**TEN**	94					
LaBrie, Brad	LAP E	**BSB**	11					
Lack, Kevin	FEN	**FB**	15					
LaClair, Kate	HOL	**VB**	16					
Ladd, Brendan	BRAN	**WR**	14	16				
Ladd, Michelle	FEN	**TEN**	91					
Lademan, Nina	FEN	**CHR**	16					
LaDuke, Scott	AIN	**GLF**	81					
LaFave, Bob	CAR	**BSB**	74	75				
LaFave, Gunnar	HOL	**TEN**	12					
LaFave, Lisa	KEAR	**SB**	11					
Lafayette, Joe	MT M	**FB**	88					
LaFee, Justin	FEN	**FB**	97	**BSK**	98			
Lafnear, Steven	OXF	**BWL**	09					
LaFrambose, Maddie	FLU	**SB**	16					
Lagios, Brendan	HOL	**CC**	08	**TR**	08	09		
Lagness, Ed	LAP E	**WR**	81	82				
Lahar, Vince	CLIO	**WR**	07					
Laidlaw, Chris	OXF	**FB**	90	**BSK**	91	**BSB**	90	91
Laidler, Autumn	OXF	**SCR**	95	97	98			
Laidler, Paul	LAP W	**BSK**	87	88				
Lainesse, Jonah	FEN	**HKY**	15					
LaJoie, Nick	CLIO	**HKY**	14					
Lake, Logan	FEN	**GLF**	18					
Lake, Olivia	DUR	**CC**	91	92				
Lamb, DJ	FEN	**BSB**	98					
Lamb, Steve	CAR	**FB**	69					
Lambart, Jason	HOL	**TEN**	04	05				
Lambert, Amy	HOL	**SB**	98					
Lambert, Brad	FEN	**TR**	87	88				
Lambert, Greg	HOL	**TEN**	02					
Lambert, Kevin	HOL	**TR**	01					

Lambitz, Jeff	FEN	**FB**	84			
Lampar, Steve	LAP W	**WR**	01			
Lamphere, Drake	LAP E	**TEN**	12	**GLF**	12	13
Lamphere, Larry	DUR	**FB**	82	83	**BSB**	83	84
Lamphere, Mark	DUR	**TR**	88			
Lamson, Reece	BRAN	**SW**	10	11		
Lanckton, Kristaa	LAP W	**SCR**	88			
Lanctot, Chad	CLIO	**WR**	08	09		
Landis, Austin	FEN	**SW**	13	14	15	
Landon, Jon	LAP W	**FB**	94			
Landrum, Evie	HOL	**TR**	80	81	82	
Landrum, Ronnell	HOL	**TR**	71			
Lane, Dave	LAP W	**FB**	82			
Lang, Emily	SW CK	**SCR**	18			
Lang, Kevin	OXF	**SCR**	86	88		
Lang, Rick	SW CK	**FB**	75			
Langdon, Kolton	CLIO	**BSK**	17			
Lange, Debbie	LAP W	**VB**	82			
Lange, Keith	LAP E	**TR**	77	78		
Langley, Bob	HOL	**FB**	75	76		
Langley, Nate	LIN	**HKY**	04			
Lannon, JD	HOL	**FB**	17			
Lansing, Tony	LAP E	**TR**	93			
Lanyi, Chris	CLIO	**BSB**	13			
Lanyi, Joshua	CLIO	**SCR**	10			
Lanzon, Jenna	LIN	**GLF**	05	07		
Lapa, Braden	FEN	**GLF**	17	18		
LaPain, Jacob	OWO	**TR**	18			
Lape, Adam	FEN	**FB**	94			
Larkin, Chris	LAP W	**TR**	04			
Larkin, Jim	MT M	**FB**	80			
LaRoy, Dave	FEN	**BSB**	96			
Larsen, Shawn	KEAR	**HKY**	15			
Lasco, Todd	FEN	**TR**	87	88		
Lasley, Jim	CAR	**FB**	69	**BSB**	69	70
Lathrop, Jim	FEN	**TEN**	75			
Latinen, Keith	FEN	**TR**	99			
Laton, Dean	AIN	**WR**	71			
Latoni, Tami	HOL	**TR**	00			
Laube, Kevin	OXF	**FB**	91			
Lauinger, Alexa	BRAN	**VB**	15			
Lauinger, Sabrina	BRAN	**VB**	13			
Launius, McKayla	CLIO	**CHR**	15	16	17	18
Launstein, Brad	LAP W	**FB**	02	**HKY**	03	
Laur, Matt	FEN	**TEN**	85	86		
Lauwers, Doug	LAP E	**TR**	96			
Lauwers, Heather	BRAN	**TR**	07			
LaVearn, Bryan	BRAN	**WR**	13	14	15	16

LaVictoire, Ryan	MT M	**FB**	91				
Lavire, Alfred	MT M	**BSB**	02				
Lawrence, Kayla	LAP E	**VB**	04	05			
Lawrence, Laurabelle	HOL	**SB**	72	73			
Lawrence, Lauren	SW CK	**SCR**	13	14	15	16	
Lawrence, Nolan	FEN	**BSB**	17	18			
Lawrence, Scott	CAR	**SW**	71				
Lawrence, Sherri	BRAN	**VB**	07f				
Lawson, Bob	LAP	**GLF**	73				
Lay, Runnell	MT M	**FB**	96				
Layman, Casey	HOL	**TEN**	99	00			
Layman, Jordan	LAP W	**FB**	05				
Layman, Quenton	HOL	**TEN**	81				
Ledington, Micheal	LAP W	**FB**	11	12			
Lee, Abby	FEN	**CC**	17				
Lee, Candice	FEN	**TEN**	85				
Lee, Dana	FEN	**TEN**	83	84			
Lee, Debbie	FEN	**TEN**	79				
Lee, Jacob	FEN	**CC**	13	14	15	**TR** 14	15 16
Lee, Joey	FLU	**TEN**	14				
Lee, Mike	AIN	**TR**	81				
Lee, Richie	LAP W	**BSB**	08				
Leeck, Roz	MT M	**SB**	74				
Leedle, Payton	LIN	**GLF**	17				
Leedle, Robin	DUR	**BSK**	86	**TR** 85			
Leeman, Toby	FEN	**TEN**	91				
Leeper, Gary	HOL	**TEN**	90	92			
LeFreniere, Barry	FEN	**TEN**	81				
Legg, Kelly	OXF	**BSK**	91				
Lehmann, Terry	FEN	**TEN**	91				
Lehmann, Todd	FEN	**TEN**	85	86	87		
Lehotan, John	LAP W	**FB**	92	93			
Leibengood, Gail	SW CK	**TR**	69				
Leid, Gayle	LKV	**TR**	82				
Leitch, Cheryl	OXF	**CC**	84	85	86	**TR** 84	86
Leitkam, Heidi	LIN	**SB**	01				
Lemere, Matt	FEN	**TR**	99				
LeMessurier, Brittney	BRAN	**CHR**	08				
LeMieux, Greg	AIN	**TR**	80	81			
LeMieux, Kyle	LIN	**CC**	07				
Lemieux, Zach	LIN	**CC**	12				
Lemond, Dilon	HOL	**CC**	12	13	14	15	
Lengemann, Jack	LAP W	**BSK**	98	**TR** 98			
Lengyel, Melissa	LIN	**CC**	03	04	05	**TR** 03	04 05
Lenhart, Amy	SW CK	**SW**	07				
Lennon, Colleen	OXF	**CC**	83	**TR** 83	84		
Lennon, Kelly	OXF	**TR**	85	86			
Lentz, Sean	LAP E	**TR**	04	05			

Lenz, Aly	FEN	**BSK**	18							
Lenzi, David	FEN	**BSB**	10	11						
Leonard, Bobby	HOL	**SW**	05							
Leone, Marlon	HOL	**TEN**	05	06	07					
Leone, Michelle	HOL	**TEN**	03	04	05	06				
Lepage, Beau	FEN	**BSK**	15							
LeRoy, John	OXF	**CC**	94	95						
Leroy, John	OXF	**TR**	95	96						
LeRoy, Karen	OXF	**CC**	96	97	98	99	**TR**	97	98	99	00
Lesch, Lauren	HOL	**TEN**	18							
Leslie, Cory	LAP E	**SCR**	00							
Lesperance, Megan	HOL	**TEN**	15	16	17	18				
Leszczynski, Laura	LAP W	**SB**	84							
Letavis, Mark	SW CK	**FB**	70	**BSB**	70	71				
Letts, Erin	FEN	**TR**	98							
Levi, Kevin	LAP E	**FB**	84							
Lewandowski, Abby	HOL	**TR**	11	12						
Lewandowski, Kate	FEN	**TEN**	14							
Lewis, Brooke	LAP W	**SB**	06	07						
Lewis, Cathy	MT M	**SB**	84	85						
Lewis, Dan	DUR	**CC**	84	**TR**	84	85				
Lewis, Jeff	HOL	**CC**	76	77	**TR**	76	77	78		
Lewis, Jenny	OXF	**TR**	90							
Lewis, Kara	LAP W	**SB**	02	04						
Lewis, Shannon	OXF	**BSK**	90	**TR**	89					
Lewis, Tyler	BRAN	**GLF**	12							
L'Hommedieu, Trevor	SW CK	**BSK**	07	**BSB**	07					
Liburdi, Marisa	LAP W	**BSK**	10	11	12					
Lich, Tom	AIN	**HKY**	84							
Liddie, Kris	HOL	**CC**	81	82						
Liddle, Dave	FEN	**WR**	73	74						
Lieber, Mike	LKV	**WR**	92	93						
Liebner, Derek	BRAN	**SCR**	07							
Lienemann, Ryan	DUR	**FB**	90	**TR**	90					
Ligeski, Erynne	LAP E	**TR**	03							
Likowski, Jenni	LAP W	**GLF**	02							
Liley, Mike	FEN	**FB**	74							
Lincoln, Ernie	LKV	**WR**	88							
Lincoln, Mindi	LKV	**VB**	95	**TR**	93	94	95			
Linderman, Jasmine	LKV	**VB**	94	95						
Lindman, Eric	LIN	**CC**	97	98						
Lindsay, Rock	LAP	**FB**	73							
Lindsay, Scott	LAP E	**BSB**	82	83						
Lindsley, Diane	HOL	**TEN**	81							
Lindstrom, Jessi	FLU	**CC**	14	15	16	**TR**	15	16	17	
Lindstrom, Keeli	FLU	**TR**	18							
Line, Prescott	OXF	**WR**	10							
Line, Zach	OXF	**FB**	06	07	**WR**	08				

Link, Jamon	LIN	BSB	16	17			
Linn, Jeremy	DUR	WR	94	95			
Linson, Robert	HOL	TR	08	09			
Linto, Bo	OXF	BSB	98				
Linton, Brett	LAP E	BSK	91				
Linton, Jamie	LAP E	TR	92	93			
Lints, Scott	LAP E	FB	87				
Lintz, Andrea	LAP W	TR	96	98			
Lintz, Craig	FEN	FB	69				
Lintz, Darryl	LAP W	FB	93				
Lintz, Jody	FEN	FB	77				
Lintz, Mike	LAP E	TR	92	93			
Lintz, Tom	FEN	FB	80				
Lipiec, Andy	HOL	SW	08	09	TR	08	09
Lipp, Stevie	SW CK	BWL	11				
Little, John	AIN	HKY	85				
Littles, Jacob	SW CK	FB	13				
Lively, Jim	DUR	FB	82	BSB	83		
Lloyd, Amy	LAP W	SCR	95				
Lloyd, John	FEN	GLF	12	13	14	15	
Lloyd, Meagan	LAP E	CHR	10				
Lobombard, Macie	SW CK	LAX	17				
Lockitsk, Aaron	HOL	BSB	18				
Logan, A. J.	OXF	WR	10				
Logan, Dan	LIN	FB	08				
Logan, John	OXF	WR	07				
Logsdon, Olivia	SW CK	CHR	18				
Loll, Vicky	LAP	SB	74				
Lomax, Rusty	AIN	WR	79				
Lomerson, Kevin	LAP E	BSB	86				
Lomerson, Kurt	LAP E	FB	92	BSB	92		
Londer, John	OXF	FB	98				
Long, Brett	CLIO	GLF	11				
Long, Bryan	CLIO	GLF	13				
Long, Jake	LAP E	FB	01	02	BSK	02	03
Long, Lisa	HOL	TEN	83				
Long, Sue	AIN	TR	69				
Longstreth, Larry	HOL	TR	69				
Longstreth, Lee	HOL	TR	79				
Lookebill, Kobe	FEN	FB	14	15			
Looman, Toby	FEN	TEN	93				
Loomis, Jason	LAP E	TR	97				
Lopez, Ted	OXF	SCR	90				
Lord, George	FEN	TR	03				
Loria, Jeff	FEN	TR	81	82	83		
Loria, Marc	FEN	TR	89				
Loria, Steve	FEN	TR	78	79			
Losh, Terry	HOL	BSK	84				

Loubert, Renee	HOL	**TEN**	02				
Lougheed, Phil	SW CK	**BSB**	09				
Lovasz, Joe	BRAN	**FB**	16				
Love, Tom	CAR	**SW**	74	75			
Lovejoy, Dwight	DUR	**TR**	86				
Lovik, Garrett	KEAR	**BSB**	09				
Lowande, Bill	HOL	**CC**	77	78	**TR**	78	
Lowande, Tom	HOL	**TR**	72				
Lowell, Glenda	SW CK	**TR**	69	70	71		
Lowman, Kim	AIN	**TR**	82				
Lozano, Javier	BRAN	**SCR**	17				
Lozano, Luke	CLIO	**TR**	17				
Lozuaway, Missy	FEN	**TR**	79				
Lucas, Becky	HOL	**TEN**	82	84			
Lucas, Jason	FEN	**SCR**	98				
Luchenbill, Connie	DUR	**TEN**	78				
Luchenbill, Ray	HOL	**SCR**	92				
Lucius, Deven	FEN	**TEN**	97				
Luck, Roger	LIN	**HKY**	89				
Luckett, Jake	LAP W	**WR**	14				
Lucky, Andrew	LIN	**TR**	11				
Ludeman, Jacqui	OXF	**VB**	02	03			
Ludwig, Mallory	SW CK	**LAX**	16				
Ludwig, Trisha	FEN	**TEN**	95				
Lueb, John	HOL	**TR**	76				
Luebke, Mike	LAP W	**TR**	93				
Luff, Lindsey	FLU	**VB**	17				
Lukas, Greg	FEN	**FB**	15	16			
Lukas, Natalie	OXF	**CHR**	07	**TR**	06		
Luke, Darius	HOL	**TR**	00	01			
Lukiankoff, Destinee	HOL	**TR**	08	09	10		
Lukshaitis, Alex	HOL	**FB**	89	**BSK**	90	**BSB**	90
Lumley, MaKenna	KEAR	**SCR**	11				
Lumm, Ed	HOL	**TR**	81	82			
Lumpkin, Darren	OXF	**TR**	10				
Luna, Gilbert	AIN	**FB**	80	**WR**	82		
Luna, Greg	AIN	**BSB**	71	72			
Lund, Blake	LIN	**BSK**	18				
Lundie, Dave	DUR	**BSK**	80				
Lussier, Mike	HOL	**GLF**	75				
Lussier, Robin	HOL	**BSK**	77	**SB**	77	78	
Luther, Maryanne	HOL	**TEN**	08	09			
Luxton, Corinne	OXF	**SB**	09	10			
Luxton, Russell	OXF	**BSB**	08				
Lyerla, Mike	LAP E	**BSK**	88				
Lynch, Chase	FEN	**FB**	14	15			
Lynch, Jessica	FEN	**LAX**	18				
Lynch, Kyla	FEN	**LAX**	18				

Name	Team	Sport			
Lynch, Pete	LAP	**FB**	74		
Lyssiotis, Andy	OXF	**SCR**	98	99	
Lyssiotis, Tony	OXF	**FB**	02	**WR** 01	03
Maas, Jenny	LIN	**CC**	87	89	
Mabery, Ali	LAP E	**BSK**	02	**SCR** 01	02 03
Mabery, Chad	LAP E	**FB**	92		
MacAninch, Taylor	HOL	**TEN**	17	18	
MacArthur, Mitchell	KEAR	**WR**	14		
MacCombs, Pat	SW CK	**CC**	69		
MacCombs, Rene	SW CK	**TR**	70		
MacDermaid, Kevin	LIN	**SCR**	88		
MacDonald, Mike	LAP W	**HKY**	00		
MacDonald, Rory	LAP E	**HKY**	06		
MacDonald, Teagan	KEAR	**BWL**	15		
MacDonald, Tom	FEN	**FB**	86	**HKY** 86	87
MacGillivray, Jami	DUR	**SB**	88		
Machak, Nick	LAP W	**HKY**	01		
Machiniak, Greg	LAP W	**FB**	06		
Macias, Austin	BRAN	**BSB**	14		
MacIntyre, Brad	BRAN	**SW**	06		
Mackey, Rachel	SW CK	**SB**	17	18	
Macklin, Zahne	FEN	**SW**	12	13	14
Macocha, Jordan	OXF	**BSB**	10		
Madden, Kenny	FEN	**FB**	68		
Madeline, Cindy	LAP	**SB**	75		
Magnusson, Anna	DUR	**SCR**	93		
Magyar, Mike	OXF	**BWL**	10		
Mahaffy, Shane	BRAN	**FB**	10	11	
Mahan, Mitchell	BRAN	**SW**	16	17	
Maher, Brittney	FEN	**TR**	05		
Maher, Josh	FEN	**FB**	17		
Maher, Sean	OXF	**BSB**	03		
Maidment, April	LIN	**TR**	93		
Maier, Noah	FEN	**SW**	18		
Maier, Tim	LIN	**SCR**	90	91	**BSK** 92
Majchrowski, Paul	HOL	**TEN**	95	96	97
Majestic, Lily	SW CK	**TR**	18		
Majewski, Jenny	MT M	**CC**	87		
Major, Michelle	HOL	**TEN**	15		
Maker, Morgan	LIN	**CHR**	11		
Maki, Scott	HOL	**TEN**	14		
Makimaa, Derek	SW CK	**HKY**	12	**GLF** 12	
Maksymowski, Matt	FEN	**HKY**	07	08	
Malaska, Janet	SW CK	**TR**	76		
Malaska, Karen	SW CK	**TR**	72		
Malito, Jack	LAP W	**TR**	94		
Mallard, Megan	FEN	**SW**	17		
Mallett, Andre	HOL	**FB**	05		

Mallory, Amber	LIN	**VB**	08					
Malmberg, Mattias	LAP W	**HKY**	91					
Malochleb, Laura	MT M	**SB**	84					
Maloney, Joel	LAP W	**FB**	07					
Mancillas, Dan	SW CK	**WR**	74					
Mandle, Quinton	FEN	**FB**	11					
Mandock, Jenny	LKV	**SB**	02					
Mangapora, Kathryn	LIN	**TR**	05					
Mangham, Artie	HOL	**FB**	86					
Mangilin, Connie	HOL	**TEN**	89	90	91			
Mankowski, Melissa	MT M	**SB**	95					
Manley, Derrick	DUR	**FB**	83					
Mann, Zack	OXF	**FB**	86					
Mansfield, Matt	HOL	**SCR**	98	**TEN**	97			
Mantei, Alexis	FLU	**VB**	16					
Mantel, Ron	OXF	**WR**	03					
Manzella, Marissa	OXF	**VB**	09					
March, Amanda	LKV	**TR**	95	96	97			
March, Sydney	KEAR	**CHR**	13	14				
Marchand, Lauren	HOL	**TEN**	05					
Marcicki, Cody	LAP W	**WR**	04	05				
Marcola, Chase	FEN	**SCR**	11	**SW**	10	12		
Mariconi, Larry	LAP W	**BSB**	76					
Marinkovski, Rich	OXF	**TR**	91					
Marion, Brandon	FEN	**FB**	10					
Marks, Cody	LIN	**FB**	07	08	09	**BSK**	09	
Marks, Trent	LIN	**BSB**	13					
Marlowe, Bill	FEN	**TR**	73					
Marney, Blaine	OXF	**HKY**	10					
Marney, Tim	OXF	**HKY**	08					
Maroun, Joe	LIN	**BSK**	97					
Marsee, Kerry	OXF	**FB**	87					
Marsh, Blayne	CAR	**TEN**	76					
Marsh, Dennis	LKV	**TR**	80					
Marsh, Ed	AIN	**FB**	77					
Marsh, Jeff	OXF	**SCR**	96					
Marsh, Ryan	OXF	**FB**	02	**TR**	02			
Marsh, Tina	FEN	**TR**	86					
Marshall, Alex	FEN	**FB**	16					
Marshall, Denise	LAP E	**VB**	93					
Marshall, Jake	LIN	**BSB**	14	15				
Marshall, Justin	HOL	**TEN**	99					
Marshall, Lucas	LIN	**BSB**	16	17				
Marshall, Stan	LKV	**WR**	94	95	96	97	**TR**	94
Martens, Sean	BRAN	**BSB**	14					
Martharst, Palle	LIN	**TR**	92					
Martin, Annie	FLU	**TEN**	15					
Martin, Connor	HOL	**HKY**	15					

Name	School	Sport	Y1	Y2	Y3	Sport2	Y1	Y2	Y3	Y4	Sport3	Y1	Y2
Martin, Greg	LKV	**WR**	95	96	97								
Martin, Heidi	HOL	**BWL**	14										
Martin, Jackie	FEN	**TR**	75	76									
Martin, John	FEN	**SCR**	92										
Martin, Mike	MT M	**TR**	80										
Martin, Nolan	FEN	**FB**	14										
Martin, Nolan	FLU	**TR**	16										
Martin, Steve	OXF	**CC**	84	85	**TR**	84	86						
Martin, Terry	MT M	**GLF**	79										
Martinsen, Jordanah	LIN	**TR**	14										
Martinus, Kyle	MT M	**WR**	02										
Marty, Gary	HOL	**FB**	71	72									
Maruszak, Shelly	LKV	**CC**	96	**TR**	94	95	96	97					
Maser, Dustin	FEN	**FB**	97	98									
Mash, Charles	HOL	**TR**	89										
Mashburn, Caroline	FEN	**VB**	88										
Masher, Andrea	FEN	**TR**	99										
Mason, Alex	LKV	**FB**	00										
Mason, Garrett	FEN	**FB**	00										
Mason, Lauren	KEAR	**CHR**	12										
Massey, Justin	MT M	**BSB**	00										
Materi, Elena	LKV	**TR**	96										
Mathers, Audrey	SW CK	**SW**	72										
Matheson, Jordyn	FLU	**BWL**	17										
Mathews, Cameron	FEN	**SW**	15	16									
Mathieson, Amy	OXF	**SCR**	88	89									
Mathieson, Andy	OXF	**SCR**	91	92									
Mathis, Keith	MT M	**WR**	92	93									
Matlock, Taylor	HOL	**TEN**	96	97	98	99							
Mattack, Bryan	OXF	**BSB**	03	04									
Matte, Brandyn	SW CK	**HKY**	13	14									
Matthews, Jeannie	FEN	**BSK**	75	**SB**	75	76							
Mattson, Kurt	FEN	**CC**	75										
Matus, Jake	FLU	**FB**	14	15									
Matvchuk, Alex	HOL	**CC**	10	11	12	13							
Matzke, Carrie	DUR	**CC**	94	95									
Maul, Larry	SW CK	**TR**	75										
Maupin, Cory	LIN	**SCR**	03	04									
Maxfield, Scott	LAP W	**GLF**	82										
Maxheimer, Madison	LIN	**LAX**	16										
Maxheimer, Payton	FEN	**VB**	11	12	**BSK**	12	13	**SCR**	11	12	13		
Maxwell, Jackson	SW CK	**FB**	12	**SCR**	12	13	**SW**	12	13	14	**TR**	13	14
Maxwell, Jared	HOL	**CC**	93	94	95	**TR**	93	94	95	96			
Maxwell, Katelynn	KEAR	**BWL**	13	14									
Maxwell, Neil	LAP E	**TR**	02										
May, Addie	FLU	**CC**	14	**TR**	15								
May, Jonathon	LIN	**SCR**	08										
Maygar, Matt	FEN	**TR**	04										

Name	School	Sport	Yr	Yr	Sport	Yr	Yr	Sport	Yr
Mayhew, John	LAP E	**TEN**	93						
Mayhew, Josh	LAP E	**TEN**	90						
Mayhew, Michelle	FEN	**CC**	91	92	93				
Mayner, Desi	LIN	**FB**	02	03	**BSK**	04	**BSB**	03	
Mayner, Dustin	LIN	**FB**	05	06	**BSB**	06	07		
Mayner, Rodney	CAR	**WR**	76						
Mays, Gerry	CAR	**BSB**	71						
Mays, Kirk	DUR	**FB**	82						
Mays, Tim	AIN	**BSK**	78	**BSB**	78				
McAllister, Craig	LAP E	**TR**	86						
McArdle, Meaghan	FEN	**SB**	16						
McCabe, Erin	FEN	**TR**	97	99					
McCain, Kevin	HOL	**BSK**	83	**TR**	82	83			
McCallum, Connor	LAP E	**BSB**	06						
McCallum, Payton	LAP E	**FB**	08	09	**BSK**	10			
McCallum, Robin	MT M	**VB**	79	80	**SB**	79	80		
McCarter, Tom	LAP E	**BSB**	10	11	12				
McCarty, Mike	HOL	**TR**	11						
McClain, Jerry	CAR	**FB**	72	**BSK**	73				
McClean, James	OXF	**FB**	07						
McClellan, Garth	KEAR	**SCR**	08	09					
McClellan, Karsyn	BRAN	**CHR**	15	16					
McClellan, Tera	LKV	**TR**	91	92	93				
McClelland, Lloyd	AIN	**FB**	75	76	77	**BSB**	77	78	
McCloud, Erik	HOL	**BSB**	05						
McClure, Jake	LIN	**GLF**	05	**HKY**	06				
McConnaughy, Steve	HOL	**CC**	98						
McConnell, Jessie	FEN	**GLF**	06						
McConnell, Tony	FEN	**GLF**	03	04					
McCormick, Joe	FEN	**TEN**	04						
McCormick, Kristen	LAP E	**BSK**	90	91	**SCR**	90	91	92	
McCormick, Mason	FEN	**FB**	15						
McCormick, Mike	FEN	**TR**	99						
McCoy, Bob	FEN	**FB**	83						
McCoy, Megan	BRAN	**TR**	07						
McCracken, Kyle	LAP W	**GLF**	96						
McCracken, Steve	OXF	**FB**	90	**TR**	90	91			
McCreedy, Josh	LAP W	**SCR**	90	91					
McCreedy, Pete	LAP W	**SCR**	87	88					
McCubbin, Nick	FEN	**CC**	00						
McDermaid, Becky	MT M	**VB**	02	**GLF**	02				
McDevitt, Chris	HOL	**WR**	90	91					
McDevitt, Paul	HOL	**WR**	88						
McDevitt, Sue	FEN	**TR**	77	78	79				
McDonald, Jasmine	SW CK	**LAX**	16	17					
McDonald, Nick	LIN	**CC**	15	17	**TR**	18			
McDonald, Nolan	LIN	**SCR**	14						
McDonald, Rachel	LAP E	**CHR**	06						

McDonald, Sean	LAP E	**SCR**	90	**TEN**	90	
McDowell, Kim	LKV	**VB**	87	88		
McDowell, Ted	AIN	**TR**	80			
McDowell, Terry	AIN	**FB**	76			
McDugald, Anthony	OXF	**TR**	10			
McEachern, Brian	LAP	**TEN**	73			
McEachern, Tom	LAP	**TEN**	73	74		
McElroy, Paige	HOL	**TR**	11			
McFarlan, Steve	CAR	**CC**	69	70		
McGeach, Lynn	SW CK	**TR**	76			
McGeary, Brian	LAP W	**GLF**	08			
McGeosch, Heather	SW CK	**TR**	71	72	73	
McGillis, Tom	MT M	**HKY**	77			
McGinnis, Jenni	HOL	**TEN**	03	04	05	
McGlashen, John	LAP	**FB**	70			
McGowan, Mike	FEN	**FB**	80			
McGowan, Mike	FEN	**BSB**	02			
McGrady, Dave	SW CK	**FB**	70			
McGrath, Evan	AIN	**CC**	85			
McGrath, Monica	LKV	**TR**	90			
McGraw, Justin	OXF	**FB**	93			
McGregor, Jeff	LAP W	**FB**	80			
McGuffie, Darcie	LAP W	**TR**	82			
McGuffie, Mike	LAP W	**FB**	80			
McGuffie, Taylor	LAP E	**CHR**	09			
McGuffin, Jim	CAR	**TEN**	76			
McHugh, Justin	LAP W	**FB**	97	**TR**	98	
McIntosh, Janeiro	MT M	**FB**	90	**TR**	90	91
McIntyre, Dayna	LAP E	**SCR**	12			
McKay, Aver	KEAR	**TR**	16			
McKay, Bob	DUR	**TR**	83	84		
McKay, Jonathon	KEAR	**TR**	15	16		
McKay, Ken	HOL	**TR**	72	73		
McKeachie, Phil	CAR	**TR**	69			
McKeachie, Stephanie	LAP E	**VB**	95	96	97	
McKee, Lilly	FEN	**LAX**	18			
McKenna, Scott	LAP E	**FB**	89	**BSB**	89	90
McKenney, Tom	HOL	**FB**	69			
McKenzie, Justin	LIN	**TR**	14			
McKeon, Emily	SW CK	**CC**	08			
McKeon, John	FEN	**FB**	08			
McKerchie, Bryce	KEAR	**BWL**	16	17		
McKerchie, Terry	MT M	**FB**	83			
McKinnon, Elizabeth	OXF	**TR**	97	99		
McKinnon, Liz	OXF	**VB**	99			
McKnight, Mike	LKV	**TR**	94			
McLaughlin, Devon	LAP W	**CHR**	06	07		
McLaughlin, Drake	LIN	**BSB**	18			

McLean, James	OXF	**BSB**	07	08				
McLean, Tom	MT M	**WR**	75					
McLemore, Jesse	FLU	**TR**	18					
Mcleod, Connor	SW CK	**HKY**	16					
McLeod, Roni	AIN	**TR**	78					
McManus, Doug	SW CK	**WR**	71					
McMillan, Kim	LAP E	**SB**	97					
McMillin, Kristine	DUR	**SB**	96					
McMullen, Lindsy	LAP W	**VB**	99					
McNab, Robin	FEN	**SB**	76	77	78			
McNab, Shelly	FEN	**SB**	78	79				
McNally, Quin	BRAN	**BSB**	09					
McNally, Tate	BRAN	**BSB**	09					
McNeely, David	HOL	**FB**	11	**BSB**	12			
McNeely, Paul	HOL	**FB**	05	**BSB**	05	06		
McNeil, Scott	AIN	**HKY**	84	85	86	**BSB**	84	85	86
McNeill, Austin	LIN	**FB**	13	14	**WR**	15		
McNew, Rick	SW CK	**FB**	69	70				
McQuigg, Cindy	FEN	**TR**	73	74	75			
McQuigg, Laura	FEN	**SB**	82					
McQuigg, Rick	FEN	**FB**	76					
McReynolds, Megan	HOL	**TEN**	16	17	18			
McRill, Kyle	KEAR	**BSB**	11					
McTaggart, Bob	CAR	**SW**	71					
McTaggert, Megan	OXF	**TR**	00	01	02			
McWilliams, Jeannine	LIN	**SB**	90	91				
Meacham, Hayley	HOL	**TEN**	02	04				
Meacham, Kevin	HOL	**TEN**	02	03	04			
Mead, McKenzie	FEN	**SW**	14					
Medamar, Shelly	CAR	**SB**	73					
Medina, Rory	LAP W	**WR**	00					
Meehan, Mike	FEN	**HKY**	74	75				
Mehlberg, Lynnette	HOL	**CC**	85	86	87			
Meinecke, Ellen	LAP W	**SB**	09	10				
Meissner, Cindi	LAP W	**TR**	96					
Melasi, Lia	FEN	**BSK**	04	**SCR**	05	06		
Mellish, Dan	LAP	**WR**	69					
Melton, CJ	LAP W	**FB**	12	**WR**	13			
Memishaj, Eva	OXF	**VB**	94					
Mendryga, Jim	LKV	**TR**	99					
Mendryga, Paul	LKV	**TR**	00					
Merewether, Laura	HOL	**TEN**	82	83	**TR**	83	85	
Mermuys, Mike	FEN	**HKY**	87	88				
Merrill, Jeff	FEN	**FB**	76	77	**WR**	77		
Merriwether, Matt	OXF	**TR**	96					
Mesack, Jim	SW CK	**FB**	69					
Mesack, Logan	SW CK	**BSB**	17					
Mesack, Scott	LIN	**GLF**	83					

Metheny, Linda	HOL	**TEN**	09			
Metievier, Tom	MT M	**CC**	97			
Metz, Tom	LAP W	**FB**	96			
Meyer, Kayla	KEAR	**SB**	15			
Meyer, Lisa	LAP W	**TR**	79	81		
Meyers, Fred	FEN	**FB**	91			
Micallef, Eric	HOL	**SCR**	09	10	11	
Micallef, Hannah	HOL	**SW**	10	11		
Miceli, Zac	FEN	**SW**	14	15	16	
Mich, Mary	HOL	**CC**	90			
Michael, Diane	MT M	**TR**	81			
Michael, Hunter	LIN	**FB**	15	16		
Michayluk, Mike	HOL	**TEN**	06	07	07f	
Middleditch, Melissa	MT M	**SB**	90			
Middleton, Amy	FEN	**TR**	88			
Mikulenas, Landon	FEN	**SW**	14			
Mikulski, Brian	LAP E	**TR**	77			
Mikulski, Mary	LAP E	**TR**	92	93		
Mikulski, Tim	LAP E	**TR**	80			
Mikus, Brad	LAP E	**TEN**	93			
Milam, Judy	AIN	**SB**	72	73		
Milam, Karen	AIN	**SB**	76			
Milam, Kathy	AIN	**SB**	74			
Milarch, Tim	FEN	**GLF**	86			
Milkos, Marty	LIN	**FB**	98			
Milkovich, Stephanie	FEN	**VB**	93			
Millard, Britt	LKV	**BSK**	88	89		
Millard, Dana	OXF	**BSK**	00	**VB**	01	
Millard, Kristi	OXF	**BSK**	95	**VB**	96	
Millard, Nicole	OXF	**SB**	93			
Miller, Aaron	OXF	**SCR**	93	94	95	
Miller, Ali	LIN	**VB**	07f			
Miller, Annie	SW CK	**TR**	17			
Miller, Brandon	FEN	**TR**	18			
Miller, Bridget	LAP W	**SB**	08	09		
Miller, Bruce	LAP	**TR**	72			
Miller, Dave	HOL	**CC**	81			
Miller, Drew	FEN	**TR**	16			
Miller, Ed	HOL	**TEN**	02			
Miller, Jason	HOL	**TEN**	88	89		
Miller, Jason	LIN	**BSK**	99			
Miller, Jennie	LAP W	**TR**	98			
Miller, Jennifer	FEN	**CC**	82	**TR**	86	
Miller, Keegan	FEN	**GLF**	15	16	17	
Miller, Kim	AIN	**SB**	76			
Miller, Kristen	HOL	**TEN**	01	02		
Miller, Mallory	LAP W	**SB**	02	03	04	05
Miller, Marv	MT M	**BSB**	85			

Miller, Melissa	FEN	**SCR**	05	06	07		
Miller, Natalie	FEN	**LAX**	16	17			
Miller, Nate	LAP W	**FB**	90	**TR**	91		
Miller, Noel	LIN	**FB**	05	06			
Miller, Pat	MT M	**CC**	81	82			
Miller, Ryan	LAP W	**FB**	07	08			
Miller, Ryan	FEN	**TR**	18				
Miller, Sandi	HOL	**TEN**	04				
Miller, Shannon	LAP W	**SB**	08	09			
Miller, Shannon	OXF	**TR**	89				
Miller, Stacey	FEN	**SCR**	01				
Miller, Tim	CAR	**BSB**	75	76			
Millerd, Kyle	OXF	**TR**	96				
Milliken, Mike	LAP W	**FB**	96				
Millington, Ed	LKV	**BSK**	92				
Millis, Cheri	LAP E	**VB**	82	**SB**	82		
Millis, Craig	LAP E	**SCR**	86				
Millis, Lisa	LAP E	**SB**	83				
Millis, Mike	HOL	**FB**	76				
Millis, Shelly	LAP E	**BSK**	84				
Millis, Tim	LAP	**FB**	74	75			
Mills, Taylor	HOL	**TEN**	10	11	12	13	**SCR** 13
Milnarich, Phil	LIN	**FB**	02				
Milne, Tom	SW CK	**TR**	75				
Milz, Katie	LAP E	**TR**	96				
Minder, Pam	HOL	**SB**	75				
Miner, Lin	OXF	**SCR**	00				
Minock, Debbie	FEN	**TR**	71	72	73		
Minock, Todd	FEN	**TR**	73	74			
Minor, Theresa	OXF	**TR**	01	03	04		
Mintz, Greg	AIN	**TEN**	77	78	79		
Miracle, Rick	LIN	**SCR**	99				
Miracle, Staci	LIN	**SCR**	02				
Miron, Andrea	KEAR	**SB**	12				
Misener, Mike	OXF	**FB**	07				
Missentzis, Scott	LAP W	**FB**	00				
Mitchell, Chris	FEN	**BSB**	90				
Mitchell, Ed	FEN	**BSB**	75				
Mitchell, Jenna	HOL	**VB**	10	**TR**	10	11	
Mitchell, Karen	LKV	**TR**	77	78			
Mitchell, McKailey	LIN	**GLF**	12				
Mitchner, Zaria	KEAR	**BSK**	18				
Mixon, Ryan	FLU	**TR**	18				
Mlinarich, Adam	LIN	**FB**	98				
Mock, Rusty	AIN	**BSB**	85				
Moffitt, Caitlin	LAP W	**TR**	01				
Moffitt, Luke	LAP W	**CC**	04				
Molesworth, Eric	LKV	**SCR**	93				

Name	Team	Sport	Yr							
Molilanean, Dan	CAR	**SW**	72							
Mollenmaker, Johan	OXF	**SCR**	95							
Moller, Leah	HOL	**TEN**	11	12	13	14				
Moller, Rebecca	LKV	**BSK**	99	00	**VB**	99	00	01	**TR**	99
Moller, Will	HOL	**TEN**	13							
Molzahn, Logan	HOL	**SW**	18							
Molzahn, Peyton	HOL	**SW**	13							
Moncrieff, Brittany	OXF	**VB**	07f	08	**SCR**	08				
Mondeau, Mike	LAP W	**FB**	93							
Monroe, Brooke	LAP E	**SCR**	93							
Monroe, Eric	LAP W	**TR**	97							
Monroe, Joe	LAP E	**SCR**	01	02						
Monroe, Melissa	LAP E	**SCR**	98							
Montague, Paige	CLIO	**SB**	13	14						
Montgomery, Bob	HOL	**TR**	70							
Montgomery, Don	LKV	**HKY**	78							
Montgomery, Tom	HOL	**FB**	71							
Montgomery, Zac	LAP W	**FB**	96	97						
Montner, Lisa	MT M	**CC**	88	89						
Montpas, Joe	FLU	**TEN**	15	**GLF**	15	16				
Montrose, Austin	FEN	**SW**	05							
Monzanares, Andres	FLU	**SCR**	14							
Mooney, Dylan	LIN	**WR**	08							
Mooney, Jeff	LAP W	**FB**	96	**TR**	97					
Moore, Aaron	OXF	**WR**	07							
Moore, Alex	CLIO	**WR**	18							
Moore, Brian	LAP W	**FB**	94	95						
Moore, Chris	HOL	**TEN**	79							
Moore, Crystal	DUR	**SB**	89							
Moore, Dan	LIN	**HKY**	03							
Moore, Darren	MT M	**TR**	82	84						
Moore, Darwin	MT M	**TR**	82							
Moore, Deana	CAR	**TR**	73	75						
Moore, Deanne	FEN	**BSK**	79	**SB**	79	80				
Moore, Derek	FEN	**BSB**	00							
Moore, Erin	LAP W	**TR**	96	98						
Moore, Gary	CAR	**FB**	71	**BSB**	71					
Moore, Grafton	HOL	**GLF**	70	**BSK**	70	71				
Moore, Jodi	MT M	**SB**	99	00						
Moore, Katie	CLIO	**BSK**	08	09	**SB**	08	09			
Moore, Laura	LAP E	**SCR**	00							
Moore, Pat	FEN	**FB**	72							
Moore, Rick	LAP	**BSK**	72							
Moore, Sherri	MT M	**TR**	83							
Mora, Michelle	FEN	**SB**	72							
Mora, Susan	FEN	**SB**	80							
Mora, Tony	FEN	**BSB**	78							
Morales, Henry	MT M	**WR**	01							

Name	School	Sport	Years	Sport	Years	Sport	Years
Morales, Ryan	BRAN	SCR	04 05 06				
Moran, Miles	LAP E	FB	04 05				
Morelli, Gabe	HOL	TR	07 08				
Moreno, Fernando	HOL	WR	73				
Moreno, Fernando	HOL	WR	91				
Morey, Abbey	FEN	SB	01				
Morgan, Andrew	CLIO	GLF	10 11				
Morgan, Devin	FLU	FB	15				
Morgan, Jamie	OXF	FB	93				
Morgan, Jesse	LAP E	HKY	90				
Morgan, Jessica	LAP E	VB	00	SCR	97 98 99 00		
Morgan, Kerry	SW CK	FB	74				
Morgan-Eller, Ashlee	OXF	TR	07				
Moriarty, Shannon	LAP W	VB	89				
Moros, Darryl	SW CK	CC	75				
Morrell, Brittany	LAP E	SCR	13				
Morris, Courtney	HOL	CC	02 03	TR	02 03 04		
Morris, Erin	FEN	CC	97	TR	97 99		
Morris, Greg	HOL	TR	77				
Morris, Kerri	FEN	SB	94 95				
Morris, Marty	MT M	BSB	80				
Morris, Mitchell	LAP E	GLF	06 08				
Morris, Ray	FEN	FB	73				
Morris, Stephanie	LAP	SW	07				
Morris, Stephanie	LAP E	TR	09				
Morris, Tyler	FLU	FB	17				
Morrison, Al	FEN	SW	05 06	TR	06		
Morrison, Amy	FEN	SW	04 05 06	VB	07	TR	04 05 06 07
Morrison, Chris	FEN	SW	08				
Morrison, Madeline	FLU	VB	17				
Morrison, Nick	FLU	SCR	16	FB	17	TR	16 17 18
Morrow, Adam	LIN	SCR	07				
Morrow, Shelby	FLU	BSK	17 18				
Morse, Chris	HOL	TEN	88 89 90				
Morten, Brady	FEN	CC	11				
Morton, Claire	CAR	TR	69				
Morton, Darcy	LAP W	SCR	92 93				
Moses, Mike	HOL	TR	74 75				
Mosley, Steve	MT M	WR	00				
Moss, Marcus	KEAR	WR	17				
Moss, Samantha	FEN	GLF	11 12 13				
Mossing, Emma	LIN	SB	18				
Mott, Justin	FEN	FB	11				
Mott, Tim	MT M	WR	92				
Moussavi, Cameron	HOL	TR	09 10				
Mowery, Eric	FEN	SCR	10	BSK	11		
Mowery, Taylor	FEN	VB	15	SB	16		
Mozader, Amanda	LAP W	SB	89				

Mrasek, Dave	CAR	**TEN**	73				
Mudar, Charlotte	FEN	**CC**	81	82			
Mudd, Kirk	OXF	**FB**	87	**TR**	87		
Mudd, Randy	OXF	**FB**	85				
Mudrak, Jenny	LIN	**TR**	93				
Mueller, Kam	OXF	**FB**	05				
Muir, Colleen	LAP E	**VB**	79	**SB**	78	79	
Muir, Laurie	LAP E	**BSK**	80	**VB**	81		
Muir, Nate	LAP E	**FB**	87				
Muir, Todd	LAP E	**FB**	82				
Mulanix, Vern	LAP W	**HKY**	81				
Mulholland, Brian	LKV	**FB**	96				
Mulholland, Mark	OXF	**FB**	84				
Mullins, Mark	FEN	**FB**	78				
Mullins, Ray	LKV	**FB**	82				
Muncy, Rick	LKV	**TR**	79				
Mundy, Brian	HOL	**TR**	90	91			
Mundy, Lorey	HOL	**TR**	85				
Mungall, Chuck	CAR	**FB**	69	**BSB**	70		
Munger, Cortney	HOL	**TEN**	11				
Mungia, Doug	LAP W	**FB**	80				
Munoz, DesRae	KEAR	**GLF**	10	11			
Muntin, Alexa	FEN	**SW**	04	05			
Murdoch, Jeff	LKV	**WR**	89				
Murdoch, Scott	LKV	**WR**	85				
Murdoch, Stephanie	LKV	**TR**	85				
Murley, Kelly	FEN	**WR**	79				
Muron, Morgan	KEAR	**SB**	10	11			
Murphy, Ann	HOL	**TR**	82				
Murphy, Brendan	FLU	**BSB**	18				
Murphy, Emily	BRAN	**CHR**	06	07	08		
Murphy, Gary	FEN	**SW**	75	76			
Murphy, Gerry	OXF	**FB**	08				
Murphy, Jim	MT M	**FB**	72				
Murphy, Karen	DUR	**VB**	92	**BSK**	91		
Murphy, Kevin	DUR	**BSK**	87	88			
Murphy, Kris	DUR	**BSB**	88				
Murphy, Lauren	FEN	**SCR**	18				
Murphy, MacKenzie	FEN	**SCR**	11	13			
Murphy, Matt	MT M	**FB**	75				
Murphy, Nick	MT M	**FB**	98				
Murphy, Pat	LIN	**FB**	89				
Murphy, Travis	BRAN	**WR**	06				
Murray, Eric	FEN	**SW**	05	07			
Murray, Kris	LAP E	**SCR**	89				
Murray, Nick	OXF	**FB**	04	05	**WR**	06	
Muskovin, Paul	FEN	**FB**	87	**BSB**	87		
Mydock, Laura	LKV	**TR**	97				

Myer, Charlie	OXF	**WR**	98	00					
Myer, Mike	OXF	**WR**	09						
Myers, LeighAnne	HOL	**SCR**	03						
Myers, Paul	LAP W	**SCR**	96						
Myers, Scott	SW CK	**FB**	74						
Mykietiuk, Kendal	FEN	**SW**	07	08	09	10			
Mykkanen, Arrtu	LIN	**HKY**	93						
Mylin, Gabe	OXF	**FB**	92	93					
Nacy, Jack	OXF	**GLF**	02						
Nagel, Bhree	OXF	**BSK**	96						
Nagy, Jason	FEN	**FB**	91						
Nagy, Marc	LAP W	**FB**	90						
Nagy, Pete	KEAR	**BSB**	12						
Nakamura, Daisuke	SW CK	**SCR**	07						
Nakkula, Brent	FEN	**SW**	13	14					
Nankervis, Don	FEN	**HKY**	75						
Nankervis, Jerry	FEN	**HKY**	80						
Napier, Damon	DUR	**WR**	80						
Napier, James	FLU	**SW**	16						
Napier, Lee	DUR	**FB**	81						
Nash, Dillon	LIN	**BSB**	11	12					
Nass, Tim	LAP E	**FB**	90	91					
Nations, Joe	MT M	**WR**	89	90					
Navarre, Nathan	BRAN	**TEN**	10	11					
Navarre, Spencer	BRAN	**TEN**	09	10	11	12			
Neal, Rachel	BRAN	**CHR**	11	12	13				
Neal, Robyn	BRAN	**SW**	12	13					
Near, Brian	HOL	**TEN**	82						
Nelder, Dan	OXF	**CC**	99	00					
Nelson, Amy	LAP W	**VB**	90	**SB**	89	90			
Nelson, Dave	LAP W	**FB**	82						
Nelson, James	OXF	**FB**	07	**TR**	06	08			
Nelson, Joel	HOL	**SCR**	01	**TEN**	02				
Nelson, Katie	LAP W	**VB**	05	06	07	**SB**	06		
Nelson, Lindsey	HOL	**TEN**	02	03	04				
Nelson, Mark	LAP W	**FB**	75						
Nelson, Russ	LAP W	**FB**	83						
Nemecek, Todd	DUR	**TR**	86	87					
Nester, Chelsea	HOL	**TEN**	00	01					
Nestor, Emily	FLU	**SB**	15						
Nettell, Kugar	KEAR	**SCR**	14						
Neukam, Terra	HOL	**TEN**	06						
Neumann, Dave	MT M	**BSB**	85	87					
Neumann, Paul	SW CK	**WR**	75	76					
Newcomb, Brock	FEN	**HKY**	97	98					
Newcomb, Chad	MT M	**BSB**	94						
Newcomb, Gerald	HOL	**CC**	92	93	94	95	**TR**	95	
Newcomb, Matt	MT M	**FB**	88						

Newcomb, Todd	MT M	FB	87	WR	87	88			
Newcombe, Shae	FEN	TR	98	99	01				
Newman, Heather	HOL	SB	02						
Newman, Lauren	FLU	BSK	15	16	17				
Newman, Paul	LAP W	BSK	87						
Newport, Dave	LAP E	WR	07						
Niblack, John	LAP	BSB	72	73					
Nicaj, Anthony	BRAN	WR	18						
Nicaj, Mike	BRAN	FB	16	17					
Nichols, Doug	FEN	FB	83	WR	82	83	84		
Nichols, Genise	MT M	VB	83						
Nichols, Jeff	FEN	FB	89	WR	89	90	TR	88	89	90
Nichols, Katie	LAP W	CHR	11						
Nichols, Scott	MT M	FB	80						
Nicholson, Bob	LKV	TR	77						
Nicholson, Brian	LKV	WR	00						
Nicholson, Lance	LKV	TR	77						
Nicholson, Randy	CAR	WR	69						
Nicholson, Terry	CAR	WR	70	71	72	73			
Nicholson, Wes	CAR	WR	71						
Nicol, Chris	FEN	FB	87	88					
Nicolai, Jamie	HOL	TEN	91	92	93				
Nicolai, Mike	HOL	TEN	95	96					
Nicolas, Sarah	LAP E	TR	05						
Nicoll, Matt	LIN	BSB	86						
Nielsen, Mary	AIN	TR	82						
Niemi, Jessie	SW CK	SCR	08						
Niles, Steven	KEAR	HKY	15						
Nixon, Davis	HOL	TR	09	10	11				
Nixon, Matt	LIN	TR	03						
Nixon, Mike	LIN	TR	02						
Nixon, Randy	HOL	CC	78						
Noble, Mike	LAP W	FB	84	BSB	85				
Noel, Steve	MT M	TR	94						
Nolan, Shane	LAP E	TR	04	05					
Nolan, Zach	LAP E	FB	10						
Nordman, Colin	HOL	WR	07						
Noren, Ashley	HOL	SB	13						
Norman, Jordan	LIN	SCR	03	04	TR	02	03	04	
Norman, Nick	LAP W	FB	03						
Norman, Ryan	LIN	SCR	02	TR	01	02	03		
Norris, Justin	FLU	FB	14						
North, Tim	FEN	GLF	74						
North, Tim	LIN	FB	02	03	04				
North, Tom	FEN	GLF	70						
North, Willie	AIN	FB	79	80					
Norton, Tina	LAP E	TEN	81						
Nosek, Madisen	LIN	BSK	12						

Novak, Sean	FEN	**SCR**	98						
Novess, Bradley	FLU	**FB**	17						
Nowacki, Brad	OXF	**FB**	98						
Nowacki, Noel	KEAR	**SW**	16	17					
Nowak, Ron	LAP W	**TR**	98						
Nuccio, Chris	BRAN	**HKY**	04	05					
Nuccio, Mikki	BRAN	**SCR**	05	06	07	08			
Nuccio, Troy	BRAN	**TEN**	06						
Nunez, Paul	LKV	**HKY**	77	**BSB**	77				
Nunn, Tyler	FEN	**GLF**	06	08	09	10			
Nuoffer, Jon	LIN	**BSK**	01	**TR**	01				
Nurenberg, JJ	LAP E	**BSK**	85						
Nurmi, Samantha	KEAR	**SB**	10						
Nyholm, Chris	FEN	**BSB**	01						
Nyholm, Jenny	FEN	**VB**	89						
Nyland, Stacy	OXF	**CC**	99						
Nyswaner, Amy	LKV	**VB**	89						
Nyswaner, Garrett	CLIO	**WR**	18						
Nyswaner, Wyatt	CLIO	**BSB**	16						
O'Brien, Caitlin	LAP W	**CHR**	08						
O'Brien, Zach	LAP W	**SCR**	12						
O'Byrne, Mike	LAP	**CC**	71	72	**TR**	72			
O'Connell, Connor	LIN	**FB**	12						
O'Donnell, Doreen	OXF	**CC**	84	85	86	**TR**	87		
O'Keefe, Emma	LIN	**VB**	16						
O'Neill, Jeff	LAP W	**FB**	89	90	**BSK**	91	**BSB**	90	91
O'Neill, Kathy	LAP W	**VB**	82						
O'Reilly, Dave	FEN	**GLF**	92	93	94				
Oakman, Cheryl	AIN	**TR**	78						
O'Brien, Joe	LIN	**FB**	86						
O'Brien, Kaitlin	HOL	**TEN**	00						
O'Brien, Steve	MT M	**FB**	97						
O'Connell, Casey	LIN	**FB**	02						
O'Connell, Connor	LIN	**TR**	12						
O'Connor, Dan	HOL	**SW**	09	10					
O'Connor, Mike	HOL	**SW**	07	08	09				
Odegard, Ed	SW CK	**HKY**	75						
Odette, Amy	HOL	**TEN**	90						
Offer, Tim	OXF	**GLF**	97						
Oginsky, Garrett	FLU	**FB**	14	15	**BSB**	15	16		
Oginsky, Robert	MT M	**FB**	88	**BSB**	88	89			
Ogle, Chris	OXF	**SCR**	89						
Ogle, Sheree	BRAN	**TEN**	06						
O'Guinn, Sean	FEN	**GLF**	04						
O'Hara, Tim	FEN	**FB**	84						
Okopien, Alex	FEN	**FB**	12						
Oland, Chris	LAP W	**FB**	97						
Oldaugh, Ralph	HOL	**HKY**	75	76					

Name	School	Sport	Year			
Olds, Marsha	CAR	**SB**	73	74		
Olds, Zach	FEN	**TEN**	99	00		
Olejniczak, Joe	LAP W	**BSB**	96			
Olive, Joel	LAP W	**SCR**	97			
Oliver, Kyle	OXF	**WR**	04			
Olivo, Ed	SW CK	**FB**	70	**BSB**	70	
Ollson, Jack	BRAN	**WR**	17			
Olney, Kent	SW CK	**FB**	72			
Olsen, Bill	AIN	**TR**	80			
Olson, Pete	OXF	**FB**	88	89		
Olszewski, Sarah	FEN	**TR**	04			
Ondovcsik, Mike	MT M	**FB**	78			
O'Neil, Pat	HOL	**TR**	82	83		
O'Neill, Rory	FEN	**BSB**	97			
Onweller, Paige	LAP E	**CC**	05	**TR**	05	06	07
Ordiway, Blake	HOL	**BSB**	12			
Orlikowski, Terri	LAP W	**TR**	79			
Ortega, Francesca	LAP W	**SCR**	11	12	13	14
Ortman, MaryAnne	LAP E	**VB**	78			
Osborn, Luke	LKV	**TR**	94			
Osentoski, Chris	LAP W	**GLF**	01	02	03	04
Osentoski, Olivia	LAP W	**CHR**	07			
Osgood, Brian	LIN	**SCR**	06			
O'Shea, Brendan	BRAN	**SCR**	15	16		
O'Shea, Bridget	BRAN	**SCR**	12			
Osmond, Ken	LIN	**HKY**	92			
Osmond, Lance	LIN	**HKY**	96			
Osmun, Ken	HOL	**CC**	85	**TR**	86	
Ostrander, Bill	LAP W	**GLF**	85			
Ostrander, Rob	LAP W	**GLF**	76	**BSB**	77	
Ostrum, Dave	LAP W	**BSB**	89			
Ostyn, Dennis	FEN	**BSB**	69			
Ouellette, Claire	KEAR	**SB**	17	18		
Ouellette, Sydney	KEAR	**SB**	14	15	16	
Owen, Colin	LAP E	**SCR**	11			
Owen, Ellery	LAP E	**VB**	09			
Owen, Sara	LAP E	**TR**	96			
Owen, Todd	LAP E	**TR**	01			
Owens, Heidi	HOL	**TEN**	86	87	88	89
Owens, Jerry	SW CK	**TR**	74			
Owens, Kaitlyn	OWO	**CC**	17			
Owens, Nicole	HOL	**TEN**	08	09	10	
Owens, Tiffany	BRAN	**TR**	10	11	12	
Owocki, Dave	FEN	**TEN**	78			
P'Simer, Chris	OXF	**BSB**	93			
Packard, Jeff	FEN	**HKY**	77			
Padgitt, Greg	LAP E	**TEN**	85			
Paese, Francesco	OXF	**SCR**	06			

Name	Team	Sport			Sport			
Paga, Jeff	LAP E	HKY	94					
Page, Bob	CAR	FB	73		BSB	74		
Page, Madison	LIN	SCR	14	15	16			
Page, Nate	LAP W	FB	11					
Painter, Duane	LAP W	FB	78					
Pais, Joe	OXF	TR	83					
Pajtas, Scott	FEN	FB	80					
Pajtas, Tim	FEN	WR	77	78	79			
Pakulak, Glenn	LAP E	FB	96	97	BSK	98		
Pakulak, Marissa	LAP E	BSK	01					
Palace, Mike	HOL	TEN	08					
Palko, A.J.	HOL	FB	06					
Palma, Ravin	KEAR	CHR	12	13	14			
Palmer, John	FEN	FB	72	WR	72	73		
Palmer, Karla	FEN	CC	01	02				
Palmer, Logan	FEN	SCR	14					
Palmgren, Amy	HOL	TEN	00	01	02	03		
Palmrose, Rick	AIN	CC	77					
Paluska, Kirk	FEN	TEN	86					
Pannick, Wally	AIN	WR	83	84				
Panzlau, Nathan	FEN	TR	06					
Pappas, Berryl	BRAN	SB	03					
Papuga, Devin	HOL	SCR	09	10				
Papuga, Evin	HOL	FB	11	12	TR	11	13	
Parcher, Ted	LIN	TR	11	12	13			
Parenteau, Gary	SW CK	CC	75	TR	75	76		
Pariseau, Elise	KEAR	GLF	16					
Parish, Halle	KEAR	SB	18					
Parker, Brandi	OXF	VB	03					
Parker, Genelle	OXF	TR	03					
Parker, Jerry	AIN	FB	84	85				
Parker, Michelle	HOL	CC	91					
Parker, Steve	FEN	WR	75					
Parkhill, Jennifer	OXF	TR	94					
Parkinson, Matt	KEAR	TR	15	16				
Parks, Jordan	HOL	SCR	12					
Parks, Kerrigan	FLU	GLF	14	15				
Parks, Skylar	FEN	LAX	17					
Parks, Sue	AIN	CC	83	84	TR	82	83	84
Parrish, B.J.	FEN	WR	95					
Parry, Olivia	BRAN	CHR	13	TR	13			
Parsons, Kendell	BRAN	SCR	16					
Parsons, Kyle	LIN	BSB	04					
Partee, Paris	HOL	FB	16					
Paschke, Terry	LAP E	TR	81					
Pashnick, Leon	FEN	TEN	03					
Pasineau, Lisa	LAP W	TEN	80					
Pastue, Mandy	LAP W	SB	93					

Paterson, Laurence	KEAR	**SCR**	09	10			
Patnode, Jim	HOL	**FB**	78				
Pattan, Rodney	FEN	**GLF**	78	**BSK**	79		
Patterson, Heidi	HOL	**SB**	95				
Patterson, Jesse	LIN	**FB**	08	09			
Patterson, Krystal	CLIO	**SB**	06				
Patterson, Mark	CAR	**SW**	72				
Patterson, Meagan	FEN	**SW**	09	10			
Patterson, Mike	OXF	**TR**	87				
Patton, Rodney	FEN	**BSB**	79				
Pavelich, Katie	KEAR	**CC**	08				
Pawelski, Helga	OXF	**VB**	97				
Pawli, Tony	DUR	**SCR**	91				
Payne, Bonnie	OXF	**TR**	98				
Payne, Lindsey	CLIO	**CHR**	16				
Peabody, Brandon	FEN	**FB**	98				
Peake, TJ	HOL	**TR**	11				
Pearce, Kevin	LIN	**HKY**	86	87			
Peariso, Shelly	LKV	**TR**	93	94	95		
Pearson, Rick	LAP E	**WR**	78				
Pearson, Ronnie	HOL	**BSK**	01	**TR**	00	01	
Pearson, Talana	BRAN	**CHR**	08	09			
Peavey, Mark	HOL	**BSB**	72				
Peck, Deb	DUR	**SB**	80				
Peck, Mike	FEN	**TR**	02	03			
Peel, Tony	SW CK	**CC**	09				
Peet, Tori	LAP W	**CC**	07	08	09	10	
Peller, Rusty	LAP W	**FB**	95				
Pellerito, Mike	OXF	**SCR**	87				
Pellett, George	FEN	**CC**	68				
Pender, Ryan	LAP E	**BSB**	03	04	05		
Penix, Dan	BRAN	**CC**	10	**SW**	11		
Pennington, Breanna	CLIO	**BSK**	11	12	13		
Penrod, Jamie	OXF	**TR**	93	94			
Penwell, Logan	FEN	**BSB**	09				
Peplinski, Stan	LAP W	**FB**	00	01			
Pepper, Jenna	HOL	**GLF**	14	**TEN**	13	14	15	16
Pepper, Kyle	HOL	**WR**	13	**GLF**	13		
Percola, Marc	FEN	**HKY**	91	92	93		
Perez, Julie	CAR	**TR**	73				
Perez, Keith	HOL	**BSB**	98				
Perez, Rey	LAP E	**FB**	91				
Periard, Tim	LKV	**TR**	85				
Perkins, Cody	LAP W	**FB**	12				
Perkins, Dave	FEN	**TEN**	85				
Perkins, Sincere	BRAN	**FB**	17				
Pero, Brett	SW CK	**FB**	14	15	**TR**	14	
Perrault, Angie	OXF	**TR**	83	84			

Perrin, Eric	DUR	**WR**	81	83			
Perrin, Jason	DUR	**WR**	93	94			
Perrin, Stacey	DUR	**SB**	95				
Perry, Breanna	FLU	**BSK**	15	17	**TR**	15	17
Perry, Dan	LAP E	**FB**	13	**WR**	14		
Perry, Jill	BRAN	**SB**	03	04	06		
Perry, Joe	LAP E	**WR**	12	13			
Perry, Joel	HOL	**BSB**	12	13	14		
Perry, John	DUR	**FB**	96				
Perry, Kris	MT M	**BSK**	74	**SB**	74		
Perry, Mark	MT M	**HKY**	74				
Perry, Rick	FEN	**FB**	01				
Perry, Rob	FEN	**FB**	03				
Perry, Todd	LAP W	**SCR**	97				
Pertier, Rick	SW CK	**BSK**	69				
Peter, Justin	LKV	**HKY**	00	01	02		
Peters, Glenn	MT M	**FB**	80	**HKY**	81		
Peters, Josh	FEN	**FB**	93				
Peters, Kurt	HOL	**WR**	93				
Peters, Stephan	FEN	**SW**	05				
Peterson, Ashlee	LAP E	**TR**	92				
Peterson, Dale	LKV	**WR**	84				
Peterson, Debbie	FEN	**TR**	76				
Peterson, Donna	LKV	**TR**	85	87			
Peterson, Erica	FEN	**SCR**	98	99			
Peterson, Joel	LIN	**GLF**	04				
Peterson, Neeley	SW CK	**GLF**	17				
Pethers, Brad	LAP W	**SCR**	90	91			
Pethers, Steve	LAP W	**BSB**	95				
Peto, Krystal	LAP W	**CHR**	12				
Petruska, Ed	FEN	**TR**	73				
Pettis, Fred	FEN	**FB**	80				
Pettis, Tristan	CLIO	**TR**	17				
Petts, Travis	LIN	**BSB**	15				
Pettus, Nola	AIN	**TR**	72				
Pettway, Kevin	HOL	**TR**	77				
Peyerk, Pat	OXF	**FB**	86				
Pfau, Doug	HOL	**TR**	79				
Pfeifer, Bryan	HOL	**GLF**	85	86			
Pfeiffer, Jared	LIN	**TR**	06				
Pfundt, Dan	CAR	**WR**	76				
Phelps, Preston	OXF	**WR**	98				
Philburn, Evan	FEN	**FB**	08				
Phillips, Chris	FEN	**FB**	83				
Phillips, Jaime	FEN	**BSK**	74	**SB**	73		
Phillips, Jeff	FEN	**BSB**	72				
Phillips, John	AIN	**BSB**	81				
Phillips, Roger	LIN	**CC**	10	11	12		

Name	Team	Sport						
Phillips, Roy	HOL	**BSB**	69	70				
Phillips, Sarah	LAP E	**VB**	13					
Phipps, Sydney	FEN	**TEN**	14	15				
Pickelman, Brian	LAP E	**TR**	81	**BSB**	83			
Pickelman, Chris	LKV	**BSB**	95	96				
Pickens, Jeff	LKV	**WR**	77					
Pickhover, Katie	FEN	**SB**	98	99				
Pickhover, Mike	FEN	**WR**	73	74				
Pickup, Kursten	HOL	**TEN**	96	97	98	**SB**	97	99
Pickup, Natalie	HOL	**TEN**	96	97				
Pierce, Jeff	DUR	**BSK**	81					
Pierce, Kylee	SW CK	**SB**	16	17				
Pierce, Lisa	DUR	**SB**	85	87				
Pierce, Madison	BRAN	**TR**	12	13	14	15		
Pierce, Tim	DUR	**FB**	83	84	85			
Pierce, Tom	DUR	**BSK**	85	86				
Pierce, Tricia	BRAN	**TR**	16	17				
Pierce, Wes	FEN	**SCR**	97					
Pieron, Dave	FEN	**BSB**	99					
Pierson, Natalie	LAP W	**SCR**	96					
Piet, Madison	LIN	**TR**	15					
Pietryga, David	FEN	**FB**	17	**BSK**	18	**BSB**	17	18
Pifer, Caden	SW CK	**CC**	16	17				
Pihlstrum, Nate	LAP W	**TR**	90	91				
Pike, Emilee	DUR	**SB**	95					
Pilar, Jayce	FEN	**BSB**	97					
Piliafas, Chris	LAP W	**FB**	94	**TR**	94			
Pillaro, Melanie	FEN	**TR**	77					
Pinagel, Garrett	HOL	**SW**	11	12				
Pinnix, Shelton	MT M	**TR**	73					
Piotrowski, Craig	OXF	**FB**	87	**TR**	86	87	88	
Piper, Mark	CAR	**BSB**	73					
Pitt, John	CAR	**SW**	71					
Pittenger, Jim	HOL	**BSB**	71					
Pittiglio, Monica	BRAN	**SW**	12	13	14	**TR**	12	
Pittman, Angie	FEN	**TR**	77	78				
Piwowarczyk, Chris	FEN	**FB**	85	86				
Piwowarczyk, Kim	FEN	**VB**	91					
Piwowarski, Joe	HOL	**FB**	10					
Place, Matt	LAP W	**FB**	13	**BSK**	14			
Placek, Matt	FEN	**SCR**	00	01	02			
Pletscher, Carah	SW CK	**SB**	12	13	14			
Plew, Gary	HOL	**TR**	70	71				
Ploof, Hannah	KEAR	**BWL**	13	14	15	16		
Ploof, Lindsey	KEAR	**BWL**	10	11	12			
Ploucha, Gene	MT M	**GLF**	72	73				
Plude, Logan	FLU	**BSK**	15	16				
Pluta, Don	HOL	**BSB**	73					

Podgorski, Jeremy	LAP W	**HKY**	09				
Podgorski, Nick	LAP W	**HKY**	05				
Podolski, Alex	LAP E	**SCR**	10	11			
Podolski, Lindsey	LAP E	**TR**	06				
Podsiadlik, Diana	OXF	**TR**	84				
Pohl, Don	OXF	**BSB**	08				
Polick, Tina	HOL	**TEN**	09				
Polidan, Drew	FEN	**BSB**	04				
Polidan, Steve	FEN	**WR**	89	91			
Polk, Julie	OXF	**SCR**	94				
Pollard, Tim	LKV	**TR**	84				
Polley, Mikel	CLIO	**BWL**	11	12			
Poniatowski, Don	LAP W	**TEN**	90				
Ponkey, Michael	HOL	**CC**	15				
Poole, Dave	CAR	**TEN**	76				
Pooler, Maggie	FEN	**TEN**	11				
Pope, Dave	OXF	**GLF**	84				
Pope, Julie	LAP W	**TEN**	79	80			
Popilek, Tom	MT M	**GLF**	87	88	89		
Poretta, Whitney	LAP E	**TR**	03				
Porter, Brian	AIN	**TEN**	79				
Porter, Rob	LAP E	**TR**	77	78			
Porzse, Kathy	CAR	**TR**	72				
Post, Brandon	LAP W	**HKY**	90	91			
Post, Brian	LAP W	**HKY**	89				
Postma, Carley	HOL	**TEN**	11	12	13	14	
Postma, Ethan	HOL	**SCR**	15	17	**TEN**	15	16	17
Potter, Scott	AIN	**FB**	76	77			
Potts, Casey	LAP W	**BSB**	10				
Potts, Tim	FEN	**BSB**	98				
Pouget, Claire	LAP W	**BSK**	90	SB	91		
Pougnet, Chad	LIN	**FB**	06	07			
Pougnet, Mike	CAR	**TEN**	74	75			
Poulson, Chase	FEN	**SCR**	17				
Powell, Amber	FEN	**CC**	06				
Powell, Deanna	FEN	**SB**	97				
Powell, Doug	DUR	**BSB**	81				
Powell, Max	LIN	**FB**	10				
Powell, Michele	LAP W	**SB**	88				
Powell, Todd	LKV	**TR**	84				
Powers, Lawrence	AIN	**WR**	78	81			
Powers, Nick	FLU	**BSB**	18				
Powers, Nicki	HOL	**TEN**	98	99			
Powers, Steve	AIN	**WR**	75	76			
Powers, Tracy	LAP W	**SB**	87				
Poyner, Buddy	FEN	**WR**	08	09			
Praedel, Kendrah	FEN	**TEN**	15				
Pratt, Jake	OXF	**WR**	10				

Prechowski, Eric	HOL	**SCR**	05				
Premo, Alex	LIN	**LAX**	17				
Presby, Rachel	HOL	**SCR**	02				
Prescott, Brianna	BRAN	**SB**	08	09	10		
Preston, Scott	HOL	**BSB**	86				
Preville, Mark	LAP E	**TR**	99				
Prevost, Dalana	MT M	**SB**	96				
Prevost, Dave	MT M	**HKY**	91				
Price, Angie	LAP W	**SB**	93	94			
Price, AnneMarie	FEN	**VB**	02				
Price, Carol	FEN	**BSK**	98	99	**VB**	98	99	00
Price, Carrie	FEN	**SCR**	88				
Price, Christie	FEN	**SCR**	90				
Price, David	LAP W	**FB**	11				
Price, Heather	HOL	**TEN**	03	05	06		
Price, Payton	HOL	**SCR**	17	18			
Price-Rose, Jayln	SW CK	**BSK**	17	18			
Priest, David	SW CK	**WR**	07				
Priestly, Debbie	HOL	**BSK**	79	80	**SB**	81	
Prieur, Mila	FEN	**SB**	96	97			
Prime, Rae	AIN	**CC**	82				
Prime, Rhonda	AIN	**CC**	81	82	**TR**	82	83	
Prime, Tim	AIN	**CC**	85				
Prince, Julie	OXF	**SB**	98				
Prince, Mackenzie	LIN	**VB**	09				
Princing, Mary	LAP W	**TR**	81				
Prine, Keenan	LAP W	**FB**	06				
Prine, Ryan	KEAR	**BSB**	09				
Pritchard, Kevin	LAP W	**TR**	98	99			
Privette, Sarah	BRAN	**TR**	07	08	09		
Prohlik, Ed	SW CK	**FB**	72				
Proper, Bart	FEN	**TR**	89				
Protas, Bridget	HOL	**VB**	99	00			
Proulx, Paul	LAP	**GLF**	74				
Pruetz, Bethany	OXF	**VB**	00				
Pruitt, Robin	CAR	**TR**	73	74	75	76	
Pryomski, Rob	HOL	**TR**	00				
Przybylowicz, Bobbi	FEN	**TR**	86				
Przybylowicz, Jenny	FEN	**TEN**	94				
Przybylowicz, Tailer	FEN	**GLF**	12	13			
P'Simer, Chris	OXF	**FB**	91	92			
P'Simer, Dave	OXF	**FB**	89				
Ptolemy, Sandy	OXF	**CC**	00				
Puckett, Lea	FEN	**SCR**	93				
Pugh, Lorie	LKV	**TR**	85				
Purdy, Mike	CAR	**CC**	71				
Purvis, Ashley	LAP E	**VB**	03	04	05		
Pushies, Rose	FEN	**SB**	78				

Pushman, Addam	FEN	**WR**	99						
Pushman, Brian	FEN	**HKY**	01	02					
Pushman, Jim	FEN	**BSB**	97						
Pushman, Marie	FEN	**TR**	75	77					
Pushman, Marv	FEN	**FB**	68	**WR**	69				
Pushman, Rob	FEN	**HKY**	97	99	**BSB**	97	98		
Pushman, Scott	FEN	**WR**	97	98	99	00			
Putnam, Caleb	LAP W	**TR**	94						
Putnam, Clay	FEN	**SW**	73	74	75				
Putnman, Tristan	HOL	**SW**	06						
Putz, Jenni	LAP E	**CC**	09						
Pyeatt, Greg	CAR	**BSB**	74						
Pyles, Bill	CAR	**FB**	70						
Pyles, Zac	LKV	**WR**	98	99					
Querio, Walt	LAP	**FB**	71						
Quick, Doane	HOL	**FB**	72						
Quinn, Heidi	HOL	**TEN**	00	01					
Quinn, Jenny	HOL	**VB**	97	**SCR**	95	96			
Quinnan, Jake	HOL	**TEN**	09	10	**SW**	08	09	10	11
Quintanilla, Eladio	HOL	**FB**	89						
Raab, Andy	OXF	**FB**	99						
Raab, Eric	OXF	**FB**	92	93	94				
Raab, Ryan	OXF	**FB**	88	89					
Rabiduc, Nicki	AIN	**SB**	76						
Raby, Andrea	FEN	**BSK**	79	**VB**	80				
Raby, Morgan	BRAN	**CHR**	16						
Rachwal, Kyle	LAP E	**FB**	13						
RaCosta, Amy	LAP E	**SB**	00						
RaCosta, Chris	LAP E	**HKY**	91						
RaCosta, Greg	LAP E	**HKY**	90						
Radcliffe, Kerry	DUR	**CC**	84	85	86	87	**TR**	86	87
Radcliffe, Michelle	DUR	**CC**	87	88	**TR**	89			
Radford, Kelly	MT M	**SB**	93						
Radford, Kenny	MT M	**BSK**	00	**BSB**	99	00			
Radford, Steph	MT M	**SB**	92						
Raffina, Kristine	HOL	**TR**	99						
Rainwater, Brad	CAR	**FB**	73	**TR**	73	74			
Rainwater, Peyton	SW CK	**CHR**	18	**SB**	18				
Raisch, Jessica	OXF	**BSK**	09						
Rajala, Jeff	FEN	**GLF**	76						
Rakowski, Elizabeth	LIN	**SB**	15	16	17				
Raleigh, Mike	FEN	**BSB**	72						
Raley, Kathy	DUR	**SB**	81						
Ralph, Dan	FEN	**TR**	76						
Ralph, Jane	CAR	**SB**	72						
Ralston, Alex	FEN	**CC**	04	05	06	**TR**	05	06	07
Ralston, Allyssa	LAP W	**CHR**	06						
Ralston, Ben	OXF	**WR**	10						

257

Ralston, James	FEN	**TR**	05				
Ralston, Tommy	FEN	**TR**	03				
Ramage, Charlie	LIN	**GLF**	86				
Rambow, Todd	LAP E	**TR**	81				
Ramey, Mackenzie	KEAR	**BSK**	18	**TR**	18		
Ramirez, Minna	FEN	**LAX**	18				
Rancik, Mike	LAP	**BSK**	75				
Randick, Tyler	FLU	**BSB**	15	16	17		
Randle, Ray	MT M	**FB**	94				
Ranger, Dave	LAP W	**WR**	96				
Ranger, James	LAP W	**WR**	99				
Ranger, Jon	LAP W	**WR**	02	03	04	**SCR**	03
Ranke, Kevin	HOL	**TEN**	07f	08			
Ransom, Adam	FEN	**SW**	10	11	12		
Raslich, Bill	FEN	**FB**	83				
Rasmussen, Kemp	LAP W	**FB**	95	96	**BSK**	96	97
Rasmussen, Kyle	LAP W	**FB**	97	98			
Rates, Scott	HOL	**TEN**	87				
Rau, Alanah	HOL	**TEN**	13				
Rau, Justin	FLU	**FB**	15				
Rauh, Kelsey	HOL	**BWL**	09				
Rawlings, Nolan	FLU	**FB**	14				
Ray, Ashley	MT M	**TR**	02				
Ray, Kelly	HOL	**TR**	13				
Raymond, Jon	LIN	**TR**	93				
Raymond, Katelin	KEAR	**SCR**	10				
Raymond, Mia	LIN	**BSK**	97				
Raymond, Noah	LAP W	**FB**	13	**WR**	14		
Rayner, Dave	OXF	**FB**	99	00	**SCR**	98	99
Rayner, Dustin	HOL	**TR**	94	95	96		
Reader, Jesse	LAP W	**WR**	01				
Readman, Eric	FEN	**BSK**	13				
Ream, Don	LAP E	**BSB**	80				
Ream, Ryan	LAP W	**GLF**	03	04	05		
Reardon, Kristen	FEN	**SB**	01				
Reaver, Ryan	HOL	**TEN**	00	01			
Reaves, Carl	OXF	**FB**	90	91	92	**TR**	92
Reaves, Mark	AIN	**BSB**	75				
Recard, Darius	SW CK	**TR**	07	08			
Redoutey, Robin	HOL	**CC**	98	99			
Reed, Alex	HOL	**TEN**	09				
Reed, Andrew	SW CK	**TEN**	11				
Reed, Ben	BRAN	**SCR**	02				
Reed, Brandon	LAP W	**BSK**	93	**BSB**	92	93	
Reed, Mike	LAP W	**HKY**	81				
Reed, Rick	LAP W	**HKY**	84				
Reed, Shelly	MT M	**SB**	81				
Reed, Tom	LAP	**TEN**	73				

Reel, Seth	FLU	**BWL**	18				
Reese, Josh	LIN	**SCR**	06	07			
Reeser, Tim	LAP W	**GLF**	83				
Reeves, Bob	HOL	**BSB**	75				
Reeves, Glen	HOL	**GLF**	71f	72	73		
Regimbal, John	AIN	**FB**	79	80			
Regnery, Matt	FEN	**FB**	01	**TR**	02		
Reichle, Jada	HOL	**TEN**	82	83	84		
Reichle, Jenny	HOL	**TEN**	86	87			
Reid, Emily	FLU	**BWL**	17				
Reid, Garrett	HOL	**TEN**	17				
Reid, Jake	KEAR	**BWL**	18				
Reid, Paige	HOL	**TEN**	14	15	16	17	
Reid, Tyler	KEAR	**BWL**	12	13			
Reidel, Todd	CLIO	**BSB**	16				
Reigle, Larry	FEN	**FB**	78				
Reinhardt, Paul	LAP W	**HKY**	86				
Remillard, Eric	FEN	**BSB**	06				
Remillard, Renae	FEN	**TR**	01	02	04		
Renaud, Pete	FEN	**BSB**	09				
Rench, Carol	LAP W	**TEN**	81				
Renehan, Cody	HOL	**TEN**	06	07			
Renehan, Shannen	HOL	**TEN**	09	10	11		
Renehan, Sydney	HOL	**TEN**	13	14	15	16	
Rennie, Corey	FEN	**HKY**	92				
Rennie, Rich	LAP W	**TR**	91				
Rennusch, Dawn	LAP W	**TR**	82				
Rensch, Bob	FEN	**TEN**	77				
Rentschler, Kirk	CAR	**BSK**	72				
Reo, Luigi	BRAN	**WR**	11				
Reuschlein, Ellie	FEN	**LAX**	16	17			
Reuschlein, Sarah	FEN	**LAX**	17	18			
Revers, Jon	LIN	**FB**	87				
Reyes, Gwen	FEN	**SCR**	98	00	01		
Reyna, Rachel	SW CK	**TR**	07				
Reynolds, Bill	HOL	**CC**	84	86	**TR**	85	86	87
Reynolds, Chloe	HOL	**TEN**	14				
Reynolds, Ellie	FLU	**CC**	17	**TR**	18		
Reynolds, Johvi	FEN	**FB**	13				
Reynolds, Maria	FEN	**BSK**	81	82			
Reynolds, Melissa	FLU	**TR**	17				
Reynolds, Rod	DUR	**BSB**	86				
Reynolds, Steve	FEN	**WR**	75				
Reynolds, Todd	MT M	**HKY**	89				
Reynolds, Wendy	MT M	**TR**	83	84			
Rheingans, Megan	FEN	**SW**	09				
Rhinehart, Delia	LAP E	**VB**	89				
Rhyndress, Matt	LIN	**FB**	86				

Rice, Greg	CAR	**SW**	71								
Rice, Jodi	LAP W	**VB**	77								
Rice, T.J.	FEN	**GLF**	02	03	04						
Rich, Hayley	FEN	**SB**	09								
Richards, Brandon	KEAR	**BWL**	14								
Richards, Colton	HOL	**TEN**	10								
Richards, Craig	HOL	**TEN**	10	11	12	13					
Richards, Danielle	BRAN	**TEN**	10								
Richards, Laura	OXF	**VB**	90	**SCR**	89	90					
Richardson, Bart	SW CK	**FB**	74	**TR**	74	75					
Richardson, Danielle	LAP W	**SB**	04	05							
Richardson, Eric	MT M	**FB**	95								
Richardson, Jamilla	BRAN	**TR**	07								
Richmond, Adam	OXF	**CC**	04								
Richmond, Brad	LAP W	**FB**	05								
Richmond, Donnie	OXF	**CC**	00	01	02	03	**TR**	01	02	03	04
Ridal, Mariah	HOL	**CC**	10	11	**TR**	09	10	11	12		
Riddell, Ian	CAR	**TR**	69								
Riddle, Riley	BRAN	**CHR**	14	15							
Ridgeway, Trey	HOL	**TEN**	17								
Riester, Brian	FEN	**TR**	99								
Rieves, Pat	LAP E	**FB**	10								
Rieves, Taylor	BRAN	**TR**	13	14	15						
Rigdon, Zach	SW CK	**BSB**	16								
Riley, Derrick	MT M	**GLF**	91	92							
Riley, Mike	OXF	**CC**	83	84							
Riley, Willie	AIN	**BSB**	72								
Rincon, Carlos	LAP W	**TEN**	00	01	02						
Rincon, Monica	LAP W	**TEN**	96	97							
Ring, Becky	LKV	**TR**	91								
Rinks, Amos	MT M	**WR**	81								
Rinks, Seth	MT M	**WR**	90	91							
Riseman, Dan	LAP E	**TEN**	90								
Risi, Dave	FEN	**FB**	82								
Rising, Troy	FEN	**TR**	90								
Risner, Jamie	FEN	**SB**	07	08	09						
Rittenbury, Jayden	FEN	**WR**	17	18							
Rivera, Ryker	LIN	**FB**	15	16	**BSB**	16					
Rivette, Ali	FEN	**BSK**	00	01							
Rivette, Christina	FEN	**BSK**	05	06	08	09					
Rivette, Gabrielle	FEN	**BSK**	08	09	10	11					
Rix, Joy	FEN	**TR**	73								
Roach, Kevin	LAP W	**FB**	09								
Robbins, Jenny	FEN	**SB**	05	06							
Robbins, Matt	DUR	**CC**	87								
Robbins, Mike	DUR	**TR**	86								
Robbins, Terry	FEN	**FB**	74	**BSB**	75						
Roberts, Christian	HOL	**TEN**	10								

Name	School	Sport	Year	Year	Sport	Year	Sport	Year	Year	Year
Roberts, Isaac	LAP E	TR	01							
Roberts, Julie	FEN	BSK	75	76	VB	77	TR	74	75	76
Roberts, Melinda	MT M	TR	77	78						
Roberts, Mike	FEN	TEN	75							
Roberts, Ralph	SW CK	WR	74							
Roberts, Ry'lon	FLU	TR	18							
Roberts, Sam	BRAN	SCR	08							
Roberts, Stacy	FEN	SB	96							
Roberts, Steffanie	FEN	BSK	87							
Robertson, Justin	LAP W	BSB	97							
Robinson, Bruce	HOL	WR	80							
Robinson, Capus	KEAR	BSK	09							
Robinson, Dwayne	HOL	TR	92							
Robinson, Jerry	MT M	FB	81		BSB	82				
Robinson, Kelsy	LAP E	GLF	09	10						
Robinson, Mike	MT M	FB	80							
Robinson, Tony	DUR	WR	92	93						
Robinson, Vinnie	SW CK	SCR	08							
Rock, James	DUR	WR	88							
Rockman, Amanda	FEN	SB	01	02						
Rockman, Beth	FEN	SB	06	07						
Rockman, Megan	FEN	SB	04							
Rockman, Pat	FEN	FB	77							
Rockman, Randy	FEN	HKY	98							
Roda, Amy	LAP W	TR	82							
Roda, Ann Marie	KEAR	SB	11							
Rodda, Bob	CAR	GLF	71							
Rodela, Ray	LAP E	GLF	80							
Rodriguez, Briana	HOL	TEN	09	10	11					
Rodriguez, Justin	LAP E	TEN	97							
Rodriguez, Maria	LAP E	SCR	02							
Rodriguez, Marty	MT M	BSB	99							
Rodriquez, Lorenzo	HOL	SCR	14							
Roe, Paul	FEN	FB	73		WR	74				
Roeder, Tom	HOL	FB	69		BSB	69	70			
Roeser, Michael	BRAN	SW	12							
Roge, Chad	LAP W	FB	01							
Rogers, Amy	FEN	TR	87	89	90					
Rogers, Frank	HOL	BSK	08							
Rogers, Paul	FEN	FB	80							
Rogers, Ted	MT M	TR	80							
Rogers, Whitney	FEN	GLF	85							
Roggentine, Kade	CLIO	WR	07	08						
Rohr, Barb	MT M	TR	77							
Rohr, Kristi	FEN	TEN	91							
Rohr, Steve	FEN	HKY	87							
Roldan, Roly	LAP E	TEN	97							
Rolison, Brina	LIN	SCR	05							

Rolison, Connie	MT M	SB	84	85				
Rolle, Chris	OXF	TR	10					
Rolle, Pat	OXF	TR	84					
Rolleston, John	FEN	FB	73					
Rollier, Josh	FEN	FB	08	BSB	08	09		
Romano, Matt	KEAR	BSK	13					
Romanski, Sara	HOL	CC	97	98	99	TR	99	
Roney, Bryce	FEN	FB	13	14				
Roof, Alexis	KEAR	BWL	16	17	18			
Rooker, Ally	FEN	VB	10					
Roop, Ron	OXF	FB	85					
Roose, Jason	DUR	BSB	94					
Roose, Sam	OWO	SCR	17					
Root, Charles	DUR	WR	79	80	81			
Root, Jamie	LKV	CC	92	TR	93			
Root, Julie	LKV	CC	88	89	90	TR	89	90	91
Root, Keith	LAP E	WR	78					
Rosebush, Keith	LAP E	TR	92	93				
Rosine, Rick	AIN	FB	76					
Ross, Eric	LAP W	FB	96	WR	97			
Ross, Mike	BRAN	HKY	04	05				
Ross, Morgan	BRAN	TR	16	18				
Ross, Nick	FEN	SCR	94					
Ross, Tim	FEN	SCR	93	94				
Rosseel, Sue	OXF	TR	87	88				
Rossiter, Tim	AIN	FB	77					
Roth, Bruce	MT M	FB	75					
Roth, Kim	MT M	SB	74					
Rothgeb, Jay	LAP E	TR	96					
Rousos, Anthony	BRAN	HKY	10					
Roussey, Ashlee	BRAN	VB	12	TR	11	13		
Rowan, Bo	LAP W	HKY	97	99				
Rowden, Michelle	LAP W	SB	84					
Rowley, Duncan	LAP E	SCR	11					
Rowley, Kyle	OXF	FB	03	WR	04			
Rowse, Parker	HOL	TEN	11	12	13			
Rubey, Heidi	LKV	VB	96					
Rubick, Samantha	LAP E	TR	11					
Ruby, Jon	MT M	BSK	95					
Ruddy, Jim	LAP	FB	68					
Rudland, Linda	CAR	TR	75					
Rudland, Ron	CAR	FB	71					
Rudland, Russ	CAR	FB	72					
Ruffini, Charlotte	HOL	CC	11	12	TR	13		
Rufli, Rebecca	LIN	BSK	03	SCR	03	04		
Ruggirello, Kailey	LIN	BSK	04	GLF	04	05		
Ruggirello, Lexi	LIN	GLF	07f					
Ruhlman, Alyssa	LAP W	CHR	10	11	12			

Ruhstorfer, Andrew	KEAR	**SCR**	16	**WR**	15	16	18	
Ruiz, Andrea	HOL	**CC**	17					
Rumbles, Megan	FEN	**SW**	09	11				
Rundall, Mike	AIN	**FB**	81					
Running, Ryan	LAP	**HKY**	14					
Runyon, Ben	LAP W	**SCR**	96					
Rusaw, Randy	HOL	**TR**	07					
Rush, Cyonna	BRAN	**TR**	13	15				
Rushton, Brooklyn	CLIO	**SB**	17					
Russell, Adam	FEN	**SCR**	01					
Russell, Jake	LAP E	**BSB**	07					
Russell, Julie	LAP E	**TR**	91	92				
Rust, Dustin	OXF	**FB**	90					
Rutenbar, Glen	CAR	**BSB**	76					
Rutherford, Carson	FLU	**VB**	14					
Rutkowski, Josh	OXF	**FB**	06					
Ryan, Marshael	FLU	**FB**	14					
Ryan, Marshael	LIN	**FB**	13					
Ryan, Mike	LIN	**BSK**	83					
Ryan, Mitch	LIN	**FB**	12	**BSB**	13			
Ryan, Tessa	BRAN	**CHR**	17					
Rybka, Haleigh	KEAR	**BWL**	15					
Ryerson, Mark	SW CK	**TR**	08					
Ryeson, Chet	LAP W	**GLF**	13					
Rykulski, Ed	CAR	**FB**	71	72	73	**BSB**	73	74
Sabo, Courtney	KEAR	**GLF**	09					
Sack, Heidi	LIN	**CC**	08	09				
Saelens, Meaghan	LAP E	**VB**	12					
Saffold, Fred	AIN	**WR**	86					
Saffold, Joe	AIN	**TR**	85	86				
Sage, Brendan	LIN	**CC**	08	09				
Sage, Ellen	FEN	**TR**	13	14				
Sage, Hannah	FEN	**TR**	14	15	16			
Sage, John	FEN	**FB**	17	**TR**	18			
Sage, Noah	FEN	**TR**	18					
Sage, Patrick	LIN	**TR**	05	06				
Sage, Sabrina	CLIO	**SB**	15	16	17			
Saidoo, Sydney	SW CK	**SB**	10					
Saiz, Tina	HOL	**TEN**	89					
Sak, Jerry	LAP W	**TEN**	80					
Salerno, Tony	AIN	**FB**	79					
Salquist, Payge	OXF	**BSK**	99	00	01	**TR**	00	01
Sammon, Dennis	LKV	**TR**	77					
Sammut, Lucas	HOL	**SCR**	15	16				
Sams, Kim	LAP W	**SCR**	01	02				
Samuel, Wayne	HOL	**CC**	68					
Sanborn, Dan	HOL	**TR**	72					
Sanchez, Anthony	LAP W	**SCR**	96	97	98	99		

Sanchez, Nick	LAP W	**SCR**	97	98	99	**TR**	99
Sanders, Kevin	FEN	**TR**	87				
Sandlin, Nic	SW CK	**BSB**	11				
Sands, Mark	SW CK	**WR**	72				
Sandstrom, Lynn	FEN	**TEN**	89				
Sandstrom, Monica	FEN	**TEN**	90				
Sanford, Brie	FEN	**LAX**	18				
Sanford, Lisa	LKV	**VB**	93	94	95	**TR**	92
Sansiribhan, Mitch	SW CK	**CC**	12				
Sargent, Dale	HOL	**HKY**	79				
Sargent, Jordan	LIN	**VB**	11				
Sargent, Niki	LIN	**TR**	13				
Sargis, Greg	DUR	**FB**	78	**WR**	79		
Sarkon, Aaron	LIN	**FB**	15	16	**BSB**	17	
Sarkon, Brady	LIN	**BSB**	14				
Sartwell, Stuart	FEN	**BSB**	91	92			
Satkowiak, Alicia	SW CK	**TR**	16				
Satkowiak, Jon	LKV	**BSB**	02				
Satkowiak, Maija	LIN	**SB**	10	12	13	**BSK**	13
Saul, Barb	HOL	**TR**	80				
Saunders, Shelly	MT M	**TR**	81				
Sauve, Jason	HOL	**TEN**	89				
Sauve, Trevor	FLU	**HKY**	16				
Savage, Chuck	FEN	**TR**	79				
Savoie, Scott	AIN	**WR**	81	82			
Sawchuk, Mike	LAP E	**FB**	09	10			
Scarbrough, Marilyn	SW CK	**TR**	69				
Schafer, Nathan	LAP E	**HKY**	98				
Schafka, Matt	LAP W	**HKY**	01	02			
Schaft, Drew	LAP E	**FB**	02	**BSK**	03		
Schaible, Bill	SW CK	**SW**	73				
Schalau, Wally	LAP	**FB**	70				
Schaller, Lindsey	LAP E	**SB**	01	02			
Schaltz, Amy	OXF	**SB**	86	87			
Scheffler, Erik	LIN	**GLF**	02				
Scheitler, Kathy	SW CK	**TR**	71	72			
Schenk, John	FEN	**BSK**	80	81	**TEN**	80	81
Schenk, John	FEN	**TEN**	78	79			
Schenk, Matt	FEN	**TEN**	85	86			
Schenk, Mike	FEN	**TEN**	76	79			
Schenk, Vickie	DUR	**BSK**	79				
Scherba, Colleen	LKV	**BSK**	85				
Scherer, Hannah	BRAN	**CC**	06	07	08		
Schettenheim, Jim	FEN	**BSB**	85				
Schian, Ashley	LKV	**SB**	01	02			
Schiebel, Chris	MT M	**BSB**	00				
Schihl, Justice	LAP E	**BWL**	12				
Schills, Kurt	OXF	**SCR**	86	**TR**	87	88	

Name	Team	Sport	Years					
Schimmelpfenning, Darwin	LAP	**BSB**	72					
Schlader, Tony	OXF	**FB**	07					
Schlak, Sergio	OXF	**FB**	05					
Schlaud, Carol	LAP E	**TEN**	78	**SB**	79			
Schlaud, David	LAP W	**WR**	00	01	02	03		
Schlaud, Evan	LAP E	**SCR**	12					
Schlicht, Eric	OXF	**FB**	85					
Schmidt, Bob	OXF	**FB**	01	**BSB**	01	02		
Schmidt, Corinne	LAP E	**TR**	92					
Schmidt, Nick	FEN	**TR**	04					
Schmidt, Ron	AIN	**BSB**	73					
Schmidt, Ruth	LAP W	**TEN**	80					
Schmidt, Samantha	CLIO	**CHR**	11					
Schmidt, Warren	MT M	**WR**	82					
Schneider, Joe	LKV	**FB**	85					
Schneider, Maggie	HOL	**CC**	12	13	14	**TR**	13	14
Schneider, Paul	LKV	**BSB**	77	78				
Schneider, Ryan	LAP E	**BSB**	84	85				
Schneider, Sam	HOL	**CC**	16	17				
Schoals, Rod	FEN	**WR**	80					
Schoenfield, Jaylen	SW CK	**FB**	12	**TR**	13			
Schoenherr, Dani	LAP W	**BSK**	09	**SCR**	08	09		
Schoenherr, Rick	LAP W	**FB**	84					
Schoenherr, Ryan	LAP W	**FB**	06					
Schons, Sommer	LAP E	**VB**	98	**SCR**	98			
Schoolcraft, Jeff	HOL	**TEN**	91					
Schooltz, Adam	HOL	**TEN**	01					
Schott, Julie	DUR	**SCR**	95					
Schrader, Doc	CAR	**BSB**	73	74				
Schrader, Donna	AIN	**TR**	78					
Schreiber, Jim	CAR	**SW**	71					
Schreiber, Rod	CAR	**TEN**	76					
Schroeder, Celeste	LKV	**TR**	77	78				
Schroeder, Hilarie	LAP E	**BSK**	93	94	**SB**	96		
Schroeder, Joel	LAP E	**TR**	95					
Schrot, Greg	LAP E	**BSB**	10					
Schuala, Chris	OXF	**TR**	90					
Schuermann, Jarrod	HOL	**TR**	13					
Schuermann, Joel	HOL	**FB**	11					
Schuermann, Nate	HOL	**FB**	06					
Schultz, Rodger	LAP	**CC**	73	74				
Schultz, Sara	HOL	**CC**	04	05	06	**TR**	08	
Schulz, Sherry	OXF	**BSK**	88					
Schumaker, Dennis	FEN	**WR**	75	76				
Schunot, Mickey	LKV	**HKY**	92					
Schupbach, Brian	FEN	**TR**	89	90				
Schupbach, Brittany	FEN	**TR**	04	05	06			
Schupbach, Chad	FEN	**FB**	10	**BSB**	10			

Name	School	Sport	Yr1				
Schupbach, Jenny	FEN	**SB**	02				
Schwerin, Luke	HOL	**CC**	10	**TR**	10	11	12
Schwerin, Ryan	BRAN	**SW**	11	12			
Schwieman, Kyle	FLU	**CC**	16				
Schwieman, Lori	MT M	**SB**	81	82			
Scofield, Brent	FEN	**GLF**	78	79	80		
Scott, Andrew	HOL	**WR**	12	13	14		
Scott, Eric	LKV	**WR**	94	95	**TR**	94	
Scott, Kent	AIN	**WR**	70				
Scott, Kevin	AIN	**HKY**	75				
Scott, Kris	LIN	**SCR**	05				
Scott, Shawn	HOL	**WR**	10	11	12		
Scowden, Tami	HOL	**TEN**	84	85	86		
Scowden, Terri	HOL	**TEN**	87	88			
Scram, Lance	HOL	**FB**	81				
Scribner, Wyatt	HOL	**WR**	17	18			
Seacrest, Aaron	LAP W	**WR**	11				
Sealey, Heather	LKV	**TR**	89				
Seaman, Leah	LAP W	**CHR**	09	10			
Sears, Bryan	HOL	**WR**	05				
Sears, Matthew	BRAN	**FB**	13				
Seavey, Dave	HOL	**GLF**	75	76			
Seavey, Mark	HOL	**CC**	76	77	78		
Seavey, Tom	HOL	**CC**	73	74	**TR**	74	75
Secrest, Aaron	LAP W	**WR**	10				
Sedlock, Paul	DUR	**FB**	93				
Seeley, Chris	SW CK	**HKY**	16				
Seeley, Megan	OXF	**TR**	08	09	10		
Seeley, Shannon	OXF	**CC**	08	**TR**	07	08	09	10
Seffens, Brooke	BRAN	**SB**	03				
Seger, Cathy	FEN	**TEN**	80				
Seger, Donna	FEN	**TEN**	78	**TR**	79		
Seger, Stacey	FEN	**TEN**	81				
Seib, Brenda	LAP W	**VB**	91				
Seibold, Nick	LAP W	**TR**	97	98			
Seidall, Ryan	LKV	**TR**	90				
Seidel, Sean	LAP W	**HKY**	04				
Seidl, Monica	OXF	**BSK**	01				
Seigle, Meaghan	LIN	**CC**	92				
Seitz, Tim	HOL	**TR**	85				
Sekulich, Anna	FEN	**SW**	04	05	06		
Self, Charlie	AIN	**FB**	77				
Selley, Ryan	LIN	**FB**	05	**WR**	04	05	06
Sells, Christian	HOL	**TEN**	17				
Sells, Makenzi	HOL	**TEN**	17	18			
Semark, Mike	SW CK	**TR**	75				
Sembler, Leah	LIN	**CC**	92	93	94	**TR**	94
Senter, Brianne	LIN	**SB**	12				

Senter, Dick	HOL	**WR**	74	76		
Senter, Eric	HOL	**BSK**	95			
Senter, Phil	HOL	**BSB**	95	96		
Sepanak, Debbie	SW CK	**TR**	72			
Sepanek, Bruce	SW CK	**FB**	73			
Serges, Kellie	CAR	**BSK**	74	75	**TEN** 74	75 76
Serges, Toni	CAR	**BSK**	74	**TEN** 73	74	75
Serven, Jan	MT M	**SB**	77			
Sesock, Jaime	HOL	**TEN**	03	04	05	
Sessink, Brad	LIN	**FB**	08	09		
Setzke, Chanse	FEN	**FB**	16	17	**TR** 18	
Severyn, TJ	FEN	**TR**	08			
Sexton, Tom	LAP W	**FB**	75			
Sexton, Tom	LAP	**WR**	76			
Sexton, Trevor	SW CK	**SCR**	13			
Seyffert, Mike	SW CK	**BSB**	11			
Seymour, Audrey	MT M	**BSK**	88	**SB** 89		
Shade, Julie	LKV	**VB**	90			
Shade, Mary	LKV	**VB**	88	89		
Shagena, Jake	OXF	**FB**	99	**WR** 99		
Shaheen, Dan	FLU	**FB**	17			
Shaheen, Steve	CAR	**FB**	73			
Shallman, Emily	LAP	**SW**	10	11	12	
Shalz, Tait	FEN	**GLF**	17	18		
Shamaly, Todd	LAP W	**BSB**	95			
Shannon, Bret	LKV	**FB**	78	**TR** 79		
Shannon, Keli	LKV	**SB**	90			
Shannon, Taylor	LKV	**VB**	02			
Shannon, Troy	LKV	**FB**	78	79		
Sharkey, Margaret	LAP W	**TEN**	80			
Sharkey, Mike	LAP W	**BSK**	76			
Sharp, Emily	FEN	**TR**	00	01	02	
Sharpe, Lynne	LAP E	**SCR**	04	05	06	
Sharpe, Mitch	HOL	**BWL**	13			
Sharrard, Alyssa	LAP W	**SB**	07	08	09	
Sharrard, Hunter	LAP W	**FB**	13	**BSB** 13	14	
Shaughnessy, Shelby	FLU	**TR**	16			
Shaver, Gale	CAR	**TR**	73			
Shaw, Haley	FEN	**SW**	09	10	11	12
Shaw, Houston	FEN	**FB**	11			
Shaw, Kenton	FEN	**SW**	08	09		
Shaw, Pete	FEN	**WR**	80	81		
Shaw, Rick	CAR	**WR**	72			
Shea, Chris	HOL	**WR**	02			
Shea, Ken	LAP E	**CC**	80	81		
Sheared, Calvin	FEN	**TR**	89			
Sheerin, Craig	AIN	**FB**	84	**WR** 85		
Shegos, Mitch	FEN	**FB**	12			

Shegos, Taylor	FEN	**SW**	15	16	17			
Shelton, Aaron	BRAN	**SCR**	17					
Shenk, Scott	DUR	**FB**	81	**BSB**	83			
Shepard, John	FEN	**HKY**	05					
Shepard, Matt	LIN	**BSB**	94					
Shepherd, Dave	HOL	**SCR**	00					
Shepherd, Doug	HOL	**SCR**	91	92	93	**BSK**	93	94
Shepherd, Josh	HOL	**TEN**	04					
Shepherd, Steve	HOL	**SCR**	93					
Sherman, Anne	LAP E	**SB**	99					
Sherman, Jennifer	BRAN	**SB**	06	07	08			
Sherman, Jessica	BRAN	**SB**	09	10				
Sherman, Molly	LIN	**SB**	13					
Sherrod, Tracy	AIN	**TEN**	79					
Sherry, John	LAP W	**FB**	05					
Sherwood, Jan	MT M	**SB**	85					
Sheyachich, Bob	LIN	**FB**	84					
Shier, Julian	LIN	**SCR**	15	16	17			
Shiffer, Char	DUR	**SB**	95					
Shipman, Chris	KEAR	**SW**	14					
Shiveley, Mark	FEN	**FB**	89					
Shooltz, Aaron	HOL	**TEN**	03	04				
Shooltz, Adam	HOL	**TEN**	00					
Shoopman, Darrell	HOL	**BSK**	81	82				
Shore, Jack	LIN	**BSB**	16	17				
Shorland, Tracy	OXF	**TR**	88	90				
Short, Mike	LAP W	**FB**	75					
Shoup, Meghan	OXF	**TR**	02					
Shown, Sarah	LKV	**SB**	99					
Shriner, Kasey	CLIO	**WR**	12					
Shufflin, Tom	OXF	**FB**	85					
Shuler, Matt	OXF	**TR**	02					
Shultz, Alex	LAP E	**FB**	11					
Shumaker, Rachel	FEN	**SB**	05					
Shuman, Terry	SW CK	**TR**	75					
Shurlow, Jim	FEN	**WR**	00					
Shuttlin, Tim	OXF	**TR**	84					
Sibilsky, Liz	LAP E	**GLF**	02	03				
Siefker, Grace	FEN	**SW**	15	16				
Siegel, Kristen	HOL	**TR**	87					
Siegle, Annie	LIN	**SCR**	95					
Sierakowski, Frank	LAP	**WR**	73					
Sierakowski, Jim	LAP W	**SCR**	01					
Sierakowski, Max	LAP	**FB**	70	**WR**	70			
Sierakowski, Nick	LAP W	**WR**	01					
Sierakowski, Paul	LAP W	**WR**	99					
Sierakowski, Tom	LAP W	**GLF**	88	89	90			
Sierakowski, Wally	LAP W	**GLF**	87	88				

Sievanen, Juha-Pekka	LAP W	**HKY**	84					
Silver, David	DUR	**TR**	95	96				
Simerau, Cameron	LAP W	**FB**	07					
Simin, KathyJo	HOL	**TEN**	83	84	85			
Siminski, Bob	DUR	**GLF**	79	80	81			
Simmons, Keith	HOL	**TR**	85					
Simmons, Robert	HOL	**TR**	85					
Simms, Joshua	HOL	**BSK**	15					
Simon, Matt	KEAR	**HKY**	09					
Simons, Nancy	SW CK	**TR**	72					
Simpson, Bridget	FEN	**TEN**	78					
Simpson, Jawan	BRAN	**TR**	07					
Simpson, Jeff	LKV	**FB**	87					
Simpson, John	FEN	**FB**	74					
Simpson, Lauren	LIN	**TR**	98	99	00			
Simpson, Mark	LAP W	**FB**	89					
Simpson, Mike	HOL	**TR**	75					
Simpson, Shannon	LKV	**TR**	85					
Simpson, Sharon	LKV	**TR**	88					
Simpson, Tom	LKV	**BSB**	90					
Sinclair, Dean	FEN	**TEN**	81					
Sines, Corbin	LIN	**FB**	17	**BSB**	17	18		
Singriel, Kevin	FEN	**TR**	76					
Sink, Danielle	HOL	**TEN**	17	18				
Sink, Dillon	HOL	**TEN**	13	14				
Sink, Mike	LAP W	**FB**	94	95	**BSK**	96		
Sipes, Tyler	FEN	**SW**	10					
Sippert, Brian	LIN	**FB**	03	04				
Sirovey, Tom	LAP	**TEN**	73					
Sisk, Courtney	LIN	**SB**	99					
Sizeland, Olivia	BRAN	**CHR**	17					
Sizemore, Noah	FEN	**SW**	15	17				
Sizemore, Terry	FEN	**FB**	69					
Skank, Dan	LKV	**BSB**	77					
Skene, Tyler	LAP W	**BWL**	12					
Skergan, Christie	LKV	**BSK**	01					
Skidmore, Kelly	CAR	**CC**	74					
Skidmore, Kevin	CAR	**CC**	71	72	**TR**	72	73	
Skinner, Ally	SW CK	**VB**	14					
Skinner, Michael	LIN	**CC**	05	06	07			
Skinsacos, Nick	BRAN	**TEN**	12					
Skubik, Katherine	HOL	**TEN**	13	14				
Skubik, Victoria	HOL	**TEN**	12	13				
Skuta, Tim	AIN	**FB**	77					
Sky, Kelly	HOL	**SW**	15					
Slaght, Brian	BRAN	**WR**	03					
Slater, Doug	AIN	**BSB**	77					
Slater, Glen	AIN	**BSB**	73					

Slater, Jake	HOL	**WR**	98	99					
Slater, Joe	AIN	**BSB**	75						
Slater, Justin	LAP W	**FB**	10						
Slater, Kari	LAP E	**SCR**	01						
Slater, Shelley	LAP E	**BSK**	96	**VB**	97	**SCR**	95	**TR**	96
Slattery, Dan	MT M	**SW**	74	75					
Slatton, Richard	CLIO	**WR**	06						
Slaughter, Adam	FEN	**BSB**	00						
Slegaines, Darryl	HOL	**TR**	81	82					
Slemons, Ricky	HOL	**TEN**	09	10					
Slieff, James	LKV	**BSB**	99						
Sloboda, Bob	CAR	**TEN**	76						
Slosar, Julie	FEN	**TEN**	85						
Slough, John	MT M	**BSB**	86						
Slusarzyk, Justin	CLIO	**BSB**	06						
Slyfield, Scott	LAP W	**HKY**	85						
Smalley, Matt	HOL	**SW**	06	07					
Smethwick, Stephanie	LIN	**VB**	86	87					
Smiecinski, Gregg	LIN	**HKY**	87						
Smiecinski, Kevin	LIN	**HKY**	86						
Smigelski, Julie	FEN	**SB**	92						
Smigielski, Troy	FEN	**BSB**	17						
Smiles, Melissa	HOL	**SCR**	10	11					
Smillie, Zak	LAP E	**SCR**	06	07					
Smith, Alex	KEAR	**BWL**	13						
Smith, Andy	FEN	**FB**	87	**TR**	88				
Smith, April	OXF	**CHR**	06	07					
Smith, Asia	FLU	**TR**	18						
Smith, Brian	HOL	**CC**	79	80	**TR**	81			
Smith, Bryan	LAP E	**HKY**	93						
Smith, Chase	CLIO	**CC**	15	**WR**	14	15			
Smith, Cynthia	LKV	**TR**	92	93	94	95			
Smith, Dave	LAP W	**WR**	78						
Smith, Debbie	LAP E	**SB**	80	81					
Smith, Dennis	MT M	**WR**	77						
Smith, Dylan	OXF	**CC**	09	**WR**	09				
Smith, Elaine	LAP W	**SB**	86						
Smith, Eric	AIN	**BSB**	84						
Smith, Gage	SW CK	**FB**	14						
Smith, Gordon	FEN	**CC**	68	69					
Smith, Greg	FEN	**WR**	77						
Smith, Hunter	FEN	**SW**	18						
Smith, Jarett	FEN	**FB**	16						
Smith, Jayce	FEN	**FB**	75	**BSK**	75	**BSB**	76		
Smith, Jon	LAP E	**SCR**	08						
Smith, Jonathon	FEN	**FB**	13						
Smith, Kaitlyn	HOL	**BSK**	14	15	16	**TR**	13		
Smith, Kelly	DUR	**SB**	84						

Smith, Kevin	OXF	**GLF**	98			
Smith, Kyle	MT M	**GLF**	00			
Smith, Lauren	FLU	**TR**	18			
Smith, Maddison	LAP W	**SCR**	10	11	12	
Smith, Marty	FEN	**HKY**	76			
Smith, Mason	CLIO	**WR**	12	13	14	15
Smith, Matt	AIN	**HKY**	81			
Smith, Nate	LAP W	**FB**	09			
Smith, Olivia	HOL	**SCR**	10	11		
Smith, Paige	LAP W	**CHR**	10			
Smith, Payton	CLIO	**SB**	17	18		
Smith, Randy	AIN	**WR**	69			
Smith, Steve	FEN	**CC**	71			
Smith, Taylor	LIN	**BSK**	15			
Smith, Trevor	LKV	**HKY**	89			
Smith, Wes	MT M	**TEN**	77	78		
Smith, Will	LAP E	**FB**	03			
Smythe, Kelly	FEN	**TEN**	78			
Snedden, Emma	FEN	**SW**	16			
Snider, Kerry	MT M	**FB**	91			
Snitgen, Cliff	HOL	**CC**	99			
Snodsmith, Ryan	HOL	**BSB**	91			
Snyder, Donny	FLU	**BSB**	18			
Snyder, Eric	LIN	**BSB**	87			
Snyder, Evan	FLU	**SW**	15			
Snyder, Terry	AIN	**CC**	81	**TR**	81	
Snyder, Tom	MT M	**FB**	79	**BSB**	80	
Soave, Thomas	BRAN	**GLF**	10			
Sobota, Dan	SW CK	**BSK**	76			
Sochor, Jan	LAP E	**HKY**	97			
Socia, Bert	DUR	**FB**	83			
Sohlden, Dave	LAP	**FB**	69			
Sohlden, Matt	LAP E	**HKY**	84	85	86	
Sohlden, Paul	LAP E	**HKY**	81			
Sohlden, Pete	LAP E	**HKY**	81	82		
Soldon, Kristen	FEN	**TEN**	88			
Somers, Dean	LAP W	**WR**	11	12	13	
Somers, Jennifer	AIN	**CC**	81			
Sondgeroth, Grady	FEN	**FB**	16	17		
Soper, Dave	DUR	**BSB**	82			
Soper, Jeff	FEN	**WR**	78			
Sophiea, Jeff	HOL	**TEN**	13			
Sophiea, Will	HOL	**TEN**	06	07f		
Sorensen, Kevin	HOL	**TEN**	89			
Sorenson, Derek	MT M	**BSK**	94	**BSB**	93	
Sorenson, Luke	CLIO	**BSK**	10			
Sorys, Paul	HOL	**BSB**	01			
Soto, Austin	SW CK	**SCR**	16			

Name	School	Sport						
Souders, Pete	OXF	**SCR**	86	87				
Southwell, Rob	SW CK	**TR**	76					
Sova, Todd	FEN	**BSK**	99					
Spain, Diane	HOL	**TEN**	77					
Spain, Marti	HOL	**TEN**	77					
Spak, Andrew	HOL	**TEN**	14	16	17			
Spangler, Gary	HOL	**TR**	72	73	74			
Spaniola, Nick	DUR	**FB**	88	**TR**	86			
Sparks, Chelse	HOL	**BSK**	08					
Sparks, Jason	LAP E	**BSB**	90					
Sparks, Kelly	LAP E	**TR**	78	79				
Spaulding, Dennis	LAP	**GLF**	71					
Spear, Robin	FEN	**VB**	87					
Spears, Fletcher	CLIO	**FB**	08	**BSB**	09			
Spees, Jason	FEN	**BSB**	91					
Speidel, Ines	LKV	**VB**	79					
Spencer, Alison	HOL	**TEN**	98	99				
Spencer, Jason	LIN	**FB**	94					
Spencer, Kelly	HOL	**BSK**	92	**VB**	92	93	**TR**	91
Spencer, Mike	AIN	**SW**	73					
Spencer, Mike	OXF	**BSK**	00					
Spencer, Mike	FEN	**WR**	95					
Spencer, Roger	LAP E	**GLF**	78					
Spencer, Sue	AIN	**TR**	76					
Spillane, Jim	SW CK	**FB**	68	**BSB**	69			
Spivy, Randy	LAP W	**FB**	85	**BSB**	86	87		
Spooner, Casey	LAP W	**TEN**	08	09				
Sporer, Jon	FEN	**TEN**	94	95				
Sporer, Kara	FEN	**VB**	94					
Spotts, Mike	CAR	**SW**	76					
Sprague, Matt	DUR	**WR**	92					
Sprague-Ross, Alexus	KEAR	**CHR**	18					
Springer, Barb	HOL	**TEN**	92	93				
Springer, Richard	HOL	**TEN**	96	98	99			
Springs, Doug	DUR	**BSB**	83					
Springsteen, Russ	DUR	**WR**	86	87				
Springsteen, Ryan	LAP E	**FB**	08					
Squires, Dennis	FEN	**TEN**	76					
St. Clair, Stacey	HOL	**CC**	06					
St. John, Ron	MT M	**WR**	83					
St.John, Jessica	LIN	**CC**	07					
St.John, Jill	DUR	**TR**	87					
St.John, Ryan	HOL	**SCR**	10					
Stack, Gary	HOL	**GLF**	69					
Stack, Matt	HOL	**CC**	78	79	80	**TR**	80	81	82
Stack, Paul	LIN	**TR**	88					
Stack, Steve	HOL	**TR**	87					
Staffne, Blake	HOL	**TR**	15					

Name	Team	Sport	Year										
Staffne, Ernie	HOL	**FB**	77										
Stahl, Jason	MT M	**FB**	93	**BSB**	93	94							
Stakewicz, Dylan	FLU	**GLF**	18										
Stallcup, Eric	FEN	**BSB**	04										
Stambaugh, Jerry	LAP E	**SCR**	86										
Stanczyk, Devon	FEN	**SB**	85										
Standal, Adam	FEN	**BSB**	05										
Standal, Mike	FEN	**BSB**	09										
Standerfer, Kelly	MT M	**BSB**	97	99									
Stanek, Blair	LAP E	**TEN**	93										
Stangler, Monta	LAP E	**FB**	11										
Stankevich, Chris	FEN	**FB**	83	**HKY**	84								
Stankiewicz, Amy	LAP W	**SB**	92	93									
Stanley, Anne	MT M	**TR**	82										
Stanley, Becky	MT M	**TR**	82										
Stanley, Karen	MT M	**TR**	82	84									
Staple, Kyle	HOL	**FB**	16										
Stark, Jim	CAR	**FB**	73										
Stark, Mandy	FEN	**SW**	04										
Stark, Sam	FEN	**SW**	07										
Starr, Jarrett	LAP E	**FB**	07	**WR**	08								
Starrs, Chris	LIN	**TR**	01										
Starrs, Danielle	LIN	**CC**	10										
Starrs, Tim	LIN	**FB**	10										
Stebbins, Kurt	FEN	**FB**	79										
Stedman, Brittany	BRAN	**BSK**	02										
Stedman, Savannah	BRAN	**BSK**	04	05	06	**VB**	05	06	07	**TR**	05	06	07
Steele, Diane	LAP W	**SB**	94										
Steenson, Amanda	BRAN	**CHR**	06										
Steffey, Kristi	LIN	**SCR**	92										
Stehlin, Christine	HOL	**SCR**	96	97	98								
Steibel, Matt	LIN	**CC**	04	05									
Steiert, Audrey	LIN	**CC**	15	16	**SCR**	17							
Steigerwald, Tabitha	HOL	**TEN**	12										
Stein, Jeff	MT M	**BSK**	90										
Stein, John	OXF	**CC**	98										
Steiner, Jim	FEN	**BSB**	77										
Steinley, Brandon	OWO	**SW**	18										
Stemczynski, Joshua	FLU	**SW**	17	18									
Stephan, Heather	OXF	**SCR**	94										
Stephen, Chad	KEAR	**BWL**	15	16									
Stephens, Carey	MT M	**VB**	89										
Stephens, Jaime	LKV	**SB**	97	98									
Stephens, Kendal	FEN	**TEN**	09	12									
Stephens, Lisa	MT M	**VB**	83	**SB**	82	83							
Stephens, Marquavian	SW CK	**BSK**	14										
Stephenson, Kurt	OXF	**CC**	89	**TR**	91								
Stevens, Brandon	OXF	**HKY**	03										

Stevens, Bryan	HOL	**TEN**	90					
Stevens, Cynthia	HOL	**TEN**	03	04				
Stevens, Gary	HOL	**TEN**	92	94				
Stevens, Matt	HOL	**TEN**	01	02	03			
Stevenson, Kay	FEN	**SB**	83					
Steward, Todd	FEN	**TR**	83					
Stewart, Shawn	CLIO	**TR**	14					
Stiles, Cameron	OXF	**FB**	99	00				
Stiles, Damon	HOL	**GLF**	84					
Stiles, Kayla	FEN	**TR**	14					
Still, Kevin	HOL	**TEN**	91					
Stimac, Curtis	BRAN	**BSB**	16					
Stimson, Mary	LKV	**SB**	86					
Stimson, Steve	LKV	**FB**	95	**BSB**	96			
Stites, Katie	KEAR	**SB**	12					
Stites, Skyler	LIN	**FB**	15	16				
Stocker, Julia	FEN	**CHR**	17					
Stocker, Leon	FLU	**TR**	17	18				
Stockero, Nick	LIN	**FB**	05					
Stockton, Carissa	KEAR	**SW**	13					
Stockton, Taylor	KEAR	**SW**	13	14				
Stoignoff, Bill	OXF	**TR**	91					
Stokes, Josh	LIN	**TR**	09					
Stokes, Rod	DUR	**FB**	85	**TR**	86			
Stoll, Nic	HOL	**BSK**	12					
Stone, Derek	LAP E	**CC**	05					
Stone, Hannah	LAP E	**CC**	03	04	05	**TR**	04	05	06
Stone, Mike	FEN	**FB**	89					
Stone, Rob	AIN	**HKY**	81	**BSB**	81			
Stone, Tedd	HOL	**CC**	82	83	84	**TR**	83	
Stone, Todd	HOL	**CC**	81	82	**TR**	83		
Stone, Zack	LAP E	**BSB**	13	14				
Stone, Zeke	LAP E	**BSB**	12	13				
Stoner, Chuck	HOL	**TEN**	82					
Stoody, Wes	FEN	**CC**	03					
Stoody, Winston	FEN	**CC**	78					
Storrs, Steve	OXF	**WR**	01					
Stout, Josh	HOL	**WR**	08					
Stover, Ray	LAP E	**BSB**	83	84				
Stowers, Ben	BRAN	**SCR**	10	11	**GLF**	12		
Strahle, Amanda	FEN	**TEN**	03					
Strahle, Catherine	FEN	**TEN**	08					
Strahle, Lindsay	FEN	**TEN**	01					
Stransky, Krista	OXF	**BSK**	92					
Stratfold, Katie	BRAN	**CHR**	06					
Stratton, Julie	FEN	**TEN**	94	**SCR**	95			
Strauss, Lisa	OXF	**SCR**	99	00				
Strawser, Terry	FEN	**SW**	07					

Streeter, Adam	KEAR	**BWL**	09	11		
Streetman, Brett	OXF	**FB**	91			
Streit, Pat	OXF	**FB**	03			
Stresen-Reuter, Tina	LAP E	**VB**	84	**SB**	84	
Strickler, Dan	HOL	**WR**	78	79		
Strickler, Eric	LAP E	**FB**	10			
Striggow, Tim	HOL	**TR**	69			
Striler, Brian	SW CK	**WR**	76			
Striler, Dennis	SW CK	**FB**	69			
Strode, Allan	HOL	**FB**	11			
Strom, Art	FEN	**HKY**	78			
Stroope, Karlyn	OXF	**VB**	07f			
Stroub, Kevin	DUR	**BSB**	97			
Struck, Danielle	KEAR	**CHR**	12	13	14	
Stuart, Mike	AIN	**TR**	77			
Studebaker, Kevin	HOL	**FB**	94			
Studer, Brianne	HOL	**TEN**	99	00	01	
Stuk, Aaron	OXF	**TR**	10			
Stumpf, Aaron	FEN	**TEN**	93			
Stumpf, Andy	FEN	**TEN**	93			
Sudberry, Kamara	CLIO	**BSK**	10	11		
Sudika, Joe	LIN	**SCR**	07			
Sugar, Darryl	CAR	**TR**	69			
Sullivan, Brennan	FEN	**SCR**	14	15		
Sullivan, Sean	LAP W	**SCR**	13			
Sullivan, Sebashton	LAP E	**FB**	09			
Summers, Alex	LIN	**BSB**	10			
Summers, Eddie	OXF	**FB**	02	03		
Summers, Liz	HOL	**BSK**	81	**TR**	80	81
Summers, Louisa	FEN	**SB**	85			
Summers, Tim	AIN	**FB**	79	**TR**	80	
Sumpter, Eric	DUR	**BSB**	89	90		
Sundell, Ray	FEN	**BSB**	74			
Sundrla, Trevor	LIN	**GLF**	16			
Supernault, Jon	LAP E	**FB**	90	**TR**	91	
Surtees, Terry	LAP	**FB**	68			
Suslich, Dale	LKV	**TR**	80			
Suszek, Chris	FEN	**FB**	87			
Sutherby, Tim	MT M	**TR**	82			
Sutherland, Jake	BRAN	**BSB**	14			
Sutika, Joe	LIN	**SCR**	05			
Sutika, Zack	LIN	**GLF**	14			
Sutkowi, Rich	FEN	**GLF**	82	83		
Sutphin, Lora	LKV	**TR**	93	94	95	
Sutton, Carrie	LKV	**SB**	77			
Sutton, Jill	LAP W	**TR**	79			
Sutton, Tanya	HOL	**SB**	87	88	89	
Svarc, Darren	DUR	**TR**	90			

Name	Team	Sport	Yr	Yr	Sport2	Yr	Yr	Yr
Svejcara, Heather	LIN	SB	98					
Svetcos, Krista	LAP W	TR	92	93				
Swailes, Marty	LAP E	SCR	86					
Swain, Matt	LAP	FB	69	70	GLF	71		
Swan, Blake	LAP W	FB	08					
Swank, Brian	LKV	TR	95					
Swanson, Kayla	FEN	TR	01	02				
Swanson, Marv	HOL	FB	72					
Sweeney, Julie	LAP W	VB	80					
Sweeney, Pat	LAP	WR	75					
Sweeney, Patricia	LAP	TR	74					
Sweeney, Steve	FEN	TR	07					
Sweet, Jack	LAP	FB	71					
Sweet, Sydney	CLIO	VB	16	17				
Sweetman, Chris	FEN	FB	84	TR	83	84		
Swegles, John	LIN	SCR	97					
Swift, Dan	HOL	TR	78					
Swims, Yolandria	LKV	TR	85	86	87			
Switalski, Dale	MT M	TR	82					
Swix, Brennan	BRAN	SCR	15	16				
Sylva, Jacqui	OXF	VB	07f	TR	05	06	07	08
Sylva, Krysten	OXF	TR	03	04	05			
Szabo, Aaron	SW CK	BSB	10					
Szafranski, Dan	FEN	FB	93	94				
Szczesny, Brandon	LAP W	FB	09					
Szczetka, David	LKV	TR	80					
Szecsodi, Mike	MT M	HKY	95					
Szedlak, Amy	BRAN	SB	12					
Szydlek, Kevin	OXF	GLF	91					
Taft, Mike	CAR	SW	71					
Takacs, Zack	CLIO	BSB	14	15				
Talbot, Linda	CAR	TR	70					
Talbot, Tom	FEN	HKY	80	81				
Taljonick, Ethan	CLIO	CC	14	15				
Tallman, Patty	DUR	VB	80					
Tallsma, Sam	CAR	TEN	76					
Tanner, Rich	DUR	BSB	94	95				
Tarrant, Lindsey	OXF	VB	04					
Tarrence, Dylan	KEAR	WR	15	16	17			
Tartt, Deniko	SW CK	SCR	15					
Tasic, Dean	FEN	SW	07					
Tatarczuk, Tiara	OXF	TR	06	07				
Tatu, Eric	LAP W	HKY	04	05				
Taylor, Brigitte	AIN	VB	82					
Taylor, Chris	FEN	SW	13					
Taylor, David	HOL	TEN	93	94	95	96		
Taylor, David	LAP E	TR	05					
Taylor, Greg	LAP E	FB	81					

Taylor, Greg	OXF	**FB**	90				
Taylor, Hannah	FEN	**VB**	09				
Taylor, Harold	MT M	**BSK**	74	**BSB**	74		
Taylor, Iamani	SW CK	**BSK**	14				
Taylor, Jason	LIN	**HKY**	00				
Taylor, Ken	HOL	**TR**	78	79			
Taylor, Lindsay	CLIO	**CC**	09	10			
Taylor, Mark	SW CK	**BSK**	75				
Taylor, Micah	SW CK	**SCR**	17				
Taylor, Paul	FEN	**SCR**	06				
Taylor, Scott	FEN	**GLF**	91				
Taylor, Steve	AIN	**TR**	79				
Taylor, Steve	HOL	**FB**	92	**BSB**	92	93	
Taylor, Todd	FEN	**BSK**	95	96	**TEN**	95	96
Teague, Kyle	OXF	**BSB**	07	08			
Teed, Madison	KEAR	**CHR**	16				
Teenier, Brandon	HOL	**BSB**	01				
Teffner, Angela	FEN	**SCR**	88				
Temple, Matt	FEN	**TR**	04				
Templeton, Kay	LKV	**TR**	78	79			
Tenbusch, Katie	OXF	**TR**	94				
Tennis, DJ	HOL	**BSB**	16	18			
Terebinski, Eric	LKV	**TR**	77	78			
Terry, Jack	HOL	**TEN**	15	16	17		
Terry, Maya	SW CK	**TR**	72				
Terry, Mike	FEN	**WR**	70				
Terry, Pam	HOL	**TEN**	95	96			
Terry, Scott	HOL	**CC**	96	**TEN**	96	97	98
Tessmer, Lisa	LAP E	**SCR**	94				
Tetlow, April	HOL	**TEN**	18				
Teuber, Andreya	KEAR	**BWL**	09				
Teuber, Andreya	SW CK	**BWL**	10				
Tews, Nolan	BRAN	**SCR**	14	15	16	**TR**	17
Thams, Lindsay	LAP W	**VB**	08				
Thayer, Dick	SW CK	**FB**	72	**BSK**	73		
Thayer, Mike	LAP W	**BSB**	92				
Thayer, Mostyn	LAP	**TEN**	74				
Theis, Jeff	OXF	**WR**	85				
Therriault, Kati	HOL	**VB**	03	04			
Thibault, Jill	FEN	**TEN**	79				
Thibault, John	FEN	**GLF**	81				
Thick, Ed	LAP E	**BSK**	82				
Thick, Gary	LAP	**BSB**	72				
Thomas, Alec	FEN	**FB**	14				
Thomas, Brooke	FLU	**GLF**	14	15			
Thomas, Colleen	LAP W	**TEN**	97				
Thomas, Craig	SW CK	**TR**	71	72	73	74	
Thomas, Damon	FEN	**FB**	12				

Thomas, Dan	LKV	**TR**	80				
Thomas, L.M.	HOL	**BSK**	70	71	**TR**	70	71
Thomas, Matt	BRAN	**SCR**	05				
Thomas, Mike	LAP W	**WR**	98				
Thomas, Scott	LIN	**SCR**	98	99	00		
Thomas, Sheila	FEN	**TR**	71				
Thompson, Amanda	KEAR	**BWL**	13				
Thompson, Danielle	LAP E	**SCR**	90	91			
Thompson, Diane	LKV	**TR**	94				
Thompson, Fred	LKV	**FB**	78				
Thompson, Hailey	HOL	**SB**	17				
Thompson, Jacara	SW CK	**BSK**	15	16	17		
Thompson, Jake	FEN	**HKY**	16				
Thompson, John	FEN	**TEN**	81				
Thompson, Josh	LKV	**WR**	94	95			
Thompson, Justin	LIN	**FB**	05				
Thompson, Keith	FEN	**FB**	83				
Thompson, Kevin	LAP E	**BSB**	14				
Thompson, Michelle	LAP E	**BSK**	86				
Thompson, Reid	FEN	**FB**	16				
Thompson, Sadie	FEN	**CHR**	14				
Thompson, Scott	LIN	**FB**	85	**BSB**	85	86	
Thomsen, Krysta	LKV	**TR**	95	96			
Thorington, Dakota	HOL	**TR**	15				
Thornton, Ben	LIN	**SCR**	12	13	14		
Thornton, Samantha	LIN	**SCR**	11	12	13		
Thornton, Sandy	FEN	**SB**	80				
Thorpe, Taylor	FEN	**CC**	09	11	**TR**	09	
Thorsby, Nicole	CLIO	**CHR**	16				
Thorton, Luke	FEN	**WR**	18				
Threet, Terry	SW CK	**TR**	73				
Thronson, Taras	BRAN	**TR**	13	14			
Thrower, Dave	SW CK	**WR**	72				
Thurlow, Scott	LKV	**BSK**	78				
Thurman, Scott	BRAN	**TEN**	06				
Tiderington, Tony	LIN	**HKY**	92	93	**BSB**	93	
Tiemann, Cambria	FEN	**CC**	15	16	17	**TR**	17
Tiernan, Maggie	FEN	**TR**	01	02	04		
Tiffany, Brent	LAP W	**SCR**	08				
Tigner, Jessica	CLIO	**CHR**	10	11			
Tilley, Megan	OXF	**BSK**	10				
Tilley, Zach	OXF	**TR**	08				
Timm, Hillary	HOL	**SB**	10				
Timm, Zach	KEAR	**BWL**	17				
Timmons, Scott	LAP E	**BSK**	79	80			
Tinsman, Dan	HOL	**FB**	82	**WR**	83		
Tinsman, Randy	HOL	**FB**	79				
Tisdale, J.D.	SW CK	**BSK**	13				

Toaso, Callie	FEN	CC	07				
Tobler, Liz	LAP W	VB	94				
Todd, Dave	LAP W	FB	88				
Todd, Jim	MT M	BSB	98	99			
Tokarski, MaryAnne	FEN	VB	83				
Tokarsky, Mike	FEN	FB	84				
Tolbert, Leo	LAP W	FB	91	92			
Tolbert, Toni	MT M	TR	97	99			
Tomasek, Kelly	LIN	SB	07				
Tomasi, Kyle	LAP W	BSK	05	06			
Tomayko, Mike	HOL	TEN	84				
Tombrella, Nick	OXF	FB	08				
Tomczak, Krystal	FEN	SB	00	01			
Tomczak, Nick	FEN	BSB	99				
Tomczyk, Clayton	LAP E	SCR	10				
Tomczyk, Kristen	LAP E	SCR	08	09			
Tomek, Steve	FEN	FB	74				
Toms, Jenni	HOL	TEN	91	92	93		
Tooley, Adam	HOL	FB	15				
Tooley, Grant	HOL	FB	17				
Toombs, Randy	SW CK	WR	76				
Toonder, Alise	FEN	TEN	81				
Toop, Pat	FEN	SW	73				
Topolewski, Amy	FEN	TR	87	89			
Torabi, Zeinab	FEN	TR	15	16			
Toriumi, Shinobu	FEN	TEN	85				
Torpey, Shannon	HOL	TEN	17				
Torres, Jesse	HOL	WR	12				
Torres, Justin	HOL	WR	97	98	99		
Toth, Brad	FEN	SCR	91				
Tottingham, Tim	LIN	CC	92	93	94	TR	94
Tougas, Jay	LAP W	HKY	01	02			
Tousley, Dan	FEN	FB	10	TR	09		
Toward, Sam	BRAN	TR	13	14			
Towner, Mary	FEN	SB	74	75			
Tran, Steve	SW CK	TR	14				
Trantham, Steve	HOL	BSB	73				
Trebtoske, Justin	SW CK	HKY	11	13			
Trecha, Steve	SW CK	TR	76				
Trecha, Thomas	OWO	BWL	18				
Treponier, Janis	SW CK	TR	72				
Treponier, Sally	SW CK	TR	72				
Trevis, Kylie	OXF	CHR	08				
Trigger, Erik	SW CK	BWL	12	15			
Trigger, Matt	SW CK	BWL	11	12			
Trim, Denise	MT M	VB	81				
Trimmer, Andrea	HOL	TEN	00				
Triplett, Chris	FLU	FB	14	BSK	15		

Triplett, Jennifer	CLIO	**CHR**	08	09			
Tripp, Mark	LAP E	**BSB**	78				
Tromble, Nicole	LAP W	**TR**	98				
Truchan, Scott	HOL	**SCR**	95				
Trujillo, Mario	FEN	**FB**	08				
Truran, Tiffany	FEN	**SB**	98				
Truscott, Brent	LAP W	**TR**	97				
Trussell, Paul	CAR	**FB**	72	73			
Tschirhart, Jenny	HOL	**TR**	99	00			
Tschirhart, Samantha	HOL	**TR**	15				
Tuck, Jan	AIN	**SB**	72				
Tucker, Brian	FEN	**BSK**	89				
Tucker, Dan	AIN	**BSB**	72				
Tucker, Emily	BRAN	**SB**	16				
Tucker, Greg	SW CK	**WR**	71	72	73	74	
Tucker, Randy	SW CK	**WR**	74	75	76		
Tucker, Rick	MT M	**FB**	76				
Tucker, Tim	MT M	**TR**	73				
Tunison, Kevin	LAP E	**TR**	04				
Turcott, Neil	LKV	**HKY**	85				
Turcotte, Dan	LKV	**HKY**	87				
Turcsak, Joe	BRAN	**BSK**	04				
Turczyn, Caycee	LAP W	**GLF**	11	13			
Turczyn, Cullen	LAP W	**BSK**	12	13	**GLF**	13	
Turczyn, Keely	LAP E	**GLF**	08	09	10		
Turk, Eric	OXF	**BSB**	07				
Turkovics, Brian	LKV	**WR**	84				
Turkowski, Heather	FEN	**SB**	97				
Turnbull, Ron	SW CK	**BSB**	72				
Turner, Chris	HOL	**WR**	02	03			
Turner, Jacob	BRAN	**BWL**	18				
Turner, Joe	LIN	**WR**	06	07			
Turner, Matt	HOL	**WR**	02	03	04		
Turner, Mike	HOL	**WR**	94	96	97		
Turner, Shelby	CLIO	**CHR**	15				
Turner, Sue	HOL	**SB**	96				
Turnipseed, Breyanna	LIN	**VB**	15	**TR**	15		
Turonek, Missy	LAP E	**BSK**	04	05			
Turonek, Scott	LAP E	**BSK**	02				
Turrentine, Brent	HOL	**TEN**	94				
Turrentine, Justin	HOL	**TEN**	93	94	95		
Tuttle, Jordan	FLU	**TR**	17				
Tweedie, Jarrett	FEN	**TR**	88	89			
Twite, Jen	LAP E	**VB**	01				
Twite, Taylor	LAP E	**VB**	00	01	**TR**	01	
Tyler, Alan	DUR	**CC**	87	88	**WR**	89	
Tyler, Buzz	HOL	**FB**	69	70	**TR**	70	71
Tyler, Jessica	HOL	**TEN**	96	98			

Tyler, Tiffany	MT M	**CC**	00						
Tyler, Tony	AIN	**CC**	83						
Tysick, Emily	LAP E	**TR**	06	09					
Uebel, Pat	FEN	**TR**	76						
Uhlmeyer, Mike	AIN	**HKY**	83						
Underwood, Kim	FEN	**TR**	89						
Upadhyay, Sanjiv	FEN	**TEN**	82	83					
Upadhyay, Suman	FEN	**TEN**	85						
Upadhyay, Sunil	FEN	**TEN**	82						
Upleger, Emma	FLU	**CC**	16						
Upshur, Mike	OXF	**WR**	06						
Upthegrove, Dave	LKV	**TR**	87	88					
Urban, Brittany	FEN	**SW**	05	06	07				
Urban, Doug	FEN	**BSB**	80						
Urban, Jenny	LKV	**CC**	95	**TR**	95				
Urcheck, Micheal	LAP E	**SCR**	98	99					
Ureche, Tom	SW CK	**BSB**	71						
Uribe, Jason	FEN	**SCR**	08	09					
Utica, Bill	MT M	**BSB**	80						
Utley, Nick	LAP W	**FB**	00						
Utley, Tom	LAP	**CC**	72	**TR**	72				
Vadovich, Paul	LIN	**CC**	00						
Vadovich, Scott	AIN	**CC**	79						
Valentine, Julie	LAP W	**SCR**	96	97	98	99			
Vallad, Scott	OXF	**FB**	86						
Valley, Bruce	LAP W	**GLF**	76						
Valley, Gale	LAP W	**VB**	77	**BSK**	75	76	**SB**	77	
Van Auken, Mike	FEN	**WR**	77	78	79				
Vana, Charlie	HOL	**GLF**	06	09					
VanAllen, Terry	LAP E	**FB**	81						
VanAlst, Mike	CLIO	**BSB**	08						
VanAtten, Ashley	OXF	**CHR**	06	07					
VanCura, Sally	LAP E	**SB**	83						
VanDam, Jay	OXF	**BSB**	98						
Vandecar, Myron	LAP W	**WR**	04	05					
Vandell, Kyle	HOL	**FB**	12						
Vanden Bossche, Eric	BRAN	**WR**	11	12					
Vanderlaan, Chad	LIN	**FB**	96						
VanDrese, Janice	AIN	**SB**	86						
VanFleet, Stacey	CLIO	**SB**	09						
VanGilder, Garrett	HOL	**TEN**	15	16	17				
VanGoethem, John	LIN	**BSB**	90						
VanGorp, Kary	HOL	**CC**	81	**TR**	83				
VanGuilder, Roz	OXF	**BSK**	85	86					
VanHorne, Marit	DUR	**TEN**	88						
VanLoon, Josh	CLIO	**BSB**	16						
VanMach, Karen	FEN	**TEN**	78						
VanOertzen, Mortiz	FEN	**TEN**	91						

VanOoteghem, Amanda	KEAR	**CHR**	18				
VanRiper, Becky	DUR	**TEN**	78				
VanSeggern, Ruth	FEN	**TR**	75				
VanSlambrouck, Nick	DUR	**WR**	86	87			
VanWagoner, Chris	LAP W	**BSB**	01				
VanWagoner, Randy	FEN	**GLF**	83	84	85		
Vanwagoner, Ron	KEAR	**HKY**	09	**BSB**	09		
VanWallagher, Brandon	HOL	**TEN**	07f	08			
VanWormrr, Garry	CAR	**BSK**	76				
Varacalli, Mikey	LIN	**CC**	14				
Varner, Brandon	SW CK	**TR**	18				
Varner, Karrah	LIN	**CC**	09				
Varner, Molly	FEN	**BSK**	10				
Varney, Joe	FEN	**WR**	71	72			
Vasha, Briselda	OXF	**CHR**	10				
Vaughn, Derek	HOL	**BSB**	99				
Vaughn, Greg	LAP W	**FB**	95				
Vaughn, Ryan	SW CK	**GLF**	09				
Veatch, Adam	LIN	**FB**	01				
Veenhuis, Brock	SW CK	**HKY**	08	**GLF**	06		
Veenhuis, Jacob	SW CK	**HKY**	11				
Vela, Jose	OXF	**FB**	06				
Venner, Kaila	CLIO	**SCR**	13				
Vergith, Aaron	HOL	**TEN**	12	13	14		
Vergith, Evan	HOL	**TEN**	15				
Vergith, Ian	HOL	**TEN**	06	07			
Verhelle, Chris	FEN	**WR**	81	82			
Verhelle, Greg	FEN	**FB**	79				
Verhelle, Pat	FEN	**FB**	70				
VerPlanck, Gregg	LAP E	**FB**	77	**WR**	78		
Verran, Jessica	SW CK	**SB**	18				
Verran, John	HOL	**CC**	06				
Vessell, Brian	MT M	**BSB**	95	96			
Vibbert, Mark	OXF	**SCR**	86	88	**TR**	88	89
Videla, Dan	FEN	**TEN**	87				
Videla, Gabe	FEN	**TEN**	86	88			
Vierk, Colleen	LAP E	**VB**	07f				
Vierk, Jenna	LAP E	**VB**	10	11			
Viik, Erik	HOL	**SCR**	90	91	92		
Villarreal, Ray	HOL	**WR**	73				
Villereal, Nate	LAP E	**FB**	04				
Vincent, Chelsey	FEN	**SCR**	06				
Vincent, Tim	FEN	**FB**	69				
Vincent, Vanessa	HOL	**VB**	00	01			
Violassi, Amanda	BRAN	**SW**	14				
Violassi, Rachael	BRAN	**SW**	12	13	14		
Vivanco, Dino	HOL	**TR**	15				
Viviano, Joe	LAP W	**FB**	03				

Name	Team	Sport	Yr	Yr		Yr		Yr	Yr
Voelpel, Nick	LAP W	**TR**	97	98					
Voelpol, John	LAP W	**TR**	97	98					
Voight, Jason	KEAR	**SW**	11						
Volek, Jim	LAP W	**FB**	84						
Voller, Tyler	LIN	**TR**	12						
Voller, Zac	LIN	**FB**	09						
Vollmar, Jack	KEAR	**GLF**	16	17	18				
Volz, Mike	HOL	**BSK**	80						
VonFintel, Chelsea	LIN	**SCR**	07						
VonKnorring, Kris	OXF	**BSB**	01						
Voss, Rehne	LAP W	**VB**	92	93					
Voyer, Kelsey	BRAN	**LAX**	17						
Wabel, Hannah	LIN	**CC**	17						
Wachowski, Joel	HOL	**TR**	96						
Waddell, Stephanie	SW CK	**BWL**	16						
Wade, Chris	LIN	**FB**	04	05					
Wade, Mike	FEN	**TR**	84						
Wagner, Chloe	FEN	**SCR**	18						
Wagner, Cylee	BRAN	**TEN**	08						
Wagner, Hannah	LAP W	**VB**	13						
Wagner, Kevin	LAP E	**CC**	79	80	**TR**	81			
Wagner, Rhonda	LKV	**TR**	95	96					
Wagoner, Shawn	FEN	**SCR**	91	92	93	94	**BSB**	93	95
Wainio, Alexys	FLU	**LAX**	16						
Waite, Krista	FEN	**TR**	73						
Waite, Peggy	DUR	**TR**	94						
Waiters, Harrison	FLU	**WR**	15						
Wakefield, Nate	MT M	**GLF**	96	**HKY**	96				
Wakefield, Ryan	MT M	**HKY**	93	94					
Walden, Karen	MT M	**BSK**	77						
Walker, Andrea	LAP W	**TEN**	80						
Walker, Ann	LAP W	**TEN**	82						
Walker, Blaine	FEN	**TEN**	94						
Walker, Doug	LAP W	**FB**	81						
Walker, Jennifer	OXF	**TR**	88						
Walker, Jenny	LAP W	**TEN**	79	80					
Walker, Jim	OXF	**FB**	93						
Walker, Julie	LAP W	**VB**	84	85					
Walker, Logan	FLU	**BSB**	18						
Walker, Mike	FEN	**CC**	01	02	03				
Walker, Randy	FEN	**SW**	76						
Walker, Sanaii	KEAR	**TR**	18						
Walker, Steven	OXF	**SCR**	08						
Wallace, Kent	AIN	**HKY**	82						
Wallace, Kraig	AIN	**HKY**	80	81					
Wallace, Sheryl	AIN	**TR**	73						
Wallace, Tony	AIN	**FB**	77						
Waller, Greg	HOL	**WR**	85						

Waller, Shaunte	OXF	**TR**	08					
Walls, Elizabeth	BRAN	**SB**	14	15				
Walls, Matt	DUR	**TR**	83					
Walls, Tyler	BRAN	**SW**	06	07				
Walrath, Ken	LKV	**WR**	85					
Walrath, Kirk	LKV	**WR**	86	89				
Walraven, Jon	KEAR	**GLF**	09	10				
Walsh, Erin	FEN	**CC**	98	99	00	01	**TR**	99
Walsh, Marshall	FEN	**BSK**	09					
Walsh, McKenzie	BRAN	**TEN**	09					
Walsh, Tom	HOL	**SW**	10					
Walt, Dave	AIN	**WR**	85	86				
Walt, Jeff	AIN	**WR**	78	79				
Walt, Rick	AIN	**WR**	83	84	85			
Walter, Nolan	OXF	**CC**	01	02				
Walterhouse, Ed	LIN	**FB**	11	12				
Walterhouse, George	LIN	**FB**	17					
Walterhouse, Grace	LIN	**SCR**	14					
Walters, Barb	FEN	**TR**	79					
Walters, Lynn	FEN	**TR**	79	80				
Walters, Steve	HOL	**GLF**	74					
Walz, Allison	HOL	**BWL**	10					
Walz, Mackenzie	HOL	**BWL**	11					
Warby, Darwin	LKV	**FB**	76					
Ward, Jim	FEN	**CC**	71	72				
Ward, Karen	SW CK	**TR**	71					
Ward, Keith	LIN	**WR**	92					
Ward, Ken	AIN	**FB**	70					
Ward, Megan	KEAR	**CHR**	11					
Ward, Missy	LIN	**GLF**	02	03	04			
Ward, Ryan	HOL	**TEN**	97	98	99	00		
Ward, Tom	FEN	**CC**	73					
Wardell, Thor	BRAN	**WR**	14					
Wardin, Kate	FEN	**CHR**	08					
Wardlaw, Cory	LAP E	**TR**	92	93				
Ware, Howard	MT M	**BSK**	77					
Ware, Margery	MT M	**BSK**	83	84	**TR**	84		
Ware, Monta	MT M	**BSK**	77	78				
Warford, Jessica	FEN	**VB**	15	16				
Warner, Amy	LIN	**VB**	87	88	**TR**	86	87	88
Warner, Chris	FEN	**TEN**	78					
Warner, Denny	DUR	**WR**	83					
Warner, Jeanette	LIN	**TR**	02					
Warner, Jeff	LIN	**FB**	88					
Warner, Ken	DUR	**TR**	84					
Warner, Sara	LIN	**TR**	89					
Warner, Steve	LAP E	**FB**	84	85				
Warner, Steve	LIN	**TR**	02	03	04			

Warner, Zac	LIN	**WR**	05	**TR**	04	06	
Warren, Christie	LIN	**SCR**	96	97	98		
Warren, Jamie	FEN	**TEN**	85				
Warren, Rachel	LIN	**TR**	03				
Warren, Scott	LAP	**GLF**	71f				
Wascha, Aaron	SW CK	**TR**	10				
Wash, Marshall	FEN	**FB**	08				
Wasylyna, Zac	OXF	**SCR**	04	05	06		
Wasylyshyn, Tara	LIN	**TR**	09				
Waterson, Dave	FEN	**TEN**	87				
Watkins, Alicia	HOL	**TR**	99	00	01		
Watkins, Greg	LAP E	**TEN**	92				
Watkins, Tim	LAP W	**BSK**	83				
Watkins, Tracy	LKV	**TR**	78				
Wax, David	LIN	**FB**	05				
Waybrandt, Lauhnna	BRAN	**BSK**	03				
Wayne, Marco	BRAN	**BWL**	10				
Weatherwax, Bryan	LKV	**GLF**	00	01			
Weaver, Savannah	LIN	**SB**	13				
Webb, Mike	DUR	**FB**	86				
Webb, Nick	SW CK	**HKY**	11				
Webb, Nicole	DUR	**SB**	97				
Webber, Lindsey	SW CK	**CHR**	15				
Webber, Steve	BRAN	**TR**	07				
Weber, Chris	LAP E	**TR**	01				
Weber, Cindy	FEN	**SB**	81	82	83		
Weber, Dale	HOL	**FB**	83				
Weber, Duane	FEN	**FB**	85	**BSB**	85	86	
Weber, Lauren	FEN	**SB**	01				
Weber, Mark	SW CK	**BSB**	71	72			
Weber, Susan	FEN	**VB**	87				
Weber, Tami	CLIO	**SB**	11				
Webster, Anton	KEAR	**TR**	15				
Webster, Janet	MT M	**SB**	93	94			
Webster, Kelly	HOL	**TEN**	02				
Wedding, James	BRAN	**HKY**	09				
Wede, Jan	AIN	**GLF**	80	**HKY**	81		
Wedel, Jamie	FEN	**BSB**	87				
Wedel, Kim	FEN	**FB**	90				
Wedel, Matt	FEN	**FB**	85				
Weeks, Lauren	LAP W	**SCR**	10	11			
Wegener, Mark	DUR	**FB**	82				
Wehnlig, Eike	LAP E	**TEN**	86				
Weier, Chris	OXF	**FB**	89				
Weiler, Kevin	SW CK	**FB**	13	**TR**	12	13	14
Weinberg, Zoe	FEN	**SW**	14				
Weine, Matt	KEAR	**FB**	13	**TR**	13	14	
Weingartz, Haley	LAP E	**SCR**	07				

Name	School	Sport					
Weingartz, Jake	LAP E	**FB**	01	02			
Weinman, Evan	LAP W	**FB**	04	**TR**	05		
Weir, Bill	CAR	**SW**	71	72			
Weir, Brandon	LIN	**HKY**	03				
Weirenga, Cayla	LIN	**SB**	16				
Weisdorfer, Brian	HOL	**CC**	91	**TR**	92		
Weisdorfer, Jennifer	HOL	**CC**	89	90			
Weisdorfer, Matt	OXF	**CC**	86	87	88	**TR**	88	89
Weishun, Keith	AIN	**WR**	77				
Weiss, Dominick	FEN	**FB**	14				
Weiss, Hailey	HOL	**TEN**	11				
Weiss, Michelle	FEN	**TR**	73	74			
Welby, Abbie	LAP W	**SB**	01				
Welch, Eric	OXF	**TR**	89	90	91		
Welch, Evan	FEN	**FB**	13	14			
Welch, Jon	LAP W	**WR**	89	90			
Welch, Lynn	FEN	**WR**	72				
Welch, Mark	FEN	**WR**	70				
Welch, Mike	HOL	**TEN**	89				
Welch, Nadeen	HOL	**TEN**	82				
Welch, Tom	LAP W	**GLF**	86	**WR**	86	87	
Welker, Dave	FEN	**FB**	76				
Welker, Julie	FEN	**SB**	97				
Weller, Jack	SW CK	**GLF**	11	13	14		
Weller, Matt	LIN	**SCR**	05				
Welling, Brandon	LAP W	**FB**	12				
Welling, David	LAP E	**SCR**	06				
Wellington, Jamie	OXF	**CC**	90	**TR**	91		
Wells, Dan	LKV	**BSB**	93				
Wells, Jeremiah	LAP W	**SCR**	95	96			
Wells, Jole	LAP W	**SCR**	97	99			
Wells, Matt	DUR	**GLF**	82				
Wells, Tyler	FEN	**TR**	09				
Welter, Jayson	OXF	**CC**	94				
Wendling, Sarah	FLU	**VB**	14				
Wendt, Dave	OXF	**BSK**	05				
Wengren, Chelsea	BRAN	**SB**	05	06	07		
Wensel, Brad	FEN	**HKY**	87				
Wenta, Bob	FEN	**FB**	73				
Wenta, Claudia	BRAN	**TEN**	10				
Wentworth, Chuck	CAR	**FB**	72				
Wenzlick, Pat	CAR	**WR**	72				
Wesolowski, Luke	CLIO	**TR**	14				
West, Karen	MT M	**TEN**	88				
West, Randy	LKV	**TR**	85				
West, Zach	FEN	**TR**	16	17			
Westfall, Shannon	HOL	**CC**	11	12			
Weston, Colleen	LIN	**VB**	83				

Name	School	Sport	Yr	Yr	Sport	Yr	Yr	Sport	Yr	Yr
Westphal, Traci	LAP W	BSK	83							
Weycker, Nick	CLIO	BWL	11							
Weygandt, Ron	AIN	TR	69	70	BSK	70				
Whalen, Jordy	MT M	HKY	78							
Whaley, Gary	SW CK	FB	69		WR	69	70			
Whaley, Mark	SW CK	WR	72	73	74					
Whaley, Tim	CAR	BSB	76							
Whatcott, Zackery	LAP E	TR	12							
Wheat, Emily	KEAR	SCR	09							
Wheat, Mike	FEN	TR	78							
Wheatley, Becki	FEN	BSK	94	95	VB	95	96	SB	94	96
Wheatley, Clayton	FEN	TR	99							
Wheeler, Brandon	KEAR	BWL	17							
Whetham, Brittany	HOL	SW	05	06						
White, Carryn	KEAR	GLF	14							
White, Christy	LIN	SCR	95	96	97					
White, Chuck	LAP W	TR	79							
White, Darryl	LAP W	BSB	87							
White, Emily	CLIO	CHR	06							
White, Jake	SW CK	SW	08	09						
White, Jenny	OXF	BSK	95	97						
White, Joe	OXF	FB	00							
White, Jordan	LAP W	CHR	13							
White, Kenny	OXF	CC	02	03	04					
White, Margaret	LAP W	TR	79							
White, Morgan	LIN	CHR	15		LAX	16				
White, Taylor	LAP W	CHR	13	14						
Whitefoot, Danielle	HOL	CC	08		TR	08				
Whitehead, Rodney	MT M	FB	82							
Whiteman, Brandi	HOL	TR	06							
Whiting, Tom	MT M	GLF	93							
Whitkopf, Taylor	BRAN	SW	17							
Whitney, Erin	LAP E	SB	92							
Whitt, Pat	FEN	SB	77							
Whittaker, Bruce	FEN	FB	84							
Whitten, Dan	AIN	HKY	86							
Wichman, Jerry	OXF	FB	03							
Wickstrom, Kevin	LAP	FB	69							
Widzinski, Phil	LAP E	FB	02		BSK	03				
Wiechert, Mark	HOL	FB	77							
Wielichowski, Kaitlyn	FEN	TR	04							
Wielichowski, Tommy	FEN	CC	01	02	TR	03				
Wiesen, Mark	FEN	FB	71		WR	71	72			
Wigard, Don	LKV	FB	77							
Wightman, Callie	KEAR	SB	12							
Wilbur, Gwen	AIN	TR	78							
Wilcox, Lance	LAP E	FB	92							
Wilcox, Monte	DUR	WR	80							

Wildfong, Travis	KEAR	**WR**	15							
Wildin, Dan	OXF	**CC**	98							
Wiley, Mark	HOL	**GLF**	75	**HKY**	75	76	77			
Wilkins, Zak	FLU	**SW**	15	16						
Wilkinson, Melissa	LAP W	**SB**	03	04						
Wilkowski, Jessica	FEN	**SW**	08	09						
Wilkowski, Katie	LIN	**SCR**	13	14	15	16				
Willett, Scott	FEN	**WR**	84							
Williams, Aaron	LIN	**CC**	90	91	**TR**	92				
Williams, Alice	LAP E	**BSK**	87	**SCR**	88					
Williams, Brent	FEN	**FB**	74							
Williams, Brian	LIN	**CC**	93	94						
Williams, Bruce	AIN	**CC**	81	82						
Williams, Cottrell	HOL	**TR**	69	70	71					
Williams, Dennis	SW CK	**SW**	73							
Williams, Eric	MT M	**WR**	96	97						
Williams, Gary	FEN	**WR**	90	91						
Williams, John	HOL	**FB**	11	12	**TR**	10	11	12	13	
Williams, Josh	BRAN	**FB**	07	**GLF**	05	**TR**	07			
Williams, Kane	CLIO	**FB**	14	**WR**	15	16				
Williams, Kelly	FEN	**VB**	85	86						
Williams, Kevin	HOL	**TR**	82	83						
Williams, Kristen	BRAN	**TR**	07							
Williams, Mark	FEN	**TEN**	78							
Williams, Mike	SW CK	**FB**	75							
Williams, Myranda	KEAR	**SB**	13	14						
Williams, Russ	MT M	**BSB**	80							
Williams, Scott	FEN	**FB**	98							
Williams, Scott	FEN	**TEN**	91							
Williams, Sue	AIN	**BSK**	76	77	78	**VB**	78	79	**SB**	77	78
Williams, Tammy	HOL	**SB**	88							
Williams, Terry	HOL	**SB**	88							
Williams, Todd	FEN	**GLF**	72							
Williamson, Greg	CAR	**FB**	68							
Williamson, Jenny	DUR	**SB**	96							
Williamson, Laken	OWO	**BWL**	18							
Williamson, Phil	DUR	**FB**	82							
Willing, Denise	AIN	**TR**	78							
Willis, Tyler	LAP W	**FB**	13							
Willoughby, Tara	LIN	**VB**	91	92						
Wills, Crissy	LAP W	**CHR**	08	09	10					
Wills, Kevin	CAR	**BSB**	76							
Wills, Steve	LAP W	**BSB**	96							
Wilmers, Steve	LAP E	**TEN**	07f	**BSK**	07	08				
Wilson, Amie	LIN	**TR**	05							
Wilson, Carissa	LIN	**SCR**	03	04	05					
Wilson, Chris	HOL	**TR**	85							
Wilson, Courtney	LIN	**SCR**	01	02						

Name	School	Sport	Year			
Wilson, Eric	LAP E	**TR**	97			
Wilson, Geoff	HOL	**CC**	73	**TR**	74	
Wilson, Jenny	LAP W	**VB**	96			
Wilson, Jeremy	MT M	**GLF**	92			
Wilson, Kelly	BRAN	**CC**	05	**TR**	05	06
Wilson, Kevin	HOL	**TEN**	08	09		
Wilson, Leigh	HOL	**TEN**	95			
Wilson, Leigh	HOL	**TEN**	94			
Wilson, Matt	BRAN	**HKY**	16			
Wilson, Reagan	FEN	**CHR**	18			
Wilson, Rhonda	LAP E	**VB**	81			
Wilson, Ryan	LIN	**BSB**	01			
Wilson, Sarah	LKV	**TR**	95			
Wilson, Steve	HOL	**TEN**	02	03	04	05
Wilson, Terence	OXF	**FB**	92	**TR**	92	93
Wilson, Tim	CAR	**FB**	69			
Wilson, Verlynda	MT M	**BSK**	85	**TR**	83	84	85
Wilson, Victoria	LIN	**TR**	98			
Winchester, Nick	MT M	**WR**	96	97		
Wingate, Renita	HOL	**TR**	09			
Wingblad, Ben	FEN	**GLF**	90			
Winglemire, John	HOL	**FB**	71			
Winiarski, Nick	FLU	**SCR**	14	**GLF**	15	
Winohradsky, Andy	HOL	**WR**	91			
Winohradsky, Dan	HOL	**WR**	91	92	93	
Winohradsky, Ellen	HOL	**TEN**	93	94	96	
Winter, Michele	LAP W	**SB**	91	92		
Winterlee, Melissa	MT M	**VB**	86			
Winterlee, Scott	MT M	**FB**	88	**BSK**	89	**BSB**	88	89
Winterlee, Stephanie	MT M	**VB**	88			
Winters, Bill	HOL	**CC**	86			
Wirostek, Ramona	CAR	**TR**	74	75		
Wiskur, Brian	CLIO	**BSB**	18			
Wiskur, Colton	CLIO	**BSB**	16	18		
Wiswell, Macy	FEN	**SW**	09			
Withers, Madeline	FEN	**LAX**	16			
Witt, Monica	CLIO	**SCR**	08			
Witt, Stacy	DUR	**CC**	96	**SCR**	96	97
Witte, Ted	HOL	**FB**	68	**TR**	69	
Wohlfert, Chris	FEN	**FB**	86	**BSB**	88	
Wohlfert, Dave	FEN	**FB**	83	**WR**	81	
Wohlford, Don	AIN	**FB**	68			
Wojcicki, Mike	LAP W	**FB**	92	**TEN**	91	
Wojciechowski, Matt	LAP W	**WR**	06			
Wojkowicz, Jaclyn	BRAN	**SB**	05			
Wolanin, Kate	OXF	**TR**	07	08	09	10
Wolbert, Dale	SW CK	**FB**	74			
Wolf, Don	FEN	**SW**	74	75	76	

Wolfe, Spencer	HOL	**TEN**	89	90	
Wolfgram, Ron	FEN	**FB**	94		
Wolford, Tim	HOL	**FB**	82		
Wolosiewicz, Adam	OXF	**SCR**	95	96	
Woloszyk, Paul	LAP E	**BSB**	09		
Woloszyk, Stacy	BRAN	**GLF**	08		
Wonch, Jeff	LAP E	**HKY**	77		
Wong, Alden	LAP W	**TEN**	92		
Wood, Amber	CLIO	**VB**	06		
Wood, Debbie	LAP E	**SB**	82		
Wood, Jeff	FEN	**HKY**	83		
Wood, Mike	LIN	**HKY**	83		
Wood, Mitch	MT M	**CC**	00		
Woodbury, Tammy	LIN	**CC**	84		
Woodcum, Sierra	LAP E	**GLF**	13		
Woodruff, Kyle	HOL	**BSK**	14	16	
Woods, Kody	LAP W	**FB**	08		
Woods, Michelle	OXF	**TR**	83		
Woomer, Samm	LAP E	**BSK**	06		
Woonton, Allison	OXF	**SW**	07	08	
Worden, Kyle	BRAN	**TR**	05		
Worden, Spencer	LAP E	**SCR**	12		
Workman, Briane	LAP W	**VB**	96	97	
Workman, Cathy	LAP W	**VB**	89	90	
Workman, Robin	LAP W	**VB**	87		
Worthing, Amy	LAP W	**SCR**	88	90	
Worthing, Arden	CLIO	**SCR**	12		
Worthing, Matt	LAP W	**SCR**	92		
Woycik, Scott	LAP E	**GLF**	89	90	91
Wray, Jenni	OXF	**TR**	02		
Wright, Courtney	BRAN	**SB**	03		
Wright, Dennis	LIN	**HKY**	89		
Wright, Heidi	HOL	**TR**	85		
Wright, Kevin	LIN	**SCR**	12	13	14
Wright, Luke	LIN	**HKY**	96	98	
Wright, Tevin	BRAN	**SW**	12		
Wright, Tom	FEN	**WR**	75		
Wright, Tyson	LIN	**HKY**	95		
Wujciak, Anna	FEN	**SW**	09		
Wujciak, Sara	FEN	**SW**	10	11	
Wunderlich, Jeannie	CAR	**TR**	71		
Wurtz, Gary	OXF	**FB**	09		
Wurtz, Phil	OXF	**TR**	84		
Wyatt, Tom	LAP W	**TR**	94		
Wycoff, Jenny	HOL	**CC**	87		
Wykes, Cal	SW CK	**BWL**	13	14	
Xiong, Ashley	HOL	**BSK**	11		
Yancho, Samantha	FLU	**VB**	15	16	

Name	Team	Sport				
Yeacker, Ben	BRAN	**TEN**	14			
Yee, Courtney	HOL	**TEN**	02	03	04	05
Yelle, Kenny	LAP W	**FB**	95			
Yelle, Matt	LAP W	**FB**	01	**BSB**	02	
Yelle, Nicole	LAP W	**SB**	90	91	92	
Yi, Chol	HOL	**TEN**	80	82		
Yobuck, Steve	HOL	**WR**	85	86	87	
Yonchow, Ron	CAR	**TR**	75			
Yoon, Aaron	SW CK	**TR**	10			
York, Chris	FEN	**FB**	16			
York, Don	FEN	**TR**	78			
York, Julien	FLU	**TR**	16	17		
York, Ryan	FEN	**BSB**	98			
Yott, Todd	MT M	**GLF**	76			
Youmans, Shance	HOL	**TEN**	95	96	97	
Younes, Alicia	BRAN	**CHR**	16			
Young, Brian	DUR	**GLF**	87	88	90	
Young, Carrie	LKV	**TR**	93	94	95	
Young, Claire	HOL	**TEN**	13			
Young, Deitrick	KEAR	**TR**	15			
Young, Jason	BRAN	**BSB**	18			
Young, Jeff	FEN	**FB**	76			
Young, Joe	FEN	**FB**	85			
Young, Karlee	FEN	**TEN**	06			
Young, Kristina	KEAR	**SB**	09			
Young, Paul	LAP W	**FB**	05			
Young, Ryan	LIN	**FB**	14	15	**TR**	15
Young, Scott	DUR	**FB**	83			
Young, Scott	FEN	**TEN**	80	81		
Young, Wendy	HOL	**TR**	83			
Younger, Darrion	KEAR	**BSK**	17	**TR**	15	
Younkin, Cal	FLU	**SCR**	14			
Yurk, Jeff	FEN	**TEN**	91			
Zacharias, Bill	CAR	**FB**	70			
Zamarripa, Rachel	FEN	**TEN**	95			
Zamora, Tim	AIN	**FB**	75			
Zauel, Adrienne	HOL	**CC**	86			
Zauel, Mark	HOL	**CC**	83	84	85	
Zayan, Maddie	LIN	**SCR**	15	16	17	
Zayler, Ken	LKV	**TR**	84	85		
Zayti, Ashley	HOL	**VB**	02			
Zdunic, Katie	DUR	**TR**	94			
Zeek, Jordan	CLIO	**GLF**	06			
Zeeman, Andy	LAP E	**FB**	90	**BSB**	91	
Zeeman, Jenny	LAP E	**BSK**	02	**SCR**	03	
Zeeman, Matt	LAP E	**FB**	03	04	**BSK**	04	05
Zeeman, Tim	SW CK	**BSK**	74	75	**BSB**	74
Zeffero, Bob	FEN	**TEN**	79	80		

Zemore, Jason	FLU	SW	16			
Zepeda, Lauren	FEN	VB	08	09	10	
Zerbal, Stacey	HOL	TR	85			
Zerka, Alicia	SW CK	SCR	12			
Ziccardi, Tyler	LIN	SCR	14	15	GLF	15
Zieske, Skyler	LIN	TR	18			
Zile, Justin	HOL	GLF	08			
Zimmerman, Luke	LIN	WR	15			
Zimmerman, Mike	BRAN	CC	10			
Zimmerman, Miranda	BRAN	SB	13	14		
Ziobro, Jim	CLIO	BSB	13	14	15	
Zmikly, John	OXF	CC	00	01		
Zorn, Jake	HOL	TR	13			
Zubrick, Jason	MT M	TR	98			
Zurbrick, Jason	OXF	FB	97			
Zyber, Ben	SW CK	GLF	11	12	13	14
Zyber, Eric	SW CK	HKY	07			
Zyber, Haylee	SW CK	GLF	08	09	10	11

ACKNOWLEDGEMENTS

Compiling 50 years of an athletic conference's history takes a lot of contributions. Among those who have had a hand in developing this record of the Flint Metro League are:

Greg Tunnicliff, journalist
Flint Metro League athletic directors during the 50th year: Chris Deines (Brandon), John Darga (Clio), Mike Bakker (Fenton), Kevin Foltz (Flushing), Deb VanKuiken (Holly), Paul Gaudard (Kearsley), Greg Durkac (Linden), Dr. Dallas Lintner (Owosso), Sue Calvo (Swartz Creek)
Cathy North, current Metro League executive director
Administrative assistants Carol Dolata (Linden), Sharon Michal (Brandon), Dallas Lesperance (Holly)
Jeff Kline, athletic director and Lisa Conrad, administrative assistant, Mt. Morris
Drew Johnson, athletic director, LakeVille
Ronda Miller, Carman-Ainsworth administrative assistant
Kathy O'Hara, Durand administrative assistant
Flint Public Library reference staff
Brittany Phalen, Curatorial Assistant, Sloan Museum
Oxford Public Library staff
State of Michigan Library staff
Lapeer Public Library staff
Linda Cheseboro-Rusaw, Fenton (Volleyball)
Scott Couch, Oxford (wrerstling)
Angela Del Morone and Claire Gentile, MIVCA (volleyball coaches association)
Kevin Fiebernitz, Linden (soccer)
Jared Field, director of communications, Lapeer
Kristi Gibson-Marshall, Oxford (competitive cheer)
Bill Hajec, Fenton

Bill Khan, journalist (hockey)

Bill Kinzer and Chad Kenny, Lapeer (soccer)

Karri Kuzma, LakeVille alumnus (track)

Clint Lawhorne, Linden (cross country and track)

Andrew McDonald, Oxford (track)

Roy Millis, Holly

Tom Mora, MHSAA official and Fenton alumnus

Sue Pittsley, Fenton alumnus (Metro League student council)

Matt Sullivan, Fenton (soccer)

Dr. Ken Wensel, Fenton

ABOUT THE COMPILER OF THIS HISTORY

When he was a freshman at Lapeer High School in 1967-68, Gary Oyster was the manager for the school's varsity basketball team. Having access to the coaches' office where the basketball inflator was located, he noticed a note card pinned to the bulletin board that read:

<u>NEW LEAGUE</u>
AINSWORTH
CARMAN
FENTON
HOLLY
LAPEER
SWARTZ CREEK

Little did he know that he would spend the next fifty years associated with that league as an athlete, coach, administrator and finally as the compiler of its fifty-year history.

Gary lettered in cross country and track his junior and senior years at Lapeer. After graduating from Oakland University he became a social studies teacher at Lapeer East High School and White Junior High, coaching girls' track and boy's and girls' cross country at East. In 1986 Gary started a 17-year tenure as assistant principal and athletic director at Lapeer East. Upon retiring in 2003, the athletic directors of the Flint Metro League asked him to stay on as league treasurer, which soon morphed into a position as the league's executive director, where among other duties Gary oversaw the development of the league's website. He has also worked as a track and cross country official since retiring as AD.

1968   1970   1979   1995   2015

27961320R00166

Made in the USA
Lexington, KY
08 January 2019